TREATING THE "UNTREATABLE"

The Isaac Ray Award Lectures

TREATING THE "UNTREATABLE"

Chronic Criminals at Herstedvester

Georg K. Stürup

✳

The Johns Hopkins Press
Baltimore

The symbol of the twisted tree
is based on a sketch by Dr. Stürup of
a tree he saw in England in the 1940's.
The crutch suggests the support that
the Herstedvester Detention Centre
tries to give to the twisted personalities
of its inmates so that they can become
strong and valuable members of society.

The Herstedvester Detention Centre at Albertslund, Denmark.

PREFACE

We like to believe that most of our actions are voluntary and we try to distinguish sharply between what is done voluntarily and that which we do by coercion or under pressure. However, anyone working with criminals detained behind high walls for the protection of society soon comes to realize that the difference between what is done voluntarily and what is done under pressure is not very clear.

For many years I have wanted to write a description of what has been done in the Herstedvester Detention Centre since I became its superintendent in 1942; several times I have started but for lack of time have been unable to finish. When the American Psychiatric Association honored me by giving me the Isaac Ray Award for 1966, I was put under heavy pressure to produce the Isaac Ray Award Lectures which are the basis of this book.

Further pressure has been exerted by Professor Norval Morris, my former chief in the United Nations Asia and Far East Institute in Tokyo, and others of my colleagues in this Institute. Especially influential was Morris' successor, V. N. Pillai, who, as one involved in practical prison work, convinced me that it was worth while to present a careful description of what we have done even if the result became a very egocentric account without comparison to other treatment experiments.

My teachers in psychology, neurophysiology, and psychiatry all stressed precision and control. I am very thankful for the care with which they taught me this, even though it inhibited my writing an account of the treatment program in Herstedvester.

I can be precise only in phenomenological description; I cannot present results of controlled experiments. Our sociopsychiatric approach to treatment is based on postulates which I can reformulate only to a limited degree as hypotheses. This presentation does not emphasize special psychiatric elements or use technical psychiatric terms because I want the book to be readable for all people interested in treating criminals.

Our basic humanitarian obligation to create a psychological climate in which life is bearable and constructive for our inmates has placed a serious restraint on attempts to evaluate scientifically which elements in our program have had the most therapeutic value. The immediate well-being of the inmates and probably their whole future depend on how well the institution functions.

Case histories have been carefully kept. Each one consists of a detailed life-story and accounts of all important interviews, including a description of the situation in which the interview was carried out and a detailed summary of what was discussed.

It is common in our time to stress that it is not sufficient to be good, considerate, and humane if the goal toward which one works is not useful. This may be true but it does not excuse the way in which we have handled most of our seriously criminal fellow citizens who present a danger to society. I hope to illustrate that humane treatment is possible within the limits of security.

Thanks to a few farsighted theoreticians and practitioners in Denmark, we have had an opportunity to carry out our work in a small closed institution.[1] Over the years it has held from 150 to 200 inmates at a time except for a short period just after World War II when the number exploded up to 330.

We have shortened the detention time from an average of over four years to between two and two and one-half years; and as we have at the same time maintained a relapse rate of about 50 per cent for each detention period, we may have been useful. Of one hundred new inmates, fifty will be brought back to us after the first parole and twenty-five after the second parole. Thus at the end of ten years only ten of those one hundred men will be in criminal detention.

We usually call a criminal who has been sentenced at least three times within a short period a "chronic criminal." If the intervals between sentences have been longer we call him an "intermittent criminal." These two types form the core of our inmate population.

Studies of the life-stories of these people usually reveal interpersonal problems of long standing. Although these problems have not been apparent before, they develop in relation to, or as a result of, the crimes and what follows in the way of blows to the self-respect of the criminals. These recidivists, as well as the psychologically deviant first-timers who are also deficient in personality for normal social life, are not welcome in society and are often hunted by the average citizen and his representatives in the legal machinery. They are also unwelcome in our mental hospitals and institutions for mental defectives. They are usually not trusted and they themselves feel

---

[1] For a history of Herstedvester, see Appendix A.

that they belong to a class of people who are different from the normal. They think that they have no chance of leading a normal social life and many people support them in this belief. It is no wonder that such men feel that their every action is conditioned by their criminal tendencies.

After many years of experience, I stress that it is possible to make a criminal believe that he can overcome the difficulties which lie ahead and lead a crime-free life. Not only may he come to believe this, but of our group—the least loved of all criminals—only about 10 per cent are institutionalized because of criminal activities ten years after they first arrived in detention. Within limits, society will finally trust and accept such a man and he in turn will have to accept these limitations. He has to realize that there are some people who should not be told everything about his past but that some, especially his future wife, ought to know his full history in order to understand and help him if inconsiderate people hurt him badly.

The more we stress that the behavior of a chronic criminal or psychopath can never be changed the more difficult it becomes for a man stamped with such a label to believe that he is not a hopeless case. Without hope he will not be motivated again to go through the ordeal of attempting to rehabilitate himself. My main hypothesis is that the chronic criminal is his own most important therapist; it is our job to help him carry out his difficult task.

For our small group we have found it possible to develop a way of life in which security considerations have never been jeopardized; we have given due regard to security as well as to development of a local milieu which may not be ideal but which is acceptable to most of our inmates. By our behavior—not only our words—we express that society does not wish to victimize the inmate further or to give him the opportunity to augment his hate for society; instead, we want to give him a chance to revise his attitude toward authority.

Our approach to the treatment of chronic criminals and criminals whose personality structures and poor adjustments to life endanger their future is based on an optimism which has proved valid. Everything that happens to the inmate in the institution may be of importance and must be integrated. Although the words we use and our mode of expression are important, the energy and the engagement which the staff puts into this type of work seems in many cases to be the greatest inducement for the inmates to change. Despite the inmates' own and other people's expressed opinions to the contrary, we have shown that about 90 per cent of our supposedly hopeless people are capable of giving up a life of crime. The individualized, integrating growth therapy which we have developed can shorten the criminal periods in a man's life; we fervently hope that others will pursue this work and improve upon it.

Chapter I of this book describes the basic principles of treatment in Herstedvester. To a large degree the description is as it was given in the first Isaac Ray Award Lecture.

Chapter II gives a more detailed description of what we actually do, and is extensively illustrated by case histories. I have avoided giving data which would make it easy to identify the individuals, but in order to present a real and truthful picture I may not have altered some of the stories beyond the possibility of recognition by people who have lived with them. Therefore this book will not be printed in Danish, and I hope that reviewers will handle the case material with discretion. I also hope that these life-stories will stimulate institutions in other countries to make experiments like ours for the benefit of society as well as individual criminals who do not like to admit, even to themselves, that they are suffering.

In Chapter III I have attempted to look at life in Herstedvester in different ways—from the inmates' and the staff's points of view and even from my own personal point of view. This section may demonstrate, especially to persons working in institutions for criminals, the differences and similarities of our institution to their own. I hope that it will convince many that the mammoth "universities of crime" that are now to be seen nearly all over the world are outmoded and should no longer be built.

In Chapter IV an attempt is made to illustrate some of our results by using life charts and case histories.

The third Isaac Ray Award Lecture was devoted to the treatment of a special kind of criminal—the sexual criminal. In Denmark there is a law which enables a Danish citizen to apply for castration when he is suffering severely from his sexual drives or is in danger of committing sexual crimes. This lecture describing the castration law and its satisfying results will be published (Munksgaard, Copenhagen, 1968).

ACKNOWLEDGMENTS

The treatment described here was made possible by the open-mindedness of the Danish authorities.

Many staff members have participated in the daily work described and have helped me collect material for this book; its existence proves the importance of this collaboration.

While I was writing the book, both in Copenhagen and in Chicago, my wife and many friends patiently listened to me, read the manuscript or parts of it, and made suggestions and offered criticisms.

My Danish secretaries, Birgit Dibbern and Esther Zeuthen-Nielsen, must be especially thanked.

At the University of Copenhagen there are still no professional courses in forensic psychiatry, no penological research, no special high-level education in penology or in the treatment of criminals; therefore the parts of this project which were carried out in Denmark were done in my own spare time. As a visiting scholar at the Center for Studies in Criminal Justice of the University of Chicago Law School, I was able to concentrate on the Isaac Ray Award Lectures and to expand them into book form. To the director, Norval Morris, and the associate director, Hans W. Mattick, I am deeply indebted for an enormous amount of time spent in polishing the content and language of the manuscript. I also received invaluable secretarial help from Anna Reuter, who, with great energy, has helped me to clarify what I wanted to communicate and to express it in a way which I hope is understandable to Americans interested in better treatment of criminals.

CONTENTS

LIST OF ILLUSTRATIONS

LIST OF FIGURES

TREATING THE "UNTREATABLE"

Chapter I

PRINCIPLES OF TREATMENT

INTRODUCTION

The work we have done over the past twenty-five years in Herstedvester has been the product of teamwork between the inmates, the staff, and various outsiders interested in our work.

During World War II, I was appointed superintendent of this special institution for emotionally disturbed, chronic criminals. Such criminals are not welcome in prisons because they are troublesome and recalcitrant; nor are they welcome in hospitals because they are neither clearly psychotic nor mentally defective. I came to this job with no practical or theoretical knowledge of work of this kind, but I had a background of general psychiatry, a special interest in social psychiatry, and some experience in handling so-called difficult children.

This was during a period when psychiatry in Denmark was beginning to take an optimistic view of what could be accomplished. The old diagnostic phase was fading away, malaria treatment had opened the way for new types of therapy, and dynamic views of personality reactions were growing.

It may be appropriate to mention that Isaac Ray himself lived in a time when there was optimism about what was then called "moral treatment." In the introduction of his *Treatise,* published in London in 1839, Spillan had affirmed how much had been achieved by this method as compared with what he called the "hopeless practices" used earlier. Isaac Ray spoke bravely and forcefully on the legal aspects of psychiatry. In Scandinavia, perhaps more than in the United States, his ideas on criminal responsibility have been accepted and applied.

I believe that we at Herstedvester have developed what was suggested by one of Dr. Ray's precursors, Dr. Benjamin Rush of Philadelphia. I knew nothing about Benjamin Rush or the Walnut Street Jail until 1955, when Negley Teeters drew my attention to him and his plans for the punisment of criminals. In Benjamin Franklin's house in Philadelphia on March 9, 1787, Benjamin Rush pleaded for more humane handling of criminals. He said, "The great art of surgery has been said to consist of saving, not in destroying or amputating, the diseased parts of the human body. Let governments learn to imitate in this aspect the skill and humanity of the healing arts."[1]

In Denmark, the value of having medical authorities handle some criminals is a well-recognized principle. As a medical man and a psychiatrist, I am in charge of a group of people removed from society because they have demonstrated by their lack of self-restraint that they are unfit to live in society. They have all been sentenced to this special institution in order to protect society. I felt that I could accept this responsibility because I had the opportunity to add new goals to Herstedvester's custodial functions—reformation of criminals and the prevention of new crime. At that time it would have been helpful to know that Benjamin Rush had already described the attachment to one's family and society as one of the strongest feelings of the human heart and that, in spite of this, he advocated the use of an indefinite term of commitment as a basis for what we now call the treatment of serious and chronic criminals.

Some years ago the late Dr. Philip Roche wisely suggested in his Isaac Ray Lectures[2] that we must develop techniques for changing the attitudes of convicted persons so that they become self-aware and thus avoid future crime. I am using his terms because they state explicitly what we have attempted to do. Let me say that this is not an attempt to overstate psychiatric claims. I never say that I cure psychopaths; I do claim, however, that during their stay in Herstedvester they have been helped to become nicer psychopaths.

Treatment in the field of clinical criminology has limited goals, the chief one being a crime-free future for the offender. Our program has always been directed toward this practical objective and we have been eclectic, intuitively using whatever approach we thought most valuable in any given situation. I have to admit that in Herstedvester we have never attempted to evaluate the results of this or that psy-

[1] Benjamin Rush, *A Plan for the Punishment of Crime,* ed. Negley R. Teeters (Philadelphia: Pennsylvania Prison Society, 1954), p. 15.
[2] Philip Q. Roche, *The Criminal Mind* (New York: Farrar, Straus and Cudahy, 1958).

chotherapeutic method. Our primary aim has been to help those unhappy, seriously criminal men who are allegedly untreatable (and are suffering from this very supposition) to feel somewhat better and to get them to dare once more to try to use the positive elements of their personalities. In focusing their attention on these positive factors and attempting individual psychotherapy, we have often felt it necessary not to aim at uncovering their basic conflicts but rather to try to make these men accept the fact that a crime-free future is not necessarily the same as a happier one.

LEGAL CONCEPTS

As early as 1912 a law concerning the special handling of criminal psychopaths was proposed.[3] This stressed that the necessity for special treatment of an offender could not be based on psychiatric classifications alone.

The decision to use severe measures is a prerogative of the court and is used both to protect the individual sentenced and to satisfy the rightful claims of society for protection. A history of penal experience may be of some value in making the classification, but the indeterminate segregation recommended for some psychopaths should be used only in cases where less severe measures are not thought to be enough. The court, although it consults the Medico-Legal Council or individual psychiatrists as to the psychiatric state of the offender, retains final responsibility as to sentencing, parole, and final release.

A law based on these principles, operating expressly for a test period, was passed in 1925. Its application was restricted to those persons who had manifested physical aggression against another person—assault, murder, and rape. Arson is also included in this category. On April 15, 1930, the law under which Herstedvester now operates received the Royal Assent; it was provided, however, that the terms should not be enforced until the beginning of 1933. This is a common practice in Denmark with its far-reaching penal legislation.

Before 1933 the criminals now sentenced to Herstedvester were termed in everyday usage as "partially responsible" offenders and were given shorter sentences than "normal" offenders, even though they presented a higher degree of risk to the community and were thought to be less positively influenced by punishment. Special measures are now used with "partially responsible" offenders but the

3 See Appendix A.

advisable extent of these measures cannot be determined in advance. This was taken into consideration in Sections 17 and 70 of the Danish Criminal Code of 1930.[4]

This law places upon the court the full responsibility for the satisfactory classification of the criminals sentenced. In the United States such classification is usually undertaken routinely at the diagnostic receiving depot of a prison system, but in Denmark this is a function of the court. Whenever the court considers it necessary, it may order a full-scale psychiatric review of a case. This may be proposed either by the prosecution or the defense, and it occurs in some 18 per cent of the cases where persons are sentenced to more than a fine, that is to prison or some other institution. A public psychiatrist or the local medical officer usually makes the report and it is presented to the court with copies for both the prosecution and defense. Such a medico-legal report contains a rather detailed case history and the findings of a physical examination as well as of the psychiatric examination. It usually takes more than a month, including many hours of interviewing, to collect this material. The purpose of these procedures is to advise the court as to the most rational action for it to take in sentencing. If the court wishes—and it usually does in serious cases—the report may be sent to the Danish Medico-Legal Council[5] for a higher level of advice. Here three psychiatrists who are experienced in legal problems review all the material which will be placed before the court and present their psychiatric views in a short summary. This summary is written in such a way that the court can easily determine which sections of the law are applicable. The Medico-Legal Council may criticize the original psychiatric report and suggest further examination in a mental hospital, by an especially qualified psychiatrist, or by one of the members of the Council itself.

Since the Medico-Legal Council gives joint advice, no single member can appear in court on behalf of the entire Council. Additional questions to the Council must be made in writing.

[4] See Appendix A.
[5] The Medico-Legal Council is an independent medical body headed by the professor of forensic medicine of the University of Copenhagen. The Council is divided into a general section and a psychiatric section. Seven psychiatrists are appointed to the psychiatric section with the professor of psychiatry of the University of Copenhagen acting as its chairman. The Council can answer questions only from official bodies such as the courts and government ministries. Three members have to participate in reviewing each case presented. In very important or difficult cases, the whole group of psychiatrists may participate.

The identification of psychotic and severely mentally defective persons is relatively easy. Once such an identification has been made, it is up to the court to decide if such a person may be considered "responsible." In Denmark this is presumed to be outside the sphere of medical competence and cannot merit psychiatric comment. In Section 17 the word "psychopath" is not used, being masked by the broad phrase, "defective development or impairment or disturbance of his mental faculties of a more permanent type."

The court, informed by the psychiatric report, decides the offender's fitness for punishment, taking proportional sentencing as well as general preventative considerations into account. If his present or former crimes are minor, stronger psychiatric arguments are required for an indeterminate sentence. When the crime is more serious from a legal point of view, the court usually finds it easier to follow medical advice suggesting that special treatment is needed. Such treatment can be applied to persons sentenced under Section 16 or 17. Section 70 makes it possible for the court to use any measure which may be appropriate, from appointment of a supervisor to placement in a hospital or in a special detention center such as Herstedvester or, since 1951, its sister institution, Horsens.

This same court will decide later, in respect to those whom it has sent to Herstedvester, when it is time to use less rigorous measures such as parole. During the parole period the sentenced person will still be under the supervision of the special institution.

The detention institution must be regarded neither as a mental hospital primarily dedicated to therapy nor as a prison dedicated to security for the most troublesome and dangerous offenders; it is a security institution, but one whose goal is rehabilitation. When Herstedvester was established, it was assumed that simple security was not enough; humanitarian considerations made it necessary to first secure protection for society and then, within these limits, to establish treatment programs.

The age of the inmates has not changed much over the years (see Figure 1). The largest number of inmates has always been younger men with peak in age range occurring at twenty-five to twenty-nine years. The curve falls off steeply before the age of forty and then declines more gradually.

The proportion of offenses leading to detention at Herstedvester has been approximately 60 per cent for property offenses, a little more than 10 per cent for aggressive offenses (including arson), and between 25 and 30 per cent for sexual offenses.

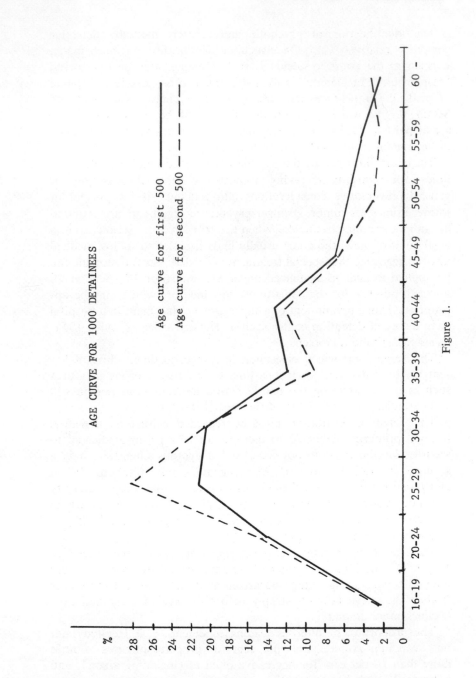

AGE CURVE FOR 1000 DETAINEES

Age curve for first 500 ⸻
Age curve for second 500 ─ ─ ─

Figure 1.

PSYCHIATRIC CONSIDERATIONS

Some of our major psychiatric concepts should now be mentioned. Psychotics and mental defectives are not discussed here because they are not accepted at Herstedvester.[6] (The inmates of Herstedvester may, of course, develop psychoses or their undiagnosed psychoses may become explicit after they are placed with us; in these cases we either temporarily transfer them, or, when more permanent hospitalization may be expected, we request the court to order their transfer to mental hospitals.) It is also unnecessary to discuss the meaning of terms such as "psychopath," "sociopath," or whatever else our criminals may have been called, as they form a hard core fitting within all the accepted definitions of these terms. Nor will I develop any sure-fire recipe for curing what I prefer to call simply "insufficiencies of personality."[7] It may be worth while, however, to stress the necessity of attempting to develop the art of drawing sufficient conclusions from insufficient premises.

The group of inmates with whom we are concerned has already been described by Tuke and later by Henderson as people who "irrespective of their will and desire are driven by impulses of thought and conduct which impel them to antisocial conduct."[8] This is a very mixed group of immature, unbalanced, spineless, sometimes unintelligent, adrift citizens whose behavior is clearly deviate. It should perhaps be stressed that they deviate so clearly in interhuman relations that they have no reason to feel solidarity with society at large. They consider themselves outcasts and find it easier to develop relationships with people who are also outcasts. This increased rate of interpersonal interaction with people of their own kind causes difficulties in their relations with conventional citizens. Consequently we must try to grasp not only the personality elements but also all the psychosomatic and social elements as a single totality despite the fact that an adequate terminology for such an endeavor is not yet at hand. We are all actors and spectators in the drama of life, as Pirandello has so clearly demonstrated. We are aware that there is only a relative stability in the patterns of reaction in all people, inmates as well as ourselves. The consequence of this is that we may not be able to differentiate sharply between the diagnostic and therapeutic phase of the treatment process; there will be a constant alternation between them,

[6] See Appendixes B and C.
[7] See Appendix D.
[8] David Henderson, "The Classification and Treatment of Psychopathic States," *British Journal of Delinquency*, 6 (1955):8.

depending upon varied situations. In any situation, the participants influence each other. Both use defense mechanisms which, in patients, may be considered new symptoms. These upset the old balance and call for new diagnoses. In any case, they call for new reactions adequate to the new situation. Many of our inmates seem to distort reality as we see it. They appear to live only for the moment, for the "here and now," feeling that what has gone before is forgotten and what is to come is of no consequence. (This syndrome of attitudes is very attractive to young women who, often in spite of high intellectual abilities, become obsessed by former inmates who, in turn, exploit them.)

Such patterns of distorted perceptions may upset realistic relations with other human beings. There are a large number of persons who exhibit symptoms of withdrawal and/or hostility similar to those found by other investigators in studies of sociocultural disintegration.[9] Nearly all of our inmates realize that they have not "made it." They feel that they have disappointed their relatives or that they were in their way. Some have felt like this since childhood and others have come to accept this view of themselves only after going through police hearings, court procedures, mental examinations, or other stigmatizing procedures. In order clearly to evaluate this part of their life-histories, it is necessary to have known the person for a long period of time and, if possible, to have followed him for several years after his experience of re-socialization, noting the changes in his patterns of reaction as he develops a new group of friends.

To understand the dynamics of different situations it may be helpful to study Figure 2. The Y axis represents accessible mental resources. The X axis represents demands on a person's abilities— what he himself and others expect of him. If few demands are made on a person's abilities, his accessible mental resources are not highly taxed and he finds himself in the sufficiency area (A). If the demands are greater, his corresponding mental resources may be just sufficient to deal with them and he will be found in the balance area (B). If the demands are very great, a person's mental resources are spread too thin, he will not be able to cope with the demands, and therefore he will be found in the insufficiency area (C). Thus as the demands on him rise, his ability to deal with them will diminish, and vice versa. If his mental resources are strengthened, a person may move from the insufficiency area into the balance area.

[9] Alexander H. Leighton, "Editorial," *Journal of the American Psychiatric Association*, 122 (1966):930.

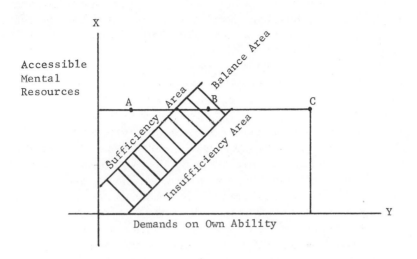

DIAGRAM OF SITUATIONAL ELEMENTS CONTRIBUTING
TO SUFFICIENCY OR INSUFFICIENCY IN THE
ADJUSTMENT PROCESS. ADAPTED FROM BENGT
LINDEGAARD.

Figure 2.

A chronic criminal is likely to perceive other people's behavior as
being directed against himself and will regard both friendly and unfriendly attitudes as being based on knowledge that others have of
him as a criminal. He may react on the basis of anticipations of what
we expect of him and this "dual experience" is a typical stereotype in
the thinking of the offender. He assumes that our expectations are
also stereotyped and that we think he is "no good." This is not a
special mechanism which applies only to an interhuman situation
between a criminal and a noncriminal, but it is also a rule for interpersonal relations in general. For instance, this double expectation
causes a nurse to act differently when she is promoted to chief nurse.
Because of her promotion she acts as she thinks chief nurses are
supposed to act.

I can illustrate this mechanism further by setting forth the relations
between persons A and B: The relations between two persons in a
dialogue are not simply between the phenomenal A and B that we
see before us, but they can be more fully described as being between

A in a situation experienced by A and B in a situation experienced by B. We can say that many people are present—A as conceived by himself, B as conceived by himself, B as conceived by A, and A as conceived by B. Further, we will have A's conception of B's conception of A's conception of himself and B's conception of A's conception of B's conception of himself. And in a recent private discussion Leonard Cottrell, Jr., pointed out that we will also have to take into consideration A's conception of B's conception of B and B's conception of A's conception of A. All this may be further complicated by the influence of other persons. This in reality means that we may well stress that we have no free choice but that our choice of behavior is conditioned not only by our former experience and internal structure which is determined but also by the situational stimuli which are dependent on the other persons' determined psychological experiences. That means that there are accidental factors in our behavior.

This means that in any particular interpersonal situation there will be an integration of at least three different elements or types of situational experience. The situation is further complicated by the different hereditary and developmental backgrounds of the participants. Patterns of perceptions and expectations are also influenced by other factors such as current (and possibly changing) emotional maturity. We are not always mature in our patterns of reactions and sometimes we need to react in childish ways, especially when we have behaved very maturely for a long time. Temporary regressions are not always unhealthy. Looking at interhuman relations with special emphasis on the relative stability of personality patterns (that is, what one may expect of a person in the future) is important for our concept of treatment.

For all practical purposes we have for examination only one of the partners in the criminal situation—the sentenced perpetrator of the crime. We try to explore his family background, childhood experiences, education, and career, then attempt to evaluate his usual level of emotional balance, his intellectual state, etc. In some cases we find a neurotic, monotonic symptomatology of hysteria and other anxiety-loaded syndromes; in others there is misinterpretation of a paranoid kind. In some cases syndrome complexes are quite varied. Many times we find a secondary depressive reaction to the serious new situation, and an analysis of the criminal situation may demonstrate the large role played by preinstitutional factors. Short-circuit reactions are not uncommon. (In Danish legal psychiatry we use the term "short-circuit" for single abnormal reactions triggered by a certain situation.)

An example of this is Arthur, age twenty-eight, who from the time he was sixteen or seventeen years old had been enough interested in sports to want to become a professional athlete. Unfortunately he suffered several brain concussions which made him unfit for such a career. He then became a farmer but kept his interest in sports. He also was a nudist and frequently ran naked in the nearby woods. One day while he was running naked he met a young girl who screamed in panic when she saw him coming toward her. He was frightened by her screaming, choked her, and hid her body with leaves. The girl's screaming triggered his "short-circuit" reaction. Because of this abnormal but not obviously psychotic behavior and some structural brain deviation he was sentenced to detention. In Herstedvester he was always a bit obsessive but continued to plan to be a farmer. Arthur was paroled after nine years and has been in no trouble since; no further complications have developed from his brain concussions. He is married and leads a peaceful, normal social life.

The interpersonal situation within which a person reacts is also important. The fact of whether he meets with insecurity or confidence, feels himself the stronger or the weaker, of equal health or similarly fatigued, in pain or not, determines to a great extent how a difficult situation can be tackled. Perception of the situation differs according to these factors. This is also true of the situation in which we examine the detainees, as the participants in the examination perceive expectations independently of what others actually expect of them. Thus it is necessary in our daily work to take these "double expectations" into consideration.

This viewpoint is in harmony with the psychological school (Murray et al.)[10] which has been working with the idea of different needs. Along with Maslow,[11] we at Herstedvester stress the importance of the interaction of different needs, the most basic of which, such as the need for food and water, *must* be satisfied. If our basic needs are not satisfied, our behavior will be influenced and if we have gone through a long period of deprivation, our behavior may be permanently influenced. Effects of this type may be called "psychic scars."

[10] Henry Alexander Murray, *Explorations in Personality* (New York: Oxford University Press, 1938).
[11] Abraham Harold Maslow, *Motivation and Personality* (New York: Harper, 1954).

Occasionally we see how people change a former pattern of behavior which has been stable for many years and substitute another;
sometimes this happens slowly and sometimes suddenly. Stevenson[12]
attempted in 1961 to investigate the important elements in so-called
spontaneous cures of nervous states and behavior disturbances; in
1965 D. Langen[13] pointed out the importance of the time factor.
Stevenson found that talking about what was painful resulted in
diminished sensitivity to this pain and that persons sometimes were
able to add newer memories to the older, more painful ones. In some
other cases, a late maturation was brought about.

We have seen such cases at Herstedvester; inmates have felt helped
when given sympathy even when that help was not provided by professional therapists. It is essential that confidence and respect be
established between the partners in a treatment situation and that
the respect be mutual. In other cases, spontaneous "recovering"
seems to be related to a new situation. A person may enter the new
situation with greater self-respect or may meet someone who loves
him and has confidence in him, giving him a feeling that he has something to live for. This is what happens in a milieu treatment where
the situational elements are strong.

In our professional work we try to help the inmates to arrive at
realistic solutions to their basic problems, and this may lead to fulfillment of some of their needs. Often it is necessary just to help a
man adjust to his surroundings, to give him security, or to assist him
in recognizing needs that he did not know he had.

When an inmate encounters a new situation, a completely new set
of reactions is called for. Sometimes this new situation helps him
form interpersonal relations, which he could not do in the rigid milieu
of his former surroundings. New forms of mental protection become
available to him and often, after his parole, he finds that his economic
situation is better than before. These factors may assist his rehabilitation.

It is useful to call "success" a human need, since one who has had
no success in life very often feels, and is felt to be, less valuable to
society than others. This view makes the chronic criminal even more

[12] Ian Stevenson, "Processes of 'Spontaneous' Recovery from the Psycho-
neuroses," *American Journal of Psychiatry,* 117 (1961): 1057–64.
[13] D. Langen, "Indikation und Kontraindikation einzelner psychotherapeu-
tischer Methoden," *Acta Psychiatrica Scandinavica,* 40 (1964): 37–49; *idem,*
"Faktoren der Spontanheilung bei Psychoreaktionen Störungen," *ibid.,* 41
(1965):428–35.

insecure. In some cases an inmate is convinced that he should move to another part of the country in order to "start over again" and we must be careful always to warn him that preliminary success in a new locale has to be followed up by continued success for some time before it is of any real significance. Outward success is less important than the inner security growing out of being able to master something that he could not do before. A realistic evaluation of his actual situation and the possibilities in the future are prerequisite to a reasonable fulfillment of the inmate's basic needs. In a welfare society the problems of hunger no longer really exist, but the needs for security and belonging and the need to love and be loved are more difficult to satisfy. One who has not obtained satisfaction of such needs for many years will not find it easy to change his pattern of life even if he arrives at an essential understanding of the necessity for such a change.

DEVELOPMENT OF THE TREATMENT MACHINERY

The varied approach to our problems, which could be called a "situational approach," developed over a period of many years. In 1942 daily life in Danish prisons was still severe, with definite elements of the classical prison system such as the inmates' having to stand silently with their faces to the wall when waiting to see the doctor or a supervisor. The atmosphere in Herstedvester was tense, but less so than in the State Prison because there was no rule of silence and because the small units made it possible to group the inmates with relatively more freedom. However, living so close together in the small units made everyone more afraid of each other.

The supervisory staff was small. As the only psychiatrist, I was responsible for the treatment of the detainees with some help from a general practitioner. I was also responsible as prison doctor to the overcrowded State Prison across the road.

From the day I arrived, collaboration between all supervisors was established. That meant daily meetings with the captain as the leader of the uniformed officers, the man in charge of social assistance, the chief nurse, and the business administrator. These conferences were aimed primarily at solving daily problems for which I had had no preparation since I had never been inside a prison or a prisonlike institution before. I had no special training in legal problems. I knew how to handle crippled people and difficult children and was well-versed in general psychiatry. (This meant that I had been taught that these selected psychopaths could not be treated.) My personal aim at that time was not to treat the inmates but rather to arrive at a better general classification made possible by the special opportunity given here to observe a large group of inmates under standardized conditions. Contrary to expectations, the daily conferences developed into a treatment system; our concept of treatment has a historical basis in these meetings.

From the beginning we attempted to classify the criminals according to the circles in which they felt at home. It was important to evaluate actual conflicts and their backgrounds early in the treatment. Fights were rather common. Discussing the backgrounds of these conflicts with inmates when they were still upset gave them and me a better insight into their patterns of behavior and often established a solid emotional contact between the aggressive inmate and myself. Out of such discussions and mutual understanding of our situations there developed ideas for improving institution life. The inmates came to the therapist with reasonable suggestions, and some of these were discussed at the daily conferences and adopted. The collaboration as seen from both sides was elaborated and consolidated.

In 1944 it became possible to acquire an open section, Kastanienborg. The inmates' interest in it was very great. A pioneering "we" feeling developed, and it became obvious that the careful integration of all possible means of influencing the inmates was essential. At the same time it was found that none of these asocial persons was satisfied with being placed outside normal society. All wanted, and still want, to be socially accepted, but their attempts had been so unsuccessful that most of them had given up, not realizing that their approach was irrational; this often brought on more new frustrations than developments in the desired direction.

CONCEPT OF TREATMENT

Our primary duty is to protect society against the danger to other people's lives and health that the inmates' freedom would create. Within these limits we attempt to influence the detainee in such a way that it becomes easier for him to manage a normal life without further crime.[14]

How does the parolee avoid committing new crimes? It is not important that the former detainee has criminal impulses as long as he does not follow them. The therapeutic result will be positive if he is not again convicted of crime.

[14] For Royal Decree of 1940, see Appendix A.

The key to all our work is a sense of reality. We call for unbiased rationality, both in our workers and in the inmates. Our treatment program is based on collaboration between all who have any potential for being active in the work, with the realization that the main burden falls upon the inmate himself, since it is his future which is at stake.

This seems simple enough, but deep prejudices may complicate the realistic integration of the inmate as a principal collaborator in the treatment. Professional therapists may wish to have the entire credit for a successful treatment.

Another complication is that often we will have to try to get the potential criminal to subdue part of what he has experienced as part of his free development; we must attempt to get him to change his way of expressing himself. The greatest problem is that he must learn that an essential change will call for continued effort when he is in the free society, and this may mean that trying to lead a crime-free life will be more difficult than his former life. It is not our object to try to reshape our criminal fellow citizens in our own image. We should not attempt to "cure" any criminal; he has to develop his own way and remain himself. It is necessary, though often difficult, to retain respect for the human beings with whom we are working. We may have an inmate who resists change. He may be right, and we feel that it may be dangerous to force a change upon such a patient. As Jung says, "Cure may act as a poison which not everyone can tolerate."

We try to help a man to understand as much as possible of his own pattern of behavior and of his own assets so that he may dare once more to believe that he will be able to avoid new crime. We must help him to realize that it is normal to feel insecure and to be lonely, and that it takes time to pass through a developing process. All of this means that we, as therapists, must be very flexible in various situations; sometimes we may even need to resist developing formal psychotherapeutical situations, in order to help the criminal in his maturation to independence. Such carefully controlled behavior by the therapists permits the inmate to develop a reasonable confidence in the persons who represent the institution. This confidence may enable him to accept the fact that we are all interested in him, even if we do not always respond to his momentary demands.

The majority of chronic criminals suffer from the fear of committing new crime, and sometimes they want to do something to prevent it. This fear may make it more difficult for them to fulfill their good intentions. As therapists we must attempt to strengthen this wish and to persuade the men to work for a realistic solution to their

problems. They have to become and remain the principal collaborators with regard to their own future. Through such collaboration, we
have the chance to follow a man's career through several years, inside
and outside our institution. In this way, and only in this way, can we
gain an understanding of how a criminal pattern begins and ends.
Through analyses of long careers we may eventually grasp which are
the more important of the differences we find between them.

One common characteristic of our inmates is that they have all
been sentenced. The other common characteristic is a result of the
first one—nearly all of them lack self-respect. By the time a man
comes to us he has already been systematically broken down. It first
happens, in some cases, in early childhood. In other cases it happens
later and for some it first happens when they feel guilty about having
committed a serious crime. The wringer of legal machinery works
upon all of them in the same way. One of the main responsibilities
of the penal authorities should be to counteract the harm inherent in
legal procedures, as well as in the penal system. Society often dis-
penses justice in such a way that the sentenced criminal will need
to be given a great deal of special assistance if he is to recover and
return to a social and bearable life.

This has not been obvious to all who work in prisons. In part this
is due to the fact that while physical damage is obvious, psychological
damage is not. Individual workers in many institutions do a good
job and often try to help inmates through difficult periods. However,
the large, Bastille-like institutions have all the undesirable qualities
of what Goffman has called "total institutions."[15] Through their
necessary mechanization, impersonality, and their very size, they
further reduce the self-respect of the inmate. In such an institution,
with a limited staff, it is impossible to develop what the sociologists
call "primary interpersonal relations" between staff and inmates. This
makes our form of therapy almost impossible in large institutions, as
it is precisely through this interpersonal relationship that the inmate
may be motivated to become optimistic enough to collaborate on his
future—that is, to collaborate with people whom, in a "total institution," he has been taught to regard as professional opponents.

Especially detrimental to the future prospects of a criminal is the
ease with which he can get naïve defense lawyers and reporters to
believe stories he has created as part of his psychological defense system or as an attempt to exploit his legal right to lie in court.[16]

15 Erving Goffman, *Asylums* (New York: Doubleday, 1961).
16 Birger's experiences illustrate this: In September, 1963, a newspaper
printed a notice under the heading, "Charge Withdrawn But in Detention."

The inmate has to learn that few people can take more than one step at a time and that after he has been paroled it will take still more time before he can feel accepted by a group of ordinary citizens. It may be years before he can come to terms with his fears and conflicting feelings regarding society. During this period he needs to avoid seeming peculiar and strange or calling unnecessary attention to himself by achieving some such public status as leading a local labor union. This is a real possibility with those paroled from Herstedvester because their group experience in therapeutic sessions has given them some social competence.

We have tried to develop a system of treatment which is individualized and which integrates all the elements that may play a role in the rehabilitative process in a given case and in a given situation. The concept of treatment is used in a broad way and includes all facets of influencing factors that are seen as contributing to this special purpose.

Let us take a concrete example. We have a man who is afraid of

---

Although this newspaper had firmly supported our rehabilitation work for a long period, it now showed astonishment that the detainee was returned to detention because he broke the parole rules, even though a charge for theft was withdrawn. (This is a well-established technical procedure to be used in cases when guilt is clearly admitted in court.) It further described how the defense lawyer had stressed that the possibilities for his treatment at Herstedvester were illusory. The accused had told him that he was left to himself at the institution and that, if he wanted some variety in his daily life, he invented a sexual problem, and then the doctors took an interest in him.

It was Birger's fifth time in detention. During former stays, he had received extremely intensive psychological assistance with complicated problems which were only partly sexual. One therapist had devoted an especially long period of time to him, and I personally had had very good contact with him.

When he came back to Herstedvester he was, for the first few days, formal in behavior and embittered to have been returned. He agreed that his life during the last parole period had been extremely unsatisfactory. A week later I more or less accidentally met him on my visit to the wards and said, somewhat ironically, that it had surprised me when I saw in the newspaper that he had to invent sexual problems in order to get contact with us. He reacted with a big smile and asserted that it was his impression that I had not taken what they wrote about me seriously before and why did I suddenly do so now? I told him that I was asked to answer his accusation publicly and that in a private letter to the chief editor I had explained that this man used his clear, constitutional right to lie in court but that I could not see any reasonable motivation for the newspaper to report what was so obviously erroneous. He answered again, "Yes, but it nearly worked. I really believed that I had caught you."

During his former stay in Herstedvester he had had facial tics. Now he was in a relaxed, friendly, and neutral mood, and once more he explained that his main problem was his feeling of loneliness and isolation which resulted from his misuse of alcohol.

everyone around him and is afraid that his freedom of movement and self-expression will be thwarted. He does not necessarily have to be aware of this at all times and is usually unable to express it. He hides his fear behind behavior which is very often disagreeable and provocative and he remains in the institution very much against his will. Outside the institution he attacked other people because he felt they challenged him. Now his surroundings are threatening to him; they create insecurity and incite aggressiveness in him. If it is now possible to expose him to a situation where he can react to his surroundings in a different way, it may be possible to diminish his feelings of insecurity. This will mean that his interpersonal relationships may change. He may then realize, more or less spontaneously, that what we might call his paranoid behavior is not inherent and he may recognize the possibility of coping with his fears. This is the beginning of a motivation for change, and the activities of the staff aiming at this goal are a part of the whole treatment. The prisoner may then start discussing his problems with a fellow inmate or staff member or with the psychotherapist with whom he worked on his life-story. This part of the treatment is individualized, but it has to be integrated with whatever else happens to the man. It also has to be geared to a maturation process so that he, himself, feels that he is his own main collaborator.

Often he will take an interest in his own problems more easily when he realizes that he must understand not only what happens in himself but also the situations in which he participates. This means that he has to understand his interaction with all other people—the group of which he wants to be a part and the group of which he is a part. At first this is experienced as something easy, but in reality it may make his life more difficult.

As the treatment becomes much more diffuse, it grows more difficult to obtain an overview, and continued integration of what happens in the ward and what happens in formal psychotherapeutic sessions becomes a necessity. This means that our concept of treatment encompasses not only all the factors that are seen as contributing to our special purpose, but also the motivation, what sustains the motivation, what helps to clear up problems, what helps to change situations, the learning processes in rehabilitation, and more direct social work. Therapists and all other collaborators use their interpersonal relations not only to treat the person but also the situation in which he participates. This treatment process includes medical elements of great importance and, at the same time, is a joint work carried out by many different persons with many types of basic training. We have called our treatment principles "individualized, integrating growth therapy."

INDIVIDUALIZED, INTEGRATING GROWTH THERAPY

In order to get an idea of what individualized, integrating growth therapy means, one must understand that adequate institutional security measures are of basic importance. If the degree of security is not sufficient to hold the man we are going to handle, he will leave. If security precautions are overdone, he will not trust officials who spend society's money in such an apparently wasteful way. Inadequate security measures will block his acceptance of the other main approaches to treatment such as psychotherapy and somatic therapy.

These methods are equally important. Psychotherapy, aiming at insight, relief from tension, and the organization and reorganization of contact with reality, may be carried out with the individual or in a group setting. Somatic therapy (physiotherapy) may help the man to relax, thus relieving tensions. He may need hormonal therapy to counteract sexual urges which have been transformed into aggressive activity or into the kind of masturbation which hurts his self-respect. Surgical therapy may be indicated for sexual problems and plastic surgery may be required for malformations.

There are two other elements—rehabilitation and social casework. Direct rehabilitation is concerned with habit-training processes, the cultivation of interpersonal relations, and some sort of industrial training. The rehabilitation elements in individualized, integrating growth therapy consist of those parts of our treatment which aim at the inmate's attitudes and his level of aspiration and include an attempt to make it possible for him to achieve a reasonable economic status. Social casework aims at these same goals while he is in the institution and during the parole years. The social aide assists the parolee to renew family relations, and to readjust to a social group, helps him to identify and avoid new criminal situations, and provides him with social support. Sometimes he needs continued help for years to find jobs and lodgings. In actual situations the social aide will often be engaged in more or less psychotherapeutical activities.

All of these activities have to be centered on the self-respecting, interested man himself—a man who must find his own balance between his capabilities and the demands placed upon him. This is especially true of those demands which he makes of himself so that he may become self-sufficient and balanced. All the different ele-

ments indicated here have to be coordinated and integrated. As far
as possible, the individual collaborators have to gear their attitudes
to the individual inmate so that whatever relevant activity takes place
in the institution may contribute to the therapeutic process.

Therefore it is of supreme importance that we organize the communication lines within the institution in such a way that everyone
receives the information he needs. The center for dissemination of
information is the daily meeting of staff members which includes
doctors, psychologists, social aides, workshop leaders, some senior
custodial officers, administrative personnel, teachers, and nurses. All
kinds of daily problems can be solved as a result of discussion by
such interdisciplinary specialists. Here a decision may be made to
transfer an inmate from one living or working unit to another. Notes
collected each day from each ward by a team consisting of a doctor,
a chief nurse, and a lieutenant are read aloud and discussed. This
group, rather than an individual staff member or the superintendent,
grants privileges. A continuous evaluation of the pattern of behavior
of each inmate, and of each group of inmates, results from these
meetings. This form of communicating and integrating relevant bits
of information takes time, but such discussions cannot be hurried if
we are to reach the ultimate goal of full-scale staff and inmate cooperation. As a result of participating in the daily conferences, staff
members develop a sense of belonging together, a respect for each
other, and a recognition of the relative value of each other's professionally biased opinions. In open discussion of a decision, positions taken can be defended by all supervisory staff members who
participate in the conference. Such decisions can then be explained
to those who could not be in the group and also to the inmates.

Each case is reviewed at regular intervals, first by the officers and
therapists working directly with the men, and then in the common
meeting. In this way the inmate's behavior in different situations is
clearly understood and, to some degree, vicariously experienced by
all who need to know about it so that a continuous evaluation of his
capabilities develops. In the meeting the social aide may learn what
kind of work an inmate can manage, what way of life he can stand,
and what observations the accompanying officers have made about
his relations to his family on six-hour leaves. His behavior during
home visits often differs substantially from that displayed during his
relatives' visits to him in the institution. These differences may give
important clues to the cause of problems that may develop in the
future. It becomes possible to judge whether and when a person is

able to realize the difficulties he will face when he leaves the institution and whether he can understand his need for help and convince himself that he should seek it. Such help is obtained through the collaboration of the institution's social aide or through the aid of another staff member such as a custodial officer whom he trusts or his therapist, who must then continue to work with him on an outpatient basis. Toward the end of the institutional phase, staff members must support the inmate more than usual and stress that his feelings of insecurity are neither unique nor peculiar. When he is paroled, he can, as others have done, continue to develop.

Finally, all evaluations of the development of the inmate have to be placed before the court that sent him to us so that the judge can decide whether the circumstances make it possible for him to follow our recommendation as to parole. It is important here to stress continuity. Generally the parole phase is looked upon as aftercare. In reality it should be looked upon as a very important part of the rehabilitation work begun in the institutional phase.

Chapter II

TREATMENT PRACTICES

RECEPTION

It is a difficult experience to arrive at an unknown institution where you are going to spend an undetermined length of time. I clearly remember my own arrival at the Herstedvester Detention Center on January 2, 1942.

The institution is located about 14 kilometers (10 miles) from the center of Copenhagen, across the road from a large State Prison. Housing more than 300 inmates, this is a very large prison for Denmark. The entrance to Herstedvester is a little, lumpy protrusion in a gray-yellow wall on the north side of the main road. (See Frontispiece.) I was met by a uniformed prison officer, dressed very much like a policeman, who accompanied me through the gate. Inside, there were—and still are—several cheaply built buildings including three living units, one accommodating sixty men and two others accommodating forty each, plus a workshop and a gymnasium, both built of yellow bricks. Instead of grass along the walls there were long rows of Brussels sprouts to supplement the winter's food.

Behind the workshop we came to the administration building with the office, security cells, reception unit, and infirmary. The office was sparsely furnished and staffed by a single male worker. In this building were also a large empty laboratory, a dispensary, and a small operating room; these were the uninspiring medical facilities. I was to be in charge of treatment, and the warden of the nearby State Prison was in charge of security and economy. My hope not to stay too long in the institution was confirmed.

This memory is undoubtedly distorted, but it has always helped me to understand the feelings of new staff members and inmates arriving at Herstedvester. The institution no longer looks as dreary as it did. Roses bloom in the summertime, the brutality of the yellow wall of the gymnasium is softened by vines, and the yard has been made into a garden. While the atmosphere is quite friendly, the new inmate probably does not really notice it because he is emotionally engaged. Usually he has been in jail for some time and does not like his indeterminate sentence to detention in Herstedvester, which means that the court has decided he has arrived "at the end of the road." Often he would have preferred a fixed sentence.

While they have been in jail and during former prison sentences, the newcomers have heard much about Herstedvester. This institution is new, this is "different." It is neither a prison nor a hospital and that means that what we do at Herstedvester has been explained in a distorted way. Usually newcomers have been told that those in Herstedvester are more or less "nuts." Others have heard inaccurate descriptions of being allowed to make their own tea and coffee or that it is like a recreation home.

When a new detainee arrives, he knows he is going to learn the truth and is very nervous and upset. He tries to hide his insecurity and anxiety in many ways—he fiddles with his buttons, looks around, stands awkwardly, and answers questions quickly and briefly in the gate office where he is first interviewed.

Others are equally nervous but are better able to hide it. They react distractedly or querulously, complain that they have not been well handled in jail and that the staff has not taken good care of their belongings, or they behave very rudely just to show off. Because of these diverse reactions, reception should never be a routine. The newcomer must be received in accordance with his own behavior but always in a peaceful, friendly, and correct way. The lieutenant of the guard presents himself to the new man, shakes his hand, and says "Hello." The quarrelsome ones get little fun out of their behavior because the lieutenant pays slight attention to their rudeness. Occasionally a man arrives handcuffed, either because of the seriousness of the crime he committed or because of his aggressive behavior in court or in jail. We have not used handcuffs in the institution for many years, and the officer in charge of the admission process may use this situation in a therapeutic way.

One of the lieutenants once told me how he said in a very sad voice to an officer bringing a new man in in handcuffs. "If you have a key to these things, I would like to have them taken off." Then he added, "We don't like them here." Behind the walls it was safe to trust this anxiety-ridden man who was not aware of the overtones in the lieutenant's remarks. He peacefully followed the officer to the isolation section and never caused any trouble in our institution.

Usually a newcomer goes to the ordinary reception section. Whatever articles he brings with him—tobacco, cigarettes, coffee, a reasonable amount of sugar and fruit, a lighter, and toilet articles— are inspected and he is allowed to bring them with him to his room. If he has been with us before, he may try to bring more than can be allowed, hoping to have enough to sell to comrades.

A man returning to Herstedvester is often more difficult to handle at the entrance than a new man. He may feel hurt by meeting officers he knew before and whom he probably assured that he would never come back. In such cases the procedure must be more formal; sometimes it is even wrong to shake hands. Most newcomers, however, like to be greeted in a friendly fashion and by their own names— certainly never by numbers.

In the reception unit the newcomer receives his uniform, eating utensils, bedding, and a copy of the rules of the institution. The senior officer—the sergeant in charge of the house where he will live— discusses the application of these rules and advises the newcomer about his future relations with personnel and fellow detainees. The officer also tells him where he can go for help with his problems.

It is important to make use of the new man's heightened receptivity during these difficult first days, and several staff members have long talks with him. On the first day the newcomer sees the doctor, who gives him a physical examination and interviews him. The doctor reports his observations the next morning at the daily conference. These supplement the impressions of the reception unit staff which are recorded in a diary.

For many years the staffs of each house and the reception unit have kept a diary. In it the ward officers record anything peculiar that happens in the ward, good or bad. The diaries are collected during each day's visit of the doctor in charge, the chief nurse, and a lieutenant and are read at the daily conference of supervisory staff members. Summaries of notes in the diaries and other comments are entered in the detainees' case records by the therapists.

During the first weeks the detainee is assigned to a therapist (either a psychiatrist or psychologist) who begins treatment by writing a chronological description of the detainee's life. Because this will form the basis of the detainee's treatment throughout his stay in Herstedvester, much time is spent to make it as accurate as possible. The therapist explores formal records with the detainee—records from juvenile institutions and prisons, court reports, and all social and psychiatric reports. The detainee is encouraged to explain fully, refute, or enlarge upon all that has been written about him. In the process, he may gain insight into his patterns of behavior. The most important result of writing this life-story is that the inmate receives the impression that we really intend to form our own opinions about him. We also evaluate his intellectual and scholastic levels and analyze his preferences among his correspondents and visitors so as to determine which ones we can permit him to keep.

In the institution's rules there are certain limits on the detainee's rights to send letters because of our obligation to society to keep him from escaping. The number of letters is seldom limited in practice, but the requirement that the detainee pay for postage and stationery for his letters to his family makes a natural limit. All letters are censored except those to the inmate's guardian, the Minister of Justice, and the Ombudsman. Those to the Minister of Justice or the Ombudsman are paid for by the state.

Sometimes during the first months of the detainee's stay we are able to make personal contact with some of his family who come to visit him. We advise the family not to make specific promises to the detainee. Although they may promise to write every day or on a special day in the week, or to visit each Sunday without fail, this may not always be possible. Several times we have seen a delayed letter or a missed visit produce panic reactions in an inmate.

The detainee may have up to three visitors every Sunday. It is amazing to see how faithfully some wives, fiancées, and mothers come, week after week. But it is also disturbing to observe how easily an inmate may develop a feeling of being insulted if a visitor fails only once to come. Such a break in a set routine can seriously interfere with the detainee's personal development. It is difficult for outsiders to understand that in a closed little world of an institution like ours there is an emotional distortion which causes small things to loom very large in the inmate's life. Outside, most small adversities are forgotten in a few days time, but this is not true in a closed institution.

At the end of four weeks the therapist prepares a report containing comments and formal statements from social workers, nurses, the school, and the workshop. It concludes with a preliminary diagnosis.

The word "diagnosis" should not be misinterpreted. At this early stage we do not consider it possible to make anything like a causal diagnosis. We aim at a preliminary evaluation of the development of the detainee from one point in his life career to the next[1] and try to correlate events and find some sort of continuity in them. Most important in this report is a short summary of the more important factors in the detainee's social and antisocial development, such as misuse of alcohol, special types of employment, use of spare time, and his attitude to institutions and authorities as observed until now.

In some cases it is desirable at this time to stimulate the inmate's interest in a social goal by indicating possible plans for his later life outside of Herstedvester. His consideration of a plan for treatment may encourage self-insight. Any plan should be tentative. Neither plan nor prognosis should be definitive because there are too many possibilities for mistakes in observation and description. We must remember that, especially in this early stage, our situation of authority in relation to the inmate makes it difficult for us to understand what he really wishes to express, and our knowledge of former events in his life is likely to influence our observations.

Subjective elements are evident not only in the daily evaluations and observations that appear in the case history but also in psychological tests. A detailed diagnostic statement that someone is a certain type of man, and that we believe that he will behave in a given way, may well prove to be self-fulfilling prophecy.

The summary of the detainee's personal development should not contain words that will be humiliating to him; it will be read to him, and he should be able to accept it as a fair description of the course of his life. We presume that the detainee's pattern of criminal behavior, as we observe it, can be described as some type of defense. It is important to stress such symptoms and their probable causes, including the detainee's reactions to court procedures, to his family's reactions to him, to newspaper reports about his crime, and his relationships to friends and employers.

Many inmates have emphasized that they have no inferiority complex but that they actually are inferior, second-class individuals. As a result, we must take into consideration in our treatment the more general problems caused by poverty and the lack of human contact which often accompanies poverty.

[1] Erik Hoeck-Gradenwitz, "Maturity and Life Stages," *Acta Psychiatrica,* 33 (1958):452–70.

In this first evaluation we should not forget that sometimes there is some special pattern which has characterized this detainee's criminal career.

To avoid too much distortion, it is important to discuss problems with the detainee before other inmates do. As early as possible he should, in therapeutic situations, express his own understanding of essential elements in his criminal career such as what he and others expected him to become and how he regards his different criminal situations. The presence of these factors in the summary indicates that the inmate has attempted to make deeper going contact with another person. This helps him to develop realistic mechanisms to approach his future life in a new way.

ORIENTATION

I have always attempted to explain to every newcomer myself how I—and I hope most of the staff—regard the institution and to explain Herstedvester's goals to him. In this way I hope to help him to profit from the time he has to spend with us. In order to help the newcomer learn to express himself in a group and not regard the authorities as too remote, I present this orientation in group meetings that are held in the reception unit and are attended by five or six newcomers together with the chief nurse and the ward officer. This allows the staff to know what information the detainees have received. In these meetings it is always stated openly that the main object of the institution is to give society reasonable protection against possible future crimes committed by the detainees and that within this limitation lies the possibilty for treatment. Because they are uncertain, newcomers are frequently aggressive in the first meeting, making derogatory comments about Herstedvester or claiming that they have been promised special treatment, such as a short detention period. When pressed to elaborate on such promises they fumble and have to admit that no promises were really made. By giving clear answers to all questions and carefully describing what Herstedvester is, I am able to calm the detainees' uncertainties; by the next meeting their aggressive attitudes are usually overcome and there is a relaxed atmosphere. Because these introductory talks cover many of the practical approaches of the institution, the following condensed version of what I say may help the reader to understand how everything we do is integrated into the total treatment.

First Orientation Meeting

I begin by saying, "Everyone attending the meeting has now obtained a preliminary impression of what detention means. All of you have been sentenced according to Sections 17 and 70 of the Criminal Code. In a few cases Section 16 has been used."

We discuss the contents of these sections,[2] and I continue, "Detention is a serious measure. The court has been convinced that you are no longer fit for punishment and that something else has to be done for the protection of society. You have had an opportunity to see our rules concerning the aims of the institution.

"It is obviously uncomfortable to be officially classified as a person with 'more permanent psychological disturbances,' but I call your attention to the phrasing. The law doesn't say 'permanent' but 'more permanent,' meaning that the disturbance is less than permanent but something more than short. Despair following a breakup with your girl friend is usually of short duration, yet it may be termed a psychological disturbance. How much is needed before a psychological disturbance is 'more permanent' is decided by the court. Medical advice is sought and is evaluated in relation to all relevant circumstances before the court makes a final decision.

"The word 'psychopath' is not used in the Penal Law, nor (since 1960) in the name of the institution. From a practical point of view we can say that the personality or character of the people sent here has not been sufficiently developed to meet the demands of their lives in recent years. It is supposed that, given your circumstances, you were not able to avoid conflict with the law, not that you cannot be a law-abiding citizen in the future.

"All of you have been medically and psychiatrically examined, and in all cases the results have been evaluated by the Medico-Legal Council. These experienced psychiatrists have found instabilities in your personality structures such as spinelessness, self-assertion, and unfounded optimism. The opinion of the Medico-Legal Council states that you fit the description of Section 17 of the Criminal Code. If such personality elements were found in the beginning of someone's criminal career, the doctor and the Medico-Legal Council may have added that they don't feel convinced that the deviation as related to the total situation was sufficient to call the person 'not fit for punishment.' This caution is often misunderstood. It may be seen

2 See Appendix A.

as a warning, indicating that the person's future career may be either good or bad. In some cases, as in yours, the Medico-Legal Council has qualified their opinion; your crimes have been so severe or have followed one another in such quick succession, or the characteristics of your personality have proven to be so constant, that it is no longer possible to expect ordinary measures to help. This means that the court may say, 'Now we have come to the end of the road.' Your indeterminate sentence means that the court wanted to postpone a decision as to when they will let you resume your existence outside the institution. I know that the most important question for you is 'When and how can I get out again?' However, only the court can decide concerning any change in the security measures now used.

"In Section 70 of the Criminal Code there is a long list of the measures which can be taken regarding people sentenced under Section 17. The offender can be put under supervision, ordered to live in a specific place, required to work in a specific place, and so on. Section 70 also has a list of different types of institutions which ends with a special institution—ours.

"What we call parole is really an application of the less rigorous measures mentioned in the first part of Section 70. A decision to parole an inmate is made by a judge sitting alone, without a jury.

"Each of you has assigned to you a special guardian who has the privilege of asking the court to consider your case for parole. He will know what is happening to you, and, if he thinks that we are keeping you too long, he may bring your case before the court on his own initiative. He has no supervisory responsibility for your behavior. He has the right to bring your case before the court if he thinks it is fully justified and to take action concerning your final discharge. If the special guardian's request is refused, he cannot request your discharge again for one year, or, in special circumstances, for six months. I *can* bring your case before the court at any time I think the risk of your committing new crime has lessened, and I *must* take action when I feel that detention is no longer necessary.

"The same is true for the Attorney General, but, as you well know, he acts on his own infrequently. Sometimes a detainee mistakenly believes the Attorney General is taking action. If a detainee writes to the Minister of Justice to ask for action, the routine answer will be that this is outside his province but that he has forwarded your request to the Attorney General. In some of these cases the Attorney General will request a report from Herstedvester. Using this

information, he decides whether he wishes to take action before the
court. As you can see, your answer from the Minister of Justice is
no guarantee that the Attorney General will take action.

"After the court has decided you should be paroled, you may be
released as soon as you find suitable work and lodgings with the
condition that you must not change these without the prior agreement
of your social aide. If you lose your work or lodging, it is possible for
your supervisor to order you to stay at a reception home or similar
institution until you find other acceptable work and lodging. We will
not discourage you from changing jobs and lodging if you can convince
us that the new ones are suitable. During parole, you must follow the
recommendations of your supervisor, and you must commit no new
crime. If you do not follow these conditions, you may be returned
to Herstedvester.

"It may seem hard on you, but we try to use our powers in a
sensible way. The reason for these regulations is the same as for
your stay inside the walls—that we must work together to plan your
future so as to limit the risk of your committing crimes again. You,
yourself, have to make a personal contribution if you want to avoid
new crime, and we believe that there is really a good prospect that you
may succeed if you work hard at it. You, yourself, must decide
whether your chances of returning to Herstedvester will be large or
small. You also have the right to decide that you prefer to stay on
here. A few have done this but usually for only a short period of
time.

"We have 170 detainees in Herstedvester and about the same number in Horsens [our sister institution in Jutland]. Of about 1,600
former inmates, more than 1,200 are outside the institution on parole
or finally discharged. About 30 or 40 have been in mental hospitals
for a long time and have been transferred to the jurisdiction of the
hospitals.

"Roughly speaking, half of a parole group return after they have
been paroled the first time. Half of this group return once more after
a second detention period, usually shorter than the first, and a second
parole. Thus it continues until, after ten years, we have approximately
10 per cent of the original parole group left in the institution. I do
not know whether this information will be of any use to you or
whether the results will be the same in the future. I hope they will be
better. I would especially like to foresee which of you will return, but
I have no way of looking into the future.

"We have had two detainees who escaped and did not come back. One died in the Spanish Civil War. The other received a long prison sentence in Berlin during World War II, and we assume that he was killed in a prison destroyed when the Russians entered Berlin. The rest of those who escaped returned, willingly or unwillingly, and their escapes resulted in a temporary limitation of privileges.

"I understand clearly that it is human to attempt to escape and that it is difficult to accept reasons for not doing so. However, the fact that all but two of those who have escaped have been returned should persuade you to find other solutions to situations in which you are under pressure and think that escape is the only answer. Sometimes you can discuss your immediate problems with persons in whom you have confidence; I hope you will find such people among our experienced staff here.

"When inmates are paroled, they usually do not plan to commit new crimes. They have been paroled because they convinced us that they would be able, with reasonable support from our social section, to avoid crime, and the inmates and we, together, have convinced the court that parole was worth trying.

"It would be simple if in my recommendation to the court I could say that parole is, or is not, advisable with a clear 'yes' or 'no.' However, I have to use the facts you give to me. It helps if there is reasonable consistency between what you say and what you do, and between your earlier explanations and later ones. If you do not provide this, it is difficult to trust you, and we must try to understand why you are inconsistent. In my recommendation I describe the things you have told us and your behavior as we have observed them.

"You shouldn't have any illusions that your life after parole will be very much easier than before. I believe that it will be more difficult for you to live without committing new crimes than it was to live as you did before. In any case it will be just as difficult as life in Herstedvester.

"To help you make an easier transition from institutional life to life on parole we have established a free unit, called 'the Hut,' within the institution. We expect the group living there to be responsible for themselves to a much higher degree than in the general units. We also have an open unit, Kastanienborg, located in Avedöre, halfway between here and Copenhagen. Many of you will be transferred there in the later part of your detention period. If nothing special is said to you about the probable length of your stay out there, you may be assured that, if everything goes well, we will go to the court to suggest your parole between three and six months after your transfer. In the few cases for which we foresee a longer detention period in the open section, we clearly discuss the matter with the inmate before his transfer takes place.

"In this open section there are many privileges. In your spare time you may use all the areas of the institution and on Sundays, your friends and family may visit you and you may go to church, to the cinema, or take a walking trip. All activities pursued outside the institution are done in groups with a staff member.

"All this may seem good, or it may be burdensome. It is difficult to live in such free conditions while waiting for your case to be sent to the court. The waiting may seem especially oppressive if you succeed in convincing your guardian to present your case to the court before we can clearly advocate your parole.

"In some cases where we have clearly discouraged parole and the Medico-Legal Council and prosecution have agreed with us, the court has gone ahead and ordered parole. Nearly all who received this type of parole got into such difficulties that they quickly succumbed to the temptation to commit new crime and were returned to Herstedvester. Of course we tried to help them but their bad luck can only confirm our skill at evaluation.

"You should remember that we have a genuine interest in making your detention period short and your time outside as long as possible. But we also try to make the detention period long enough so that few inmates will get into trouble again. In most cases the court will follow our suggestions for or against parole, but there are some exceptions. In the so-called big cases which reach the front pages of the newspapers, the courts are not very eager to agree when we propose an early parole.

"Let me tell you how we decide that a man can now manage on parole and that we should take his case to the court. Some detainees believe that if they turn up at the therapist's office often enough to tell us how happy they are here, we will soon be convinced that they are miraculously changed. Some of them really believe that we are foolish enough to be influenced by all these nice words. It is possible that now and then we are taken in, but we are aware of the problem and should we forget it, you may be sure that some of your comrades will call it to our attention; pure envy will guarantee that. Your words are not always as important as the way they are said, and professional ears may hear how much or how little truth there is in what you say.

"We will work together to analyze and understand what went wrong in your life, why you committed your crimes, why they took the particular form they did, and so forth. After such an analysis it may be possible to build realistic plans for your future. I believe that it is impossible for you to change so that you will have no criminal impulses under any circumstances. Many ordinary people have such impulses but don't follow them. If you feel an impulse to commit a criminal act but do not carry it out, I am satisfied. It is what you do that counts. In order to understand your criminal situations you must realize first of all that it is not all your fault or all the fault of the societal system that you were unable to manage your life without committing crime, but that there was a combination of many factors.

"We will help you to analyze your personal relations to your surroundings as they are, have been, and will be, and to learn to live a life without crime, but daily living and planning your future are your own problems. Our duty is to analyze your plans critically and to see if they are just day-dreams. We know that you are alone in the decisive moments of your life but we hope that we can convince you to call for help when you are in a dangerous situation, in time to keep from committing a new crime.

"Some detainees think that I, as superintendent, should manage the problems of all the detainees myself, but unfortunately I cannot do all the work myself. So please go to your therapist with your problems and analyze them together with him or her. If you and the therapist have some special problems, or you have a criticism of the institution, you may discuss it with me.

"Please remember that all of us usually react basically the same way in so-called small situations as in serious ones. Most of us use a limited number of procedures for solving our daily problems. These methods can be used with greater or lesser care, and often we do not see the similarities in the pattern. Here in Herstedvester you may get valuable help from your therapist and learn by trial and error to find better ways to cope with your difficulties in daily life than the ones you used before."

This first orientation usually closes with a discussion of sexual criminals.

Second Orientation Meeting

In the second meeting there are usually more questions than at the first one, and the sequence of content therefore varies from meeting to meeting. We usually mention that there are other difficult problems besides sexual ones, such as massive loneliness or failure to believe that it is possible to live a crime-free life after detention. This leads me to further explanation:

"Experience shows that many people have been able to manage these difficulties, but it is wise to be prepared to meet problems and disappointments along the way. These shouldn't force anyone to lose initiative, either here in the institution or while on parole. The important thing is to learn to use the opportunities that come to you and to master your problems slowly, step by step. Some former detainees strive to get on too fast. It is as if they try to climb a steep ramp without realizing that for a former detainee the ramp is greased and slippery. They will have to slant the ramp less steeply if they want to avoid slipping and hurting themselves. No one should give up hope entirely, but some of one's biggest goals should perhaps be postponed, and one should try to be satisfied with smaller ones at first.

"I repeat that many people like you have found it possible to live a satisfactory social life. It is probable, of course, that you will have to overcome the same kinds of difficulties, time after time. Some you may create yourself by your own behavior. Hans Christian Andersen has called attention to this, and to the necessity of not running from oneself, in several stories. Both in social life and in marital relations you can count on receiving benefits only in proportion to what you give of yourself.

"You will have a chance to go through your life-story and correct what has been said about you. If someone has wrongly or rightly said that you are lazy, it is important that we hear your own explanation of the situation. Why was this said then? Why not sooner or later? We are willing to believe what can be proven and to question what doesn't fit with our own observations of you. That's why we also try to discover whether you are suffering from any diseases which could be cured or made less troublesome.

"Our workshops are not as good as those in some of the older prisons, as most of you know very well. When Herstedvester was built it was wrongly supposed that we would not need larger ones.

"We may give you the opportunity to do stupid things more frequently than you are used to in prisons. For example, we know that some of you use card games for gambling but we haven't stopped card playing in general. I should mention that the staff has a daily conference in which we spend about one hour discussing information from the different units concerning what you do in your spare time as well as what happens during your working hours. We pay attention to any of you who apparently intend to win a great deal at playing cards as well as to others who are prepared to manage their economic problems in a more reasonable, or perhaps we should say, "socially acceptable," way. Occasionally we prohibit individuals from playing cards.

"The specialized treatment staff members are not snooping when they try to coordinate observations about your daily life in the workshops and the wards with our own observations. This is done to try to find an inner continuity in your way of reacting to varied situations rather than to annoy you. Let us take some examples: a person may take out a disappointment on someone around him: at home, on his closest family; here, on comrades or staff. Sometimes one is having difficulties—a visit has gone badly, a letter hasn't arrived, and so forth—and the next day his irritation may result in his destroying his own belongings, provoking a conflict with an innocent bystander, or having a serious argument with a staff member. In such situations we are not free to do whatever we like. We must consider the other people living in the institution and, of course, the people living outside. To make living together easier, we must ask you to obey the rules of the house.

"When you do not follow the rules, we may sometimes just tell you to be more careful. In other cases we must keep you isolated from the others as long as there is any reason to believe that you cannot comply. We do this in spite of the fact that we know very well that you live under great pressure here. But you must learn that pressure will also exist after you leave us.

"Often one of you tells me that someone has promised you one thing or another, perhaps that court action should be taken in your case or that you should have this or that opportunity in the workshops, and so forth. It should be quite clear that we cannot promise you anything about when you are going to be paroled. We may decide at some time that your condition has improved and we can advocate parole, but the decision must be made by the court.

"Whether or not an inmate should be transferred from one ward to another will usually be discussed in the daily staff conference, and some information may turn up which would make the proposed transfer impossible. Therefore a single member of the conference cannot promise you a transfer. If a staff member wants to promise you anything and believes he can produce it, he has to enter it in your case history. If there is a promise in the case history, we will try to keep it; if it is not recorded there, I don't recognize it.

"Newspaper accounts are sometimes used as proof of inequality in the way society handles criminals, but you cannot rely upon the accuracy of the reporters' information. They are not skilled in criminology, and they may not even know the difference between imprisonment and detention. Detention is still a new thing—still rather mysterious—and that may be why a spectacular relapse is more often reported as related to detention than to imprisonment. Headlines are especially guilty of giving wrong impressions.

"Some years ago several newspapers mentioned a man who had committed a serious sexual crime in a forest just north of Copenhagen. They inferred from the court hearing that he had been in detention. One of the papers reported questions and answers that indicated that he had been paroled from Herstedvester. In fact, he had never been in an institution on this island, and certainly he had never been in detention. He had been in a prison outside Zealand for some minor property crimes, but he had never before committed any sexual attack. When I complained about the misinformation to the director of these newspapers, he told me that the information came from a usually reliable informant, but that they would be more careful in the future. This case hit the front page and that was why I took action. Most of the newspapers' mistakes are more difficult to catch.

"It is not always easy to decide what we ought to count as a successful or unsuccessful result of our work. We are happy to know that very few serious criminals have committed serious crimes after they left Herstedvester. If one of our 'big boys' does not succeed socially for some time, he may ask to enter our open institution, Kastanienborg, to get a fresh start. I believe that our treatment can be considered successful even if a former inmate commits a rather unimportant property crime instead of a serious one. I have used the big cases as an example because the very good results we have obtained in these cases indicate that it isn't correct to say that a long stay in Herstedvester is always dangerous.

"Sometimes detainees try to explain to me that if they are kept longer it will be more difficult for them when they get out. I mention this now because the question does not apply to any of you at this moment, and not one of you needs to think that I'm talking about you. This is my general point of view. But when I say this, I should also mention that relapse, meaning a new sentence for a new crime, will almost always result in returning to Herstedvester."

We often discuss drifting from workshop to workshop as well as the difference between the earning capacities of those who work in workshops and those who work in their rooms. I tell the newcomers that "If men working in their rooms sometimes earn more than the men in workshops, it may be because they work more than eight hours a day. We do not always think it right for a man to overload himself with work. We regret that our workshops are not big enough to accommodate everyone and that some of you will have to work in your rooms. We once hoped to get some more modern workshops and to have a greater variety of work, and may get them yet.

"You are all aware of the statement in the marriage law that a person who is a psychopath to a 'higher degree' mustn't marry without obtaining a special permit. The purpose of this law is to insure that the partner be informed of the history and condition of the person she intends to marry. We try to inform the future partner of this in the presence of the detainee, but suggest that you inform her yourself first. We do this because we believe that honesty is the primary condition for a good marriage.

"We cannot help it that sometimes a fiancée talks to the social aide alone. She may tell him that she has become interested in someone else but doesn't dare to tell you. If, after she has talked with the social aide or the doctor, she informs you that she wants to break up with you, you may think we are responsible for destroying the relationship. We don't always feel it is right for us to say more about her motives than she wanted to say herself, but we really think that, if a fiancée wants to break off a relationship, she should do it while you are here and not after you are paroled. We have observed too often the enormous difficulties a man meets when he comes home and suddenly realizes that another man has been in his place and has moved out only temporarily.

"You need to know about six-hour leaves. The rules state that you may obtain permission to go on six-hour leaves after twelve months of good behavior. A sentence for a severe crime may raise the limit to three years. To be placed in the open section, Kastanienborg, you must be eligible for six-hour leaves or be a castrate. In exceptional cases, we may transfer people to the open section before permission for six-hour leaves has been granted."[3]

Long discussions of the six-hour leaves and the open section usually close the second orientation meeting.

DAILY LIFE

Development of the Integration Concept

The primary objective of Herstedvester is to protect society against the disturbances of peace and order which the inmates supposedly would create if they were living in free society. Within these limits the secondary aim is to influence the detainees in such a way that they will be better able to live a crime-free life in free society. This means that we must motivate the inmates to attempt to develop an acceptable way of social living. The more weight we give to the first of our purposes, protection of society, the easier our job is. The more weight we give to the second, resocialization, the more we need to individualize our treatment and the less satisfied we can be with simply providing a peaceful life inside walls. Somehow we have to create a reasonable balance between what suits the individual and what suits the group. This makes daily life more complicated for both staff and inmates.

The demand for security is more or less absolute. The demand for treatment calls for an evaluation of which factors increase or diminish the risk of new crime. In planning the inmate's daily life, even when we consider individual variations, our main purpose is not to have in mind a final psychiatric personality diagnosis but to have a clear impression of the latent possibilities which may be stimulated by the inmate's situations in the institution.

When I arrived at Herstedvester with no knowledge of penological problems and no burden of prejudices about methods of control, what impressed me most was the anxious tenseness evident in the interpersonal relations of most of the inmates and staff. I would have to learn many things and my closest colleagues would obviously be my teachers.

We formed a council consisting of the supervisors: an academically trained man in charge of social aid, the business manager, the captain, the nurse, and myself. We met daily and talked about how to answer

<hr/>

[3] For further description of six-hour leaves, see page 61. For more about Kastanienborg, see pages 108 and 192.

letters that came to the institution and letters from inmates to the staff. We also discussed all that had happened in the institution since the previous meeting. I made no decisions about problems before bringing them up in this group. The members' steady correction of my psychiatric point of view resulted in a swiftly diminishing interest in the final diagnosis. As I was the only psychiatrist, it would have been useless to concentrate my limited psychiatric resources on diagnostic considerations even though, according to the usual psychiatric point of view, these should have made the most demand on me. Here we had a clientele of chronic criminals, all of whom were supposed to be hopeless. Those for whom we did not dare to suggest parole stayed before our eyes and became the most serious challenge to our abilities. They were constantly there to remind us that we had evaluated them as so dangerous to society that their parole was not defensible. This emphasized not only their insufficiency but also ours. While I was influenced by my staff, they were influenced by my dynamic point of view, and we realize more and more clearly the relationship between "our" attitudes and those of the detainees.

It soon became obvious that we had to place our charges under as much social strain as they could stand so that they could have an opportunity to learn their own limits. This treatment is quite different from that which is needed in a general mental hospital where the emphasis is placed on lessening stress and strain. The psychopath placed there is normally in the minority within the larger group of psychotics. In hospitals one is accustomed to seeing a psychopath's pattern of reaction repeat itself. We are forced to try to find some way to influence a psychopathic inmate to give up the acting-out pattern or to modify it so that it will be acceptable in some circumstances or situations. In hospitals these patients are often considered burdensome, and they are dismissed with a light heart when they want to leave. But we must keep our charges as long as they make trouble or there is any reasonable risk that they would be really troublesome for society at large when paroled.

Here we meet some important difficulties. The daily life of a detainee in Herstedvester is much different from the daily life he will have to live in society. We have to infer from difficulties we observed here what difficulties he will meet in very different situations outside the institution. If he has conflicts later, we must ask ourselves what part we played, what influence the institutional situation exerted, and especially what effect his relationships to other inmates or staff had in developing his behavior.

Staff Meetings

As I have said, the daily staff meeting consisted of only five persons in the beginning. Now a minimum of twenty to twenty-five persons participate: five doctors, four psychologists, three teachers, the chief nurse, sometimes one of the two other nurses, representatives from the social section, the deputy warden, the captain, some of the lieutenants, the business manager, some workshop leaders, young people in training for psychological or social work, and guests. The meeting is still held in my office, which is now very crowded.

These meetings, which still are the heart of the institution's life, have encouraged collaboration between academically and practically trained staff members. We all try to learn about whatever happens in the institution and to use it for treatment purposes. The daily meeting makes it neccessary for the larger group of variously trained supervisory staff to understand all the different kinds of technical language used. We need to support each other and learn what difficulties confront the nonacademic as well as the academic collaborators.

It is impossible for every staff member to be at the daily conferences, but the captain and the lieutenants do come and become fully informed about every aspect of life and problems in the institution. They learn why each decision has been made, and it is their job to make sure that staff members who could not attend get the necessary information.

We start each meeting with a discussion of the daily mail. Then the doctor, who has visited the different wards with the chief nurse and one of the lieutenants, reads what is written in the daybooks collected from the houses. In some cases, decisions on questions raised in the daybooks are made on the spot. In others, decisions are postponed until further information is obtained. Because of the mixed participation, tension between people with disciplinary and treatment points of view is brought into the open. Interestingly enough, members of the conferences are not at all consistent in supporting one or the other of these attitudes. A therapist may hold a disciplinary point of view or a uniformed staff member may defend clear, therapeutical considerations. Their positions depend on a series of sometimes incomprehensible circumstances related to how the questions are raised. Sometimes there is a temptation to make a quick and clear decision, especially when an inmate's problem is seemingly commonplace, but in many cases it is important to allow time for abreaction.

Our consideration of Christian's difficulties is typical. He had created a long series of problems while working in free society and still living in the institution. The question of his parole was awaiting a court decision, and it was expected that parole would be granted in about a month. Day after day we had discussed whether or not this man had pressed his "rights" too far. He had complained that he had not received his pay for outside work in accordance with the going rate, but a thorough investigation proved that he had received the proper amount, in accordance with union rules. At the same time, however, it was found that he had been absent from work one day, several months before. The staff agreed that this infringement of regulations was too serious to be overlooked and that something had to be done. When we had nearly decided to bring the problem to his attention, someone voiced indecision. This was an old situation and the value of making a decision on the issue of rule-breaking at this stage was doubtful. Would it not be worse if we took disciplinary action which would mean stopping Christian's outside work? We discussed whether or not he would keep his job when paroled; his general laziness was well-known and many thought he would not, but no one dared to exclude the possibility that he would. If we broke his relations with the factory, he would think it was our fault if he lost a job which he had worked at for longer than usual and with which he seemed satisfied.

I decided that we should defer a decision until the following day when we might be less emotional and more objective. In this case, as in many others, we agreed that we should wait and see what would happen in the future. Christian managed without further known trouble, was paroled, and has avoided crime for a rather long time.

Once a week, on Tuesday, the daily conference is expanded, and the warden and the chaplain participate. In this meeting, which usually lasts about three hours, we systematically review our periodic reports. The first basic evaluation of an inmate is made one month after he arrives, and he is re-evaluated every six months. The therapist collects information from the wards, the workshops, the nurses, the school, the social section, and the letter control. This, combined with his own observations, gives him the background to brief the whole group on a particular case. We have considered supplementing these reports with small group discussions among representatives of different sections who have daily contact with each man, but this would consume a great deal of the therapists' time and is not yet done on a regular basis.

We also discuss drafts of recommendations to the court concerning parole and to the state's attorney concerning six-hour leaves. These discussions may take a long time and usually end with some sort of group vote, which is usually included in my own formal recommendation. The draft is prepared by the therapist after he discusses his opinion with representatives of the unit where the man lives, the workshop, the social section, his escort on six-hour leaves, and the nurse. Such "pre-meetings" are merely informative, not decision-making, and the results are entered in the case histories.

The Tuesday staff meeting ends with the usual daily conference. Every week two younger representatives of the ordinary officers are invited to attend so that they can observe what really happens in the daily conferences.

Every Monday afternoon there is a training session based on cases with which the personnel work and in which they are interested. This began as an open-house meeting for staff who wanted to hear what had happened during the previous week or who had questions. The idea of the open-house grew out of criticism from the personnel that nothing was done when they reported something about a detainee. We decided to go through every report for anyone who wanted to attend and invite critiques of decisions. After a few years the interest in these reports diminished, as did the general staff's more stereotyped demand for fixed disciplinary punishment.

On Wednesdays, the administrator and the captain meet with the sergeants and lieutenants for a discussion of practical daily problems and plans for the institution which might affect work in the wards.

Staff Training and Integration of Work

In addition to training on the job and in meetings, more formal training is offered by psychologists and doctors. This is most effective when carried out in groups whose discussions are based on actual institutional problems or on case histories which have been followed for many years. Such discussion groups obtain the best results when each meeting is reported by the participants, one after the other, and the report distributed to the other participants. This form of reporting is especially important when the group is a mixture of academically and nonacademically trained people because it presents an opportunity to control the specialized viewpoint of each member. It has often been possible for the staff to obtain a "we" feeling and share information on how the lives of the inmates are progressing. This form of training has been used adequately until now, but it must be expanded to follow the lead of business and interest the personnel and give them a stimulating role in the functions of the institution.

The personal characteristics of the staff influence training methods. I think we must not employ people with prejudices—those who are unfriendly or directly hostile to people who belong to a particular group. Strongly opinionated persons usually have prejudices against criminals that make it difficult for them to participate in our treatment work. This work is burdensome and in some cases may intensify a new staff member's feeling of insecurity because he will constantly ask himself, "Was I right in this situation?" Some years in the work usually result in a feeling of being of value to the community and a personal involvement which makes the work mean more to the employee than just collecting a salary. We all share happiness and responsibility when one of our parolees succeeds, especially if his chances were small. Our Monday staff meeting includes reports of our successes.

It is probably impossible to avoid prejudice completely, but it seems that any of the staff who have had prejudices against criminals have found that they wore away. Living together breaks down the staff's prejudices against criminals as well as those of the inmates against authorities. The personnel for whom this is not true leave us for other work.

The Ward Officer

It is very important that the ward officer be well-trained. He is the first person to observe when a man stops work, complains about something, is impatient, and so forth. He must have a reasonable knowledge of welfare regulations and penal law. He does not have to give legal advice, but he should know at least as much about the Danish legal system as the inmates, many of whom have had long criminal careers and therefore a good deal of experience with the law. He must also know enough about social work and the principles of day-to-day treatment to advise his charges responsibly. He must be able to explain the therapist's answers to an inmate's questions or encourage him to ask further questions if he did not understand the first time. Like most people, many inmates do not like to admit that they need further clarification when something has already been explained once.

The ward officer must also take care of security problems and be involved in the daily life of his group. If he is just and reliable, the detainees will respect him. There may be momentary disturbances, and someone may think that a decision is not fair, but, if the ward officer acts quietly and calmly, such differences of opinion will usually not leave permanent marks. The ward officer is better situated than any other staff member to recommend to an inmate that he discuss a serious problem with his therapist, and his description of what is going on outside of formal therapeutical situations may be of the utmost value for evaluating what the therapist observes.

A successful ward officer seems to be able to subdue the asocial atmosphere which often develops around chronic criminals who have grown up in other institutions and are proud to be able to "take it." Because they often look upon society as their enemy, they are apt to try to be the center of a group which does not dare do anything but admire their asocial stand. It is not uncommon to see this type of inmate change his attitude completely, first in relation to one officer, then to authorities in general.

THE WARD

In each ward two staff officers are in charge on a shift basis so that each officer serves during the first half of the day on one day and the other half the next day, alternating with his colleague. In this way they both become well acquainted with their group of inmates and the inmates with them.

A sergeant is in charge of each house and its four ward officers. The sergeant would like to have the freedom to make such small decisions as how to move the detainees around inside the house. But if the integration of everything that happens in the institution is to succeed, even these small decisions must be based on discussions with the therapists and other practitioners intimately acquainted with the personality problems of the individual detainees. Thus such small actions are usually discussed at the daily conferences where the staff constantly weigh the interests of the inmate, the unit, the house, the institution, and society.

If each man's daily life is to have a positive value, a number of common interests must be attended to. Of importance to the individual detainee is the room in which he has to stay and where he can be alone, devote himself to his own interests, and lick his wounds. The group with whom he will have to spend his working hours and spare time is also important. He wants to live in peace with his comrades and therefore is willing to have reasonable but not authoritarian, prisonlike discipline. He prefers, of his own will, to share in maintaining peace and order in the ward. It is of great value to cultivate the interplay between each inmate in the ward and the ward officers. To achieve this, the officers must be flexible but not compliant. A ward officer must be competent to make decisions in crises. This means that, if necessary, he must act firmly to keep peace and order in his unit in order to break up quarrels before they develop into fights. In such cases he has the right to direct a man to stay in his room alone until further notice. (In other words, the ward officer has the power to isolate inmates.) He must then enter a description of what happened in the daybook, and, if more serious incidents occur, he must write a separate, full report to which he refers in his daybook note. When there are especially serious incidents, he may call for help from a colleague in a neighboring unit or from the sergeant of the house, and they may, after a serious disturbance, move a man to the isolation section. In such cases it is usually necessary to obtain assistance from the lieutenant's office so that the final decision to move a man to the isolation section is made by the lieutenant on duty.

The Inmate's Room

Because "domestic" surroundings greatly influence everyone's experiences of himself, it is important that each inmate's room can be furnished so that he has one place in the institution where he can set his personal mark on his environment and make a "home" where he will feel comfortable. An empty, narrow room with an open or closed toilet, or with iron bars dividing the cell from the corridor as if it were a zoo, arouses aggressive and vindictive thoughts and does not give the detainee any chance for real relaxation. It is also important to have a wash basin in each room so that inmates who are irritable in the morning can avoid early contact with their comrades.

Experience has shown that a maximum of fifteen rooms per unit, with one room empty, is most convenient. The empty room makes it possible to move a man from one unit to another without disrupting a settled man.

During leisure time the doors to the rooms are open so that the inmates can easily go to the toilets and showers, to the common room, to meetings with comrades, and so forth. This also provides opportunities for exchanging casual remarks with the ward officer and establishing a natural social contact with him.

An inmate in his room at Herstedvester.

Decorations in the rooms vary according to the interests of the inhabitants. Some detainees have furniture that they have made in their spare time, and many decorate their walls with art reproductions, travel posters, or pictures of pinup girls. We try to give as much freedom as possible in room decoration, but sometimes we have to help the personnel decide when the limit of decency is overstepped. Reproductions of certain works by recognized artists, such as a very popular Danish poster of a nude mother breast-feeding her child, will undoubtedly be allowed. But we have established a basic rule that external genitals or pubic hair must not be visible in the pictures on the wall—a rule that exists in order to have standards that can be practically enforced. Thus all the ordinary pictures of half-naked girls from the weeklies are allowed. We pay little attention to the fact that a lightly covered body is perhaps a greater sexual stimulant than full nakedness.

Pornography in a Closed Institution

Because we try to give our detainees many of the same freedoms that they had in free society, some staff members have advocated trying to limit censorship in the area of pornography. It has never been proven that crude descriptions of sexual behavior cause detectable harm in ordinary humans, and it is doubtful that general society profits by prohibitions on pornography that increase curiosity. The recent undermining of the old strict laws concerning pornography must, from a mental hygiene point of view, be considered an advantage to society in general. However, the situation is quite different in a closed institution where there are a great many insecure and anxiety-ridden persons with extraordinary sexual problems. Our setting restrains normal sexual activity. Experience has shown that long isolation without sexual stimulation diminishes sexual desire and the frequency of masturbation. However, there are some exceptions to this rule; if an inmate's sexual drive is accompanied by active sexual life which upsets him, we help to diminish it by giving him estrogen injections (5-10 milligrams weekly). This treatment is continued as long as the inmate wants it.

The purpose of pornographic and other erotic literature is sexual stimulation. It is my opinion that in a closed institution such as ours it is necessary to forbid detailed erotic literature, setting our limits without considering artistic value. We also forbid the reading of instructive descriptions of criminal patterns, but ordinary thrillers and mysteries present no risk.

Another argument against experimenting with further liberalization in these areas is the risk that a detainee who commits a sexual crime while on parole may attempt to arouse sympathy by claiming that he has been stimulated by pornographic material during his stay in detention.

An example of this is David, a chronic criminal who specialized in burglarizing vacation houses. He had been with us for some time and had received very intensive therapy. He was paroled and later apprehended for several small thefts. Because the police would not keep him in jail, he was placed in our open unit, Kastanienborg, at his own request. In the evening of the day he left Kastanienborg, he saw a woman on a lonely road, threatened her with a kitchen knife, raped her, and choked her.

His first excuse for the rape was that he felt sexually tense as he passed her on his bicycle. Later he explained that he had nurtured the idea of "doing something serious, something aggressive, against a woman," for some time and that this was the reason he left the open unit.

He was given a new mental examination and explained to the psychiatrist that the atmosphere in the detention institution was very erotic. He claimed that there was continuous talk about sexual relations and perversions so that, after some time, he became "somewhat curious." Dramatic newspaper coverage focused excessive public attention on these remarks.

David had never been brutal or aggressive before. He explained to the psychiatrist that he had never consciously, before or after the rape, had fantasies concerning aggressive acts. He did admit that he had been prone to tell stories but would not agree that he could be called a mythomaniac liar. There seemed to be a lack of confidence in his attitude toward sexuality and women.

He was returned to detention and admitted to us that what he had told the court about his experience in Herstedvester was untrue. Four months later it was noted that the officers had suspected for some time that he produced sadistic, pornographic drawings of sexual relations. When questioned, he admitted that he had produced many such drawings at the request of other detainees who specified the motifs and paid for the pictures. He insisted that he got no sexual satisfaction from the drawings. It seems that he began producing them after he was recognized by other inmates who had read in the newspaper accounts of his case that he was interested in pornography. This interest, which was not observed during his first period in Herstedvester, continued for several years and caused considerable conflict in relation to the female personnel to whom he sent anonymous dirty letters.

ASSIGNMENT OF WORK

It is not only important for a paroled inmate to obtain work, but also to keep it. Therefore training in work habits as well as in techniques is vital for the inmate's future. All inmates are required to work unless they are physically unable to do so, and this means that the institution is obliged to provide work for them.

When Herstedvester opened in 1935, it was supposed that only some of the inmates could be occupied in productive work. Therefore the workshops were planned on too small a scale and were ill-equipped. This caused great dissatisfaction among the staff and increased the inmates' irritability so that, after only two weeks, the furniture shop had to close because of continuous aggressive disturbances. This situation has improved, and disturbances in the workshops are rare.

We have workshops to do printing and bookbinding, and to produce furniture and paper objects such as boxes. We also have a group of so-called small trades such as the production of Christmas decorations, tobacco pouches, and assembling and packing small items for industrial firms. Outside the walls there are market gardening and some farming. All of these are fields which do not cause conflict with labor unions.[4]

Detainees are paid either by the day or by the piece; bonuses may be added for work on Sundays and after hours. We have a forty-five hour week and the daily pay (in 1966) is between 4.20 and 4.70 kroner (about one dollar in buying power). The highest bonus varies between 1.29 and 1.41 kroner per day. This type of reward is used most with detainees working for the institution.

On June 1, 1966, there were thirty-five inmates working for the main institution and eight for the open section, Kastanienborg. Half of these were working in the library and school or were employed in maintenance work or gardening. The other half cleaned the wards or worked in the storeroom. In 1966 there were eighty-one detainees working in the workshops, on farms, and in the market gardens. Fifty-four of these were employed by state institutions in the big workshops for furniture, printing, bookbinding, and paper work. The piece wage is usually between 5.31 and 7.14 kroner per day, and some men earn substantially more than others. On the day of the last survey, four men were employed outside the institution and nine were not working because of illness or disciplinary problems.

In the regular workshops, production is now at such a high level that we have established a therapeutically oriented occupational or sheltered shop for a small group of detainees, usually five or six, who cannot keep the pace set in other workshops. They are paid the same wages as the others.

At the open section, Kastanienborg, there are ample opportunities for overtime work because it is never filled to capacity with inmates

[4] We seldom have conflicts with unions or employers' organizations. The prison system has a joint board with representatives from the management of these organizations to help us in fixing reasonable prices and in getting adequate equipment.

and there is intensive market gardening. Daily wages are higher there than at Herstedvester—12 to 14 kroner per day.

One-third of the detainee's income must be saved for his parole period; one-third may be used freely for food, newspapers, cigarettes, stamps, books, and so forth; and the last third may be spent for durable goods such as new clothes, if this is agreed upon in the daily conference.

Selecting trades to follow in the institution has been very difficult at times. Employers and labor unions in private industry have often asked, "Why is our work, our type of trade, used in a prison?" Every year a larger proportion of those paroled will be employed in mechanical or industrial occupations. It is, therefore, very unfortunate that we have no real mechanical workshop in the institution and that our workshops are too small to employ all the inmates who would benefit by working in them.

For many years we have needed new workshops with adequate storage space. Having suitable storage would help us to keep production rates steady and thus maintain an even amount of available work as part of our treatment program. As it is now, the amount of work fluctuates directly with the demand for the product and this has resulted in substantial treatment difficulties.

Unfortunately, detainees trained as office workers or businessmen cannot always be suitably employed because we have found it impossible to give detainees jobs which would give them access to official information about fellow detainees. The workshop accounts would make suitable work for these people, but they have only recently been put under our direction. Previously all bookkeeping was done in the State Prison. A few intellectual or literary detainees have been employed to copy and index materials from one of the state archives.

The hours he spends working must be of real importance to the detainee so that he will feel that work is an acceptable part of his future re-socialization. It is not enough to guarantee him forty-five hours of any kind of work per week; the work must also not be too dull. On the other hand, one should not forget that we are dealing with a group of asthenic, flabby, and spineless people who are always tired and who are well-suited to routine work. Some of them are well satisfied with an assembly line routine—the more repetitious the better. Those of us who do not like such work should remember that others may find it advantageous to avoid taking a responsible attitude to the working process. Some want to avoid situations of selection and may love to perform some small function or task to perfection. This means that, from a treatment point of view, we must provide job opportunities which are as diverse as possible and have plenty of room in the workshops so that no one has to work in his room unless special therapeutical consideration calls for it.

We have had as many as twenty detainees working in their own rooms, and that is definitely too many. Some are oversensitive or noisy persons who must be protected against too intimate contact with other detainees. It would be advantageous to have cubicles where these people could work by themselves but still be a part of a workshop. This would allow the inmate to feel he was going to work, and it would also make it easier for us to find satisfactory work for those who need to work alone. As it is now, in assigning jobs that can be done in an inmate's room, we have to avoid anything which has an odor, is too dirty, or calls for regular professional instruction and control. We also have to avoid jobs requiring expensive materials which could be destroyed in fits of anger. On the other hand, completely omitting room jobs would also mean stopping all overtime work. Generally speaking, working after hours is not a good thing, but sometimes it is valuable for an inmate to use work as a sort of anesthetic.

In the workshops we use typical technical equipment so that the detainees can become acquainted with the equipment most commonly used in free society. It is not necessary for an unskilled laborer to work with exactly the same machine as the one he will have to use in industry, but he should know the operating principles of that type of machinery as seen from the workman's point of view. If he understands his machine, and if he works steadily, it is easier to counteract the characterological handicaps which hamper his keeping a job.

Our tailor[5] and furniture shops have been suitable for training apprentices, and several people have received their full four years of training and fulfilled the theoretical requirements, partly in the institution and partly in the local apprentice school. We have also completed the apprenticeship of a few masons.

Training inmates as journeymen can give excellent results if the right persons are selected, but its usefulness in preventing new crime should not be overrated. Because of the relatively short period spent in the institution by most inmates, the four years of apprenticeship can only be finished by a minority. However, an occasional inmate has

[5] This no longer exists.

continued and finished an apprenticeship which he had started before coming to the institution. Furthermore, it must be remembered that journeymen will serve as foremen and in many cases will have to supervise unskilled laborers. This requires a special personality structure which is rare among our inmates.

In each of the bigger workshops, three or four professional workers act as instructors. When considering competition with industries in the free market, one ought to realize that one such professional would be able to produce a large part of what the fifteen or sixteen inmates do. The prices of our products are set by the business manager in accordance with standard rates so that we cannot be criticized for unfair competition.

One of the risks we face is that our demand for good work may make the inmate become too perfectionistic. We have had a well-trained furniture-maker who could work better and faster after his parole than his colleagues in a free workshop. This caused him to lose several jobs but did not harm him, in the long run. Another paroled furniture-maker was so skilled that he became a foreman in a large workshop. He was unable to tolerate the incompetence of some of the journeymen, became irritated, and gave up his job as foreman in order to return to making furniture himself.

Another risk is that, in trades such as bookbinding, some people may believe that working for some time in the institution will enable them to establish shops of their own. Unfortunately, we cannot give good enough training for this.

Working outdoors at physical labor is very satisfying to some, and it is important to have enough flower beds, hedges, and lawns inside the walls to give useful occupations to people who, for security reasons, cannot be allowed to work outside the walls. The space inside the institution is too limited for market gardening, and such work is reserved for those who can be allowed to work outside the walls. In summer three groups (in the winter, two), each with a maximum of eight inmates, work in the market gardens raising vegetables to sell on the free market.

The atmosphere in the workshop is of great importance, because an inmate may regard the work period as a time of relaxation when he can concentrate on something outside himself. We often see people who have not been accustomed to regular work, or who have felt that work is something to be suffered, come to feel happy not only because of being paid weekly but also because of being regularly occupied.

The supervisor's actions are very important. He needs to have professional expertise, because detainees often study trade books in order to ask him difficult technical questions. They like to prove that there is something which he does not know about his profession. If the supervisor stands up to such testing, he gains the respect of the inmates and can be sure that his authority will not be disputed.

In the workshops, we must treat detainees as much as possible as we expect them to be treated in a workshop in the free community. If one does something wrong, he must be criticized individually. For a man who has been in a workshop for some time, criticism may be given in sharp, obvious words. The beginner, however, cannot be expected to understand clearly the workshop supervisor's responsibility and demands for quality in production. Until he learns this, criticism of his work may have to consist of repeated and very detailed explanations.

Because of our situation as an annex to the State Prison, we have shared their business manager to oversee all the workshops, determine prices and production levels, and so on. This work has in practice been done by an assistant manager, free to act very independently. Constantly changing people in this position have pointed up how important it is, not only for the inmates, but also for the staff, to have continuous direction. This is especially true because these managers come from general prison work and do not realize how independently each member of our staff is accustomed to working. It takes time for them to learn this and to know not only the staff members but also the inmates and participate constructively in our group deliberations.

EDUCATION

In theory, the concepts of education and therapy should be kept separate. With us, this is difficult because we define treatment as anything which attempts to improve the individual inmate's chance for living a crime-free life in society. Our teachers' work is socio-pedagogic and forms a part of our whole therapeutical atmosphere along with the work of the rest of the staff. I am not trying to differentiate between education and psychotherapy but to describe how our school staff functions.

We have three full-time teachers. Seventeen other people teach for a few hours a week, and thirteen of these are full-time staff working in their spare time. Two officers take charge of getting students to and from classes and controlling the library so that the teacher on duty there can relax and talk about books with the inmates.

The teachers, of course, teach at an individual or class level, but they also have the opportunity to talk casually, without any direct therapeutical aim, with the detainees. It is important to have some people who have time to chat informally with the detainees about things which interest them, and this burden should not fall entirely on the ward officer. A teacher can often help an inmate to improve his social contacts. Thus the teachers join the staff members in their rehabilitation work and help develop a therapeutical atmosphere in the institution.

The work of the school has developed slowly, over the years. The subjects taught have depended largely on the interests of the teachers. Inmates enjoy and continue to attend classes and seminars on the relationship of the citizen to society, but their interest in foreign language classes often fades away and the classes have to be closed.

The library is part of the school and is located in the open unit inside the walls which we call the Hut. It has about 7,000 volumes, and several detainees are employed to process the books and supervise the inmates' access to the shelves.

Our first teacher was interested in theoretical criminological problems and helped to record case histories based on chronological descriptions of the inmates' careers. These gave him and the rest of the staff an opportunity to analyze carefully the decisive influences in each inmate's life and suggested individualized opportunities, both therapeutical and educational. The case histories also helped the inmates to see their own lives in new perspectives.

Labor-Technical Teachings

Our second teacher had graduated from a teachers' college and had taught children. He developed what was called "labor-technical teaching" and taught in collaboration with the workshop leaders. One purpose of this type of teaching was to rid the school of all similarities to grade school because many of our detainees would associate that with one failure after another in their earlier education. This method attempted to combine the inmates' experiences at work, in school, and during spare time into a harmonious total by using daily practical work as a basis for theoretical teaching. The goal was not to give technical training in a trade but to help the semiskilled worker to develop a better understanding of the work he was doing and to broaden his interests in many directions. In this way we could counteract the daydreaming which often accompanies the stereotyped kind of work commonly done in institutions. We tried to teach each detainee to fill out his own weekly work report and to construct a profit and loss account based on the weekly production in the workshop and his weekly pay, thereby learning to manage his own income. After that, many of them developed a technical interest in the sources of materials they were using, such as paper and wood, and in many other subjects.

Mathematical training resulted from questions which arose in farming and soil improvement: How does one calculate the amount of earth dug up when a ditch is made? What is the method of leveling an area of ground? How do surveying instruments work? From this the student may go on to making and using technical drawings.

It is important to teach at the level of the pupil, and this is often lower at Herstedvester than the teacher has been accustomed to finding in free society. Many of our inmates have practically no education, and they lack any experience that would prepare them to accept new and logical ideas. After they acquire this attitude of acceptance, they learn workshop processes more easily and become more adept at handling their machines. This gives them a feeling of self-respect that is probably the most important result of this teaching method.

Another important element in labor-technical teaching is giving the pupils an appreciation of the forms and histories of the tools they use. The historical development of modern machinery arouses the interest of most inmates. Writing a description of his own work procedure gives a detainee experience in using the Danish language and will make him use handbooks, analyze workers' hygiene, decide what clothing is most suitable for different types of work, and so forth.

Teaching Art and Culture

Our third teacher was interested in general culture and had many connections among artists. He stimulated interest in the artistic development of inmates and, after some time, most labor-technical teaching disappeared. His teaching counteracted the inmate's feeling that "it is somebody else's job to cure me." He encouraged each man to develop a sense of personal responsibility and a feeling of self-respect. Time after time, he was the first to understand that a supercilious, arrogant inmate, diagnosed as a psychopath, had devaluated himself inside his shell and was really trying to hide his feeling that he was not as good as other people. After the teacher helped him to break through this shell, we could transfer him to specialized therapy.

For a time we did not realize the danger of making a detainee more curious and interested in art than the group to which he would return. We know now that we must warn an inmate not to talk much about books or classical music in the workshops until he has tested his comrades' reactions carefully.

In some people passivity and shyness express a lack of self-respect. Our first theater performance, a revue given in March, 1943, was very helpful to people of this sort. A very charming inmate, who had been convicted of fraud, initiated plans for a series of revues portraying life in the institution. Recognizing a chance to assert himself, he organized a group of detainees, some of whom had been in detention for a long time, to sing and act. These performances soon degenerated from spontaneous demonstrations of happenings in the institution into the usual light style of the theater of the time and lost their usefulness for our purposes.

In 1947 and 1948 one of the inmates presented some very cleverly done puppet shows which he produced as a hobby. Other inmates helped him to write and improvise scenes which showed institutional life, family situations, events during World War II, and so forth. For example, in one puppet show a funny-looking judge told a character, "Now you are to be placed in an institution where you cannot be influenced by anyone or anything." This satirized the court as well as the indeterminate sentence and our treatment attempts. It is important to use such incidents for abreaction.

Extemporaneous Theater

For some years Kaj Nielsen,[6] an author interested in drama, taught study groups about the theater. To stimulate and develop the inmates' obvious interest in theater, he taught a course in the history of dramatic art and an acting course based on the Stanislavski method. The acting course encouraged the inmates to be more spontaneous and taught them to improvise; it was soon possible to get them to act in some predetermined pattern like children playing "house" or "cowboys and Indians."

Their next step was improvising a whole play from an idea taken from J. B. Priestley's *The Rose and the Crown*.

[6] Kaj Nielsen, "Teater på en ny måde, de første, forsøg de første resultater," *Mentalhygiejne* (April, 1955); *idem*, "Ekstemporalteater," *Herstedvesteriana* (Copenhagen: Privately printed, 1955); *idem*, "Extemporalspil som led i resocialiseringsarbejdet i forvaringsanstalten i Herstedvester," *Faengselsfaglige Meddelelser*, 61 (March, 1961).

The characters are ordinary people who frequent a dirty bar in the slum section of a large town. This milieu gave several of the inmates a chance to step directly into fictitious situations while keeping their own individual characteristics. They performed strongly and excitingly without the slightest trace of amateurism and with an involvement which would put many professional actors in the shade.[7] As the actors rehearsed this play, they became so engrossed in discussing the problems raised in it that several evenings passed with no discussion of theater at all.

The audience is made up of inmates and staff and a tradition of active collaboration between audience and players has developed. After a short extemporaneous play, the audience breaks up to sit in circles with the actors and discuss the theme of the play. Usually the evening ends with one of the psychologists summarizing the discussions and trying to evaluate the different points of view presented. In order to participate in the evening of drama, an inmate is required to be active in some school function; in this way we use the extemporaneous theater to stimulate school work.

The extemporaneous plays consist of two or three short scenes about ten minutes long. Each illustrates a single clear chain of situations such as escaping, adapting to employment after parole, going home on six-hour leaves, and so forth. Not all aspects of the problems are presented, and this one-sidedness stimulates audience discussion. It is interesting to see that staff as well as inmates participate in the debate, thus breaking down barriers between the two groups.

Our form of extemporaneous theater is not the same as Jacob L. Moreno's "Psycho-drama,"[8] because we use rehearsals—preferably not more than three or four for each production. During these rehearsals we eliminate the risk of acting-out too strongly. We get the actors to concentrate and sharpen their critical sense, thus giving them some self-discipline. Very often the person who has proposed a problem concerning a conflict of importance to himself does not play his own role in the performance, but gives it to a comrade who is familiar with chains of situations of a similar kind.

Kaj Nielsen later used this technique in many types of organizations outside Herstedvester. Supported by the Danish Organization for Mental Hygiene, he made tape recordings dramatizing criminal situa-

[7] This first purely extemporaneous production was performed on May 11, 1951, and was called *A Visit to a Bar*.
[8] Jacob L. Moreno, *Psychodrama* (New York: Beacon, 1946).

tions as they are experienced by the people involved. The police collaborated with Mr. Nielsen and members of juvenile clubs who had themselves been delinquent usually acted the parts. These tapes present such activities as shoplifting and joy-riding, showing the background of the crime and frequently ending with the participants being caught. The tapes have been used in schools and juvenile clubs to promote discussion among young people about the dangers to society and risks for themselves that result if they become involved in illegal activities.

We learned later of Maxwell Jones's work with socio-drama in Belmont Hospital south of London. It seems to be very similar to our extemporaneous theater.[9]

Not everyone wants to present his own problems in public. Some of the more insecure detainees have used the puppet shows because they find it easier to be concealed in the theater and let the puppets present their problems. Because it takes a long time for them to make puppets, they have ample time to discuss and collaborate on what subjects they will present and on technical details of the puppets' appearances, costumes, and so forth. We often have two directors of the puppet theater in order to give one of them training in group work and to assure complete continuity in group activities.

Recent Educational Methods

During recent years the school has been directed by men who have previously been clinical psychologists at Herstedvester and are familiar with all phases of the work. The acting chief teacher, Per Rindom, describes six areas of teaching as follows:

1) *Special teaching.* Inmates hampered in their daily life by insufficient general knowledge need individualized teaching. In an investigation about ten years ago, Asger Hansen[10] used the same intelligence and knowledge tests that the Danish army and navy use and found that 20 per cent of our inmates were so backward in their knowledge of the Danish language, and 30 per cent so lacking in arithmetical skills, that special teaching was necessary. About 10 per cent were so unskilled in the language that they had to be called word-blind.[11]

[9] Maxwell Jones, *Social Psychiatry; a Study of Therapeutic Communities* (London: Tavistock, 1952).

[10] Asger Hansen, "Treatment of Educationally Retarded Offenders," *Bulletin de la Société Internationale de Criminologie* (1960, 2e semestre): 312–19.

[11] Knud Hermann and Edith Norrie, "Is Congenital Word-Blindness a Hereditary Type of Gerstmann's Syndrome?" *Psychiatria et Neurologia,* 136 (1958): 59–73.

This is a reading problem, unrelated to intelligence level, which makes it difficult for the affected person to understand and use printed or written symbols. In a country where almost everyone can read and write, this causes serious problems. Special teaching for word-blindness, as developed by Edith Norrie, must be done on an individual basis at first but two students may be taught at once, later.

One of our obviously word-blind men attempted to be a store clerk. He had great skill in getting people to write down their names and addresses themselves "in order to insure that the address is perfect," but he had such difficulty in adding bills that he could not continue the work.

There is another group of inmates who have lacked instruction because of childhood illnesses, constant shifting from one school to another, or severe emotional disturbances. Teaching some of these people must also start with individual sessions to protect them from being made fun of by other inmates. This is especially important for those who have been considered backward or mentally defective. Some of these seem to suffer basically from disturbances of perception. When these so-called former mental defectives overcome their perception problems, they may gain normal knowledge rapidly.

It is difficult to motivate many inmates to try again to be taught. They say, "I have managed very well so far. Why should I take the trouble? Every attempt until now has shown how hopeless it is."[12]

Most of these remarks are based on anxiety because they do not want other inmates to see how little they know. When they have made some progress with individual teaching, they frequently want to move to classroom teaching. We regularly test the level of the pupil's accomplishments so that we can show him that he has made progress. In some cases, especially with word-blind people, it is necessary to continue to teach them after parole, partly in order to prove to the detainee that we really will take care of him and his interests.

Teaching these special people is done during working hours, but teaching that is not prescribed as necessary is carried on in the inmate's spare time, just as it will be in the free community. We prefer not to force education on any detainee in order to avoid giving punishment for nonattendance.

[12] Asger Hansen, "Treatment of Educationally Retarded Offenders," *Bulletin de la Société International de Criminologie* (1960, 2ᵉ semestre): 312–19.

2) *General teaching.* For those interested in learning more than they actually need in their daily lives, we have a number of study groups devoted to such topics as the role of the citizen in society, parole, discussing of radio programs, producing extemporaneous theater, and studying music. A painting class is directed by a staff member who is an artist. There is also a specialized class in drawing for furniture makers and a class to prepare inmates for the high school equivalency examination. It is important that inmates participating in the study groups or taking correspondence courses maintain their personal stability and workshop productivity at a reasonable level, and it is one of the teacher's jobs to protect the detainee from setting unrealistic goals for himself. Sometimes, however, he must find out for himself that he has set his sights too high.

3) *Motivating varied interests.* Inmates who have too few interests or are dominated by a tendency to escape from reality must be motivated to develop new and varied ones. The labor-technical teaching has been valuable for this purpose, as have courses such as driver training that give the inmate better job opportunities.

4) *Athletics.* We have facilities for handball, badminton, soccer, and table tennis. During the year, outside clubs are invited to compete with our inmates and such contact with free society is highly valued by them.

5) *Spare time activities.* The school is responsible for obtaining materials and providing instruction for a hobby shop in each ward. Bridge and chess tournaments are organized (and the staff has difficulty in preventing poker playing). Controlling the hobbies is very difficult. On one hand, we want to encourage the inmates' interest in making things, caring for their aquariums and birds, collecting stamps, and so forth; on the other hand, we must be careful that the hobby is not developed into a business with other inmates hired to do maintenance work and the contractor making a good deal of money. This would encourage illegal trading.

Spare time activities also include the organization of entertainment and the selection of films.

6) *Special support to small special groups.* During recent years we have had a group of Eskimos who have many difficulties with a foreign language and cultural climate. To teach them Danish, it has been necessary to ask for extensive assistance from people who can speak Greenlandic. They acquire ordinary, everyday language quickly, but it is difficult for them to express something about their emotional states.

RELIGION

Interest in religion is limited in Herstedvester. In the State Prison 10 to 15 per cent of the inmates participate in study circles which discuss religious questions with great interest and clarity. The sectarian religious people are usually not interested, and, if they do participate, they show little enthusiasm. In Herstedvester, those most interested are the older first-timers and some of the sexual criminals who have difficulty in seeing their relationship to existence in general.

We share the chaplain with the State Prison. He comes to us once a week, and, if he had more time (which he expects to have later when he gets an assistant), he believes he could develop a religious discussion group.

Divorce problems, which usually give the chaplain a reason to contact the detainees, are not very common here. Few of our detainees are married. If one is married, his wife is not likely to have a varying attitude toward her husband—she probably has a definite positive or negative reaction, or no reaction at all, to his unusual personality and chronic criminality.

Unfortunately we have no chapel and must hold Sunday services in the gymnasium. More suitable surroundings would undoubtedly stimulate interest in religion.

CONTACT WITH THE OUTER WORLD

All detainees have access to newspapers and radio broadcasts and may receive visitors every Sunday. They may also see their special guardians without supervision on working days. As already mentioned, all letters are censored except those to the guardian, the Minister of Justice, and the Ombudsman. The Ombudsman's reply is delivered to the inmate in a sealed envelope, and a copy goes to the institution. Besides these general opportunities for contact with the outer world, we have the so-called leave that is one of our most important treatment tools.

Leave under supervision has been practiced since the temporary institution began in 1925. It is important for the detainee to maintain contact with the outside world and especially with his family. It is also important for the institution to make an early contact with the detainee's family. At this point they still remember what life was like with him, and they often tell the social aide how happy they are that he is in Herstedvester. Frequently they do not hide the fact that they feel most secure when they know that he is behind walls. A year or two later, if he is still here, the same relatives are apt to forget the difficulties he caused and present a completely different point of view. By studying these changed points of view, we can be objective in evaluating the detainee's family, the possibilities of his getting along with them, and his general social possibilities.

During the first years of Herstedvester's operation, each man's leaves were supervised by his special guardian. This did not provide adequate security as the guardian sometimes left the detainee without supervision, the guardian having suggested a meeting time and place so that they could return to the institution together. After several unfortunate episodes, this system was abandoned and two people were employed to serve as escorts. This also was not successful because in the beginning of the 1940's we started more intensively individualized treatment and these escorts, who had no other connection with the institution, could not help with therapy. Next we added six-hour leaves to the program of the social section and the social aides acted as leave escorts. This was very successful, but the social work increased and the number of six-hour leaves grew to the point where the social aides no longer had time to act as escorts. Then some of the uniformed staff took over the six-hour leaves, and this helped them to get insight into the inmate's total situation. For a time only one officer did this job, later two. Because it is very difficult for the officers to go on six-hour leaves day after day, an inmate must now find one who is willing to go with him. This means that he must build up confidence in at least one officer. Our new scheme has probably prevented several attempted escapes, but it should be stressed that the job of supervising six-hour leaves is very burdensome.

Six-hour leaves are a privilege and are not granted automatically. The rules call for twelve months of good behavior and diligent work before an inmate becomes eligible for six-hour leaves. For persons who return to Herstedvester, or who have escaped or attempted to escape, the minimum time before a six-hour leave is granted is two years. For persons who have committed such crimes as homicide, robbery, arson, or dangerous sexual or property crimes, the length of time is three years. These regulations, introduced in 1941, are easy to attack from a theoretical point of view. To use time limits in an institution that is by principle without time limits is not logical, and in practice this arrangement has been difficult to work with. But now, as recidivists to Herstedvester stay less than two years, we have been allowed to ignore the two-year rule.[13]

Uniform instructions concerning six-hour leaves are given to the inmate, to the escort,[14] and to the relatives and friends whom they will visit. Leaves are closely related to our treatment program and should be used to lessen the severe pressure which accompanies detention for an indeterminate time. They give the detainee a realistic contact with outside life that helps him to evaluate his chances for the future and to maintain important contacts with relatives and friends who may want to help him. Furthermore, leaves show our confidence in the detainee and indicate to him that it is valuable for him to honor this confidence by not trying to escape from his escort. It is the duty of the escort always to have the detainee under his direct surveillance, which means that the leave does not relieve any of the inmate's sexual pressures.

The detainee must not drink. This rule is difficult to enforce because relatives and friends want to be especially hospitable to the detainee and in Denmark it is natural to serve beer with meals. Unfortunately we cannot allow detainees to drink even beer because we have alcoholics with a danger point of one single drink, which means that taking even a small amount of alcohol may result in an urge to drink more, increasing the risk of escape.

For many years the ordinary length of leaves was eight hours but for economic reasons it is now limited to six hours. First leaves always take place during the day. After six leaves, one may go on leave in the afternoon but he must return before nine o'clock in the evening. The detainee may go shopping during the leave, visit relatives and friends, go to the cinema, or visit museums and libraries. Some detainees find it difficult to take a sustained interest in cultural activities, and to them shopping means a great deal, even if they buy things that could be bought in the institution. They may go anywhere except to bathing beaches and they must avoid crowds. The inmate himself must account for money he uses, and his relatives are not allowed to give him more than five kroner (a little less than one dollar) for his leave.

[13] Since January, 1961, the superintendent permits six-hour leaves after obtaining consent from the local state's attorney. If there is disagreement, the question is brought before the Minister of Justice, who formally has the final decision.

[14] Instruction of October 24, 1955.

One officer, Sergeant C. J. Sondergaard, has acted as escort for more than a thousand leaves. He writes about his experiences as follows:

"An escort has formal authority over the detainee, but his personal qualifications condition how and when he uses it, if at all. Depending on a relationship of mutual confidence between the companion and the detainee is preferred. Being with the detainee's family and friends often gives rise to a human attachment that is quite different from the usual relationship between a staff member and a detainee and it minimizes the value of authority. It is important that these two people, who will be together for many hours, know each other beforehand.

"The rule that the detainee must find his own leave escort makes it common to have the escort be an employee in the detainee's ward. This ensures that they know each other well. But, because he deals with many types of detainees—some very immature and hypersensitive, with insufficient self-control—the escort has to be prepared for them to react in a surprising way on very slight provocation. The detainee may feel especially insecure during a leave, causing a great risk of unusual reactions. It is important, therefore, for the escort to be well-acquainted with his charge's personal problems, his situation in the ward and workshop, his family relations, and his case history in general.

"Most detainees try to use the leaves as systematically as possible. According to the ways they use their time, three groups can be distinguished:

"The first and largest group consists of detainees having stable relationships with relatives, sometimes in several families, or with their special guardians, and they spend most of their time with these people.

"The second group consists of people with less stable relationships with relatives and more businesslike contacts with their guardians. They usually divide their leaves between visits to relatives and other interests such as the cinema.

"The third and smallest group consists of detainees with no contact with relatives or friends because of emotional or geographical distance. They use their time to walk around, to attend exhibitions, to go to the cinema, or to eat and have a cup of coffee in a restaurant.

"Most of the people who receive detainees in their homes try to be friendly and understanding, and to demonstrate that they still like them, in spite of their criminal careers. In a few cases an inmate is met with cool indifference or open dislike. Sometimes relations

improve if visits are repeated from time to time; in other cases the
detainee gives up the relationship. It may take several visits to overcome a skeptical, negative attitude toward an inmate, but sometimes the escort can intervene and create a clearer understanding or
even a positive attitude.

"These monthly visits outside the walls are of great importance to
the detainee. It is difficult for people who have not been isolated from
society for a protracted period to understand the feelings of inmates
on six-hour leaves. One inmate explained during his first leave,
'Putting one's hands in one's own pockets and finding real money, or
buying a train ticket, may become some sort of holy act.' This
demonstrates the importance of a gradual adaptation to the real
world. Furthermore, the leave may help a detainee remember events
which were of importance in developing his present situation. Returning to old scenes in a new emotional state may help him recognize
and evaluate some of his long-term conflicts. In his isolation in the
institution, an inmate is apt to build up a dream world of unrealistic
proportions and expect too much when he returns to the free world.
In the institutional regime we try to correct such dreams, but the
inmate's experiences on leaves are more persuasive than anything we
can tell him. In any case, he returns from leaves with new perspectives
for his own speculations.

"Every single leave has its own atmosphere depending on the
personalities of the two persons, the mood of the inmate, and what
happens in the places he visits. The family group's manner of accept-
ing the escort is important, but the detainee expects that, however
the escort is affected, he ought to be alert to the inmate's point of
view and ready to discuss it with him. These expectations put physical
and psychological pressure on the escort. He has to be informed and
adaptable to new situations."

In many cases the leave escort can give important help to the
social section. His evaluation of the way in which offers of work or
lodging are given may indicate how reliable they are. His impression
of how the family lives may also be important if the detainee insists
that he could live at home. These and other questions are recorded in
the escort's report and may indicate important treatment problems.

GROUP WORK AND GROUP THERAPY

The detention institution opened in 1925. At that time it was very
small and held a relatively homogeneous group of sexual and aggres-

sive criminals. This temporary unit, which functioned until 1933, was established under such conditions that small groups developed naturally and were the inspiration for building the permanent institution around small sections with independent houses. The first two houses each had four units with ten single rooms each. Then a new house was built which, for economic reasons, housed fifteen men in each of the four units. Later, in the open unit inside the walls, we tried having eighteen people, but this large number proved unsatisfactory and this unit now has only fourteen members.

In the first few years after 1935, in the new institution, attempts were made to reserve special sections for sexual criminals, young criminals, older criminals, difficult and quarrelsome people, and newcomers, but it was hard to maintain this kind of classification and at the same time have groups of people who could get along with one another. When I arrived in 1942, it was difficult for me to tell which unit was which, because it had been necessary to place some of the quieter, older detainees in units with more aggressive youngsters in order to maintain peace and order. This is an example of making use of the influence of detainees on each other.

Contrary to what is generally supposed, the younger inmates more often have a bad influence on the older ones than the other way about. The older inmates are usually more interested than the young ones in receiving help from the staff and are therefore more eager to support them in their efforts to develop a peaceful and comfortable atmosphere. These reactions, confirmed by observations in the small workshops (those having a maximum of fifteen workers) and especially in the infirmary, led to the development of a kind of group organization with uniformed officers as leaders. The same ward officer or workshop leader serves the same unit, year after year.

A more formal type of group work was developed using the academically trained therapists as supervisors either for individuals or groups of staff members. I should mention that I avoid using the word "supervision" to mean anything other than teaching, lest supervisory members of such interpersonal relationships feel superior and the supervised regard themselves as inferior. Such precaution is especially necessary where new forms of group collaboration, based on different types of special training mutually supplementing each other, are under development.

The different kinds of coordination groups already mentioned offer numerous possibilities for discussing and clarifying observed problems. Through such group work, the leaders developed an understanding of interpersonal relations that they were able to share with other collaborators. Group experience has been the backbone of our treatment work. Since the mid-1940's, attempts have been made at exploring group activities in still other ways.

The first systematic attempt to establish an independent, small group of inmates with the common goal of a crime-free future was the establishment of the open section, Kastanienborg, in November, 1944. A small, selected group of detainees and staff members were transferred to the new unit. In private and group conversations these men had been convinced that they could see it as their special mission to be pioneers in an experiment to prove that psychopaths were capable of managing a difficult existence. The experiment became even more difficult than we had expected because it started just at the time when the Germans removed all Danish police in the autumn of 1944.

In March, 1946, a more specifically therapeutic experiment was carried out. A selected group of detainees met as a study group with a professor of penal law, Professor Stephan Hurwitz (later the Ombudsman), to discuss the problems of chronic criminals as seen from their own point of view. The participants stimulated each other by honest descriptions of their own problems, and the discussions developed very quickly into our first attempt at active group treatment. That I, myself, was intimately acquainted with the life-story of each participant may have helped to assure a high degree of truth in what the inmates told. Everyone seemed eager to give this highly respected lawyer the best possible insight into the complicated life situations that produce and result from a criminal career. This relatively short series of meetings motivated nearly all of the group to continue and elaborate their individual consultations. From this group we learned that some detainees are embarrassed because their own criminality did not stem from the socioeconomic difficulties described matter-of-factly by the majority of their comrades.

In 1945 and 1946 further experimentation was forced upon us. The institution was almost completely taken over to house war traitors who were being tried at that time. With only a few hours of warning, we had to move our inmates across the main road to the State Prison.[15]

[15] Herstedvester has always been an annex of the State Prison, sharing its business and security administration. Since 1945 this has not substantially hampered our feeling of being an independent institution, free to experiment.

After the inmates were moved to the State Prison, we saw how a group of latent aggressives may explode when faced with strain. The relaxation they had developed during the previous two and one-half years disappeared in a few hours. In one of the large wings of this prison, our 150 detainees were placed two or three to a cell with only a few in the single cells they were used to. Spontaneous groups developed very quickly. With a clear application of the pecking order, some energetic men exerted dominating power and strong influence on the more passive and weak ones. The inmates were thrown together and had to rely on themselves, and they felt let down by the staff which had not prevented this disaster. In spite of these handicaps, the inmates' confidence that a change in conditions could be achieved by negotiation survived and resulted in a very dramatic confrontation between six of the more dominating spokesmen, the captain, and myself. In this meeting we agreed to try to get at least a part of our institution back as fast as possible. Soon we were able to move the most domineering and psychopathic detainees to our infirmary which was still under our jurisdiction. This ended the attempt at organized protest.

We had not realized, until we were moved to the prison, that we could not manage our inmates in one large group, but that by using small groups as we did in Herstedvester, we could break the influence of the asocial inmates. Here we had established groups so small that the personnel could really know and be known by each inmate. We explored this experience with small groups further. Study circles connected with the school developed and some, centered around social problems, are now the oldest formal groups in the institution. Others were shorter-lived groups that discussed films or radio programs. Other groups developed the extemporaneous theater and the puppet theater. All this group work was preparing a basis for more formal therapy groups under the direction of psychologists and psychiatrists.

In 1947 and 1948 several groups worked intensively toward particular goals. One group planned and helped to make a film about life in Herstedvester. Another group, with some of the same members, established an open section inside the walls, in spite of opposition from the staff. This new unit, called the Hut, was placed in an empty wooden building left over from the time of the "traitors." It was remodeled by the pioneer group of detainees and has been one of our most successful experiments.

A few months later the state broadcasting system wanted to do a program on Herstedvester and a group of detainees participated very constructively in the production. Some of them had been rather negative and aggressive but, together with the staff, they helped the interviewers who moved around in the institution for some time.

From 1948 to 1951, overcrowding made it necessary to use a temporary unit in a wing of a reception prison in Copenhagen. Here attempts were made to set up circles to study mental hygiene. The text book used was Karl M. Bowman's *Personal Problems for Men and Women*.[16] Each meeting concentrated on a chapter and discussion soon became very dynamic with all participants attempting to interpret patterns of behavior. There were ample opportunities for supportive therapy. As only a small number could participate in this group therapy, complications developed like those in the women's section described below.[17]

Some years later, at our women's section housed in the Women's Prison, group therapy was initiated with a male psychiatrist and a female psychologist as leaders.[18] Most of the detainees in the unit at that time were aggressive. Shortly before this therapeutical attempt, the women had been moved from the old State Prison opposite Herstedvester where a cozy and relaxed atmosphere had been built up. Although the detainees moved to physically better surroundings in the women's prison, it was located about forty kilometers from the main institution and the pleasant climate was destroyed. Severe tension developed between our staff and the ordinary staff in the prison; this has been only partly solved and still causes difficulties.

Judged by theoretical standards, the direction of the group meetings in the women's section was passive to a high degree and rather severe expressions of aggression developed. The phases this group passed through were not those to which we were accustomed. Verbal and physical aggression between the inmates began almost immediately after the meetings began.

After two months of disturbance, the majority of the detainees passed from aggressiveness to an irritable depressive phase. It was

[16] Karl M. Bowman, *Sindshygiejne til hverdagsbrug,* translated into Danish by Elisabeth and Georg K. Stürup (Copenhagen: Schønberg, 1940).
[17] J. Finn Larsen, "Forsøg med gruppepsykoterapi på et mandligt forvarings-klientel," *Nordisk Tidsskrift for Kriminalvidenskab,* 44 (1956): 217.
[18] Ebbe Linnemann, "Studier i Gruppepsykologi," *Herstedvesteriana* (Copenhagen: Privately printed, 1955), p. 1–11.

as if their discharge of aggressions had diminished their sadomasoch-
istic impulses against authority, and the more normal softer emotions that had been suppressed until now came to the surface. Then
they passed into a third phase colored by transferences which were
difficult to handle because of the mutual jealousies which developed.
Because the group leaders were a woman psychologist and a male
psychiatrist, they came to represent *parents imago* for the patients. In
this phase a clear regression phenomenon of therapeutical value was
observed.

In this large group it was reasonably easy to pacify aggressiveness.
The usual mechanisms were observed—identification, projection,
sublimation, and especially the scapegoat phenomenon. Practical
reasons made it necessary to divide the group in half and this caused
new difficulties. One group's aggressive feelings were displaced and
projected upon the other, and it became obvious that it is easier to
hate outsiders than members of one's own group.

This is not the place to review the history of group therapy. We
have, following Klapmann,[19] attempted to consider different points of
view, and we have especially stressed re-education. We have also
had to consider the fact that our detainees are forced to live together
for a long period of time in a very limited area where they cannot
avoid contact with each other. Therefore, in the groups, we have
usually preferred to avoid too deep a psychotherapeutical investigation into the individual inmate's early history.

We stress that crime is an interpersonal problem, and we combine
the group approach with individual therapeutical interviews. We
see each of these elements as part of the total therapeutical work.
Individual supportive therapy between group sessions has been of
practical importance, especially to weak inmates, because when they
begin to participate in active therapy they may have difficulties with
comrades who attack them too strongly, not only inside but also
outside the group meetings. Contact with the therapist may give
the needed support in such cases. If this is not available, other inmates
may give poor and uncontrolled advice between group meetings. It is
our experience that the best therapeutic response results if we discuss
actual situations in the institution and work on problems related to
them. This gives the detainees less chance to "prepare" meetings
and attempt to arrange "testimony" in order to attract favorable

[19] J. W. Klapmann, *Group Psychotherapy*, 2d ed. (London: Grune and
Stratton, 1959).

notice for themselves. It is true that such attempts are often disclosed
in the meetings, but, until this happens, such "conning" retards the
group work and may keep someone who needs therapeutical support
from trying to get it in the group because he does not believe in its
effectiveness. Inmates know that some comrades have talked about
"conning," and it is difficult for them to understand that these people
are often caught in their own nets and discover that this behavior is
of no value to them.

How to select members for a group has been discussed frequently.
It is our impression that the groups which function best are created by
therapists who have good contact with their inmates and can get them
to help in choosing the group.

Our generally practical attitude means that we have made little
attempt to find out what single elements work in the treatment but
have been satisfied with seeing it as a whole. We are interested in
the total pattern of reaction of the single individual and find it
reasonable to operate with this pattern when and where it appears.
We are comforted by comparing what happens in the institution with
our own lives, where we regularly see how a relatively small occur-
rence can develop into some sort of chain reaction and result in a long
series of new evaluations and changes in our perceptions and reactions. This is what has been called the "ah-hah" experience.[20]

I do not advocate any special technique for group therapy; rather,
I prefer that each group therapist use a technique which suits him
and the group with which he works. If his preferred technique does
not work, he must try to adapt it to his particular situation or find
and use another, even if it is less comfortable for him. It is especially
necessary not to stress the therapeutical aim of the group too
strongly but to mask it in some way. Thus we often speak of study
circles in order to make it easier for persons who have not yet
formally accepted therapy as something in which they need to
participate.

The inmates in the open unit inside the walls, who have great
freedom in their daily life, act as spokesmen for the detainees in
general. They meet once a week with the superintendent and the chief
nurse. After some years we introduced a rule that a record of the

[20] Georg K. Stürup, "Gruppeterapi og andre nyere behandlingsmetoder overfor lovovertradere," Nordisk Tidsskrift for Kriminalvidenskab, 45 (1957):
95–104; idem, "Group Therapy with Chronic Criminals," Acta Psychothera-
peutica (1959): 377–85.

meetings must be entered in a notebook so that there can be some continuity in the discussions. This group of older inmates and the didactically run group of newcomers have undoubtedly increased the ease with which the inmates usually get over the negative aggression phase in new groups of other kinds.

Some therapists stress the importance of the special rules of play that they repeat to each new group, such as the rule of not discussing what happens in the group session outside the meetings. They believe that this is very important for the development of the solidarity necessary for internalizing new norms in the group. One of our group leaders, the psychologist Feldman, has reported that several participants have said that this is valuable.[21] Through this feeling of solidarity inmates come to regard certain acts as absolutely unacceptable. These include new crime, misuse of alcohol, the general tendency to blame others, self-deceit, hysterical reactions, dependency, and sins of omission against the rules of the group. Feldman has worked on a combination of Carl R. Rogers's nondirective methods with direct and active work on attitudes. Keeping strictly to nondirective methods seems to allow the detainee to slip too easily into a discussion of innocuous topics. Several therapists, with special permission from the detainee, have taped individual conversations concerning sensitive subjects and later used the tape—with the consent of the inmate—as an introduction to a group discussion. The discussion has usually made important corrections to the initial presentation.

We try to use the institution as a training place for group work. Because each individual inmate mirrors each of the others,[22] we may vary and repeat arrangements of problems and situations to a degree which is absolutely impossible in free society. In this way an inmate may learn to handle types of situations which have proved difficult for him in free society.

Another important element in group therapy, as well as in other types of group work (reminiscent of the type used by Norman Fenton under the name of "group counseling"), is that it may be possible to get the criminal to recognize that he is not a very good criminal.

Since 1950 we have been in frequent contact with Norman Fenton, who visited Denmark in 1952 for a few months, spending most of his

[21] Wulff Feldman, "Group Psychotherapy with Psychopaths at Herstedvester," *Bulletin de la Société Internationale de Criminologie* (1960, 2ᵉ semestre): 293–311.
[22] Georg K. Stürup, "Gruppeterapi og andre nyere behandlingsmetoder overfor lovovertraedere," *Nordisk Tidsskrift for Kriminalvidenskab* (1957):98.

time at Herstedvester. In 1954 he published his book, *Observations on the Correctional System of Denmark* (San Quentin, California State Prison). During his visit in Denmark and a visit of three weeks that I made to see the California prison system, I received much inspiration from him. Since then I have followed the development of group counseling with interest.

At a seminar in Brussels in 1962, I stressed that "the differences between the form of group work now under consideration [group psychotherapy in special wards for the most difficult to handle prisoners] and group counseling is first of all the [use of the] specialized therapist as the leader."[23] The therapist has the best opportunities for breaking down the inmate's protective mechanisms and then giving him a chance to rebuild some of his personality elements. But in counseling—with "less disturbed" people—we may also aim at some self-acceptance and self-realization through self-awareness gained in emotional experience and emotional insight.

Few people know how others regard them, and they are usually surprised and sometimes irritated when they find out. When it becomes obvious that each inmate's personality is mirrored differently in perhaps seven or eight different mirrors, the plasticity of the role he fulfills can be accepted more easily, and it may also be recognized that nothing in the mask he uses is quite accidental. Good results develop when the inmates in a group attempt not to fight each other but to help work on each other's attitude. Through such work, a "we" feeling of mutual honesty inside the group may develop, but it is necessary to warn the participants against similar openness outside the group. Such openness may irritate outsiders who sometimes look upon a group member as one of the "saved people" and may therefore tease him to despair. This may be avoided if the promise of secrecy is kept.

There is a close connection between schoolwork and some of these forms of group activity. This is especially true with the extemporaneous plays which may be used as a part of ordinary group work. In them we reproduce traumatic situations in dramatic form and objectivize them, often destroying their paralyzing effect. Feldman has described how a detainee told about his father's alcoholism: It was a hard blow to the child when he first saw his father coming home

[23] Georg K. Stürup, "Group-psychotherapy and the Other Elements of Therapy in Penology," International Penal and Penitentiary Foundation, International Colloquium, Bruxelles, 26–31 March, 1962. *Report* 4, p. 6.

drunk, and he ran away from home to avoid the teasing of his comrades. After discussing this situation, the group acted it out. The detainee first performed the role of his father, then himself as a child, with another inmate playing the role of the father. His presentation of his father was especially alive and aroused wild hilarity which seemed to help him to get rid of his conflict, as if it had been laughed out.

The advantages of group work are as follows:

(1) The detainee has a chance to give vent publicly to inner situations which have been bothering him, and his misunderstandings and mistakes can be discussed and corrected.

(2) The critique comes mainly from fellow detainees and therefore is easier to accept.

(3) Norms acceptable to society are internalized through the team work with other group members. An inmate can see others doing right as well as wrong, just as a child does during normal development.

(4) A participant can feel a sense of belonging to a group with socially acceptable goals and norms.

(5) Loyalty and collaboration are demonstrated in a social group with a recognized social goal, and loneliness may thus be lessened in a socially acceptable way.

(6) The criminal, who has suffered many defeats himself, gets a chance for abreaction of related difficulties, stimulated by the good fellowship of people who have had similar experiences.

Dissolving a group is sometimes difficult. We find it best to limit group work to one or two meetings per week for a stipulated number of months. Some groups have continued after part of the members have been transferred to the open section or have been paroled. Such meetings allowed those not yet paroled to become acquainted with the difficulties met by the parolees. In some cases it seemed as if those paroled felt that if they did not do well it would be more difficult for the others to manage on parole. They tried to live up to such a responsibility and became an essential support of the social readaptation of their comrades.

In a few groups, the leader has accompanied an inmate to his home during six-hour leaves and thus established a sort of subgroup with family members. For a while some family members came to group meetings in Kastanienborg. In the groups where this was tried there was extraordinary group cohesion, and paroled group members participated in attempts to find and stop friends who had started drinking sprees. They knew better than the staff where they could be found, and some weeks later it might be the other way around— that the searchers were being helped by the ones they had helped before.

In recent years social aides have directed groups considering parole problems, and in the open section one of the sergeants has worked as a group counselor and social assistant. He had a strong influence in developing the good atmosphere in the institution during this period.

Normal group counseling has been possible here where no special officer is in charge of a ward. In our small units where the same personnel work year after year with the same group of inmates, the officers cannot agree that some colleague responsible for another unit should take some of "their" inmates for a counseling group. Therefore it has not been found workable to train some of them as specialists in the field of group counseling. Our goal must be to develop a sensitivity in each ward officer and every sergeant so that he can step in with his own group at the right moment and establish individual or group contacts when problems need to be discussed. Personnel such as lieutenants and nurses who are not responsible to any particular unit can take on group counseling more easily, and in some cases this has been attempted.

The group in the Hut has for a long time been the only one continuing from year to year. The overlapping of this group with some of the more intensive psychotherapeutical groups has in some cases proven very valuable because of the close collaboration of the group leaders in the daily conference.

One should not forget that our form of group work has moments of risk. The extent of intimate contact achieved during group sessions cannot easily be experienced in free society. Some people feel that this can lead to a serious and frustrating conflict between the ideal and reality. It is expedient therefore for a group therapist not only to draw his group participants up the mountain to where they can look out over all the glories of life but to help them down the mountain again so that they can walk out in life with a matter-of-fact acceptance of reality. I should also mention that we have to be careful not to take borderline psychotic detainees into group work. The repeated confrontations with their own and others' problems may activate their disease processes, and it is difficult to get these people to accept the termination of such an active therapeutic attempt.

SPECIAL PSYCHOTHERAPY

Up to now I have been describing the structure of the special community that we have established at Herstedvester and the development of a therapeutic climate in the many small areas where special psychotherapy may be able to function. The therapeutic climate has a long historical development, beginning with Pinel's and Tuke's deliberate efforts "to use to the fullest possible extent in a comprehensive treatment plan a contribution of all staff and patients." (Martin, 1962, cited by Clark, 1965.)[24]

My postponement of the discussion of our special psychotherapy is quite deliberate because the different forms of psychotherapy must always be seen in the context of the total work. With chronic criminals we face special problems; it is often difficult to establish deep emotional contact with our inmates because many are primitive, some are not intelligent, and the majority are spineless and unaccustomed to any form of observation of their own emotional reactions. These are acting-out people. Only in some cases is it possible for the therapists to participate in situations in which they can help an inmate to recognize clearly and fully the insufficiency of his usual pattern of reaction and to see his own situation in a new light. Help in these situations may be given by the officers on duty.

In spite of this difficulty, there is no reason to despair. The therapeutical work that I have described during the reception phase and, later on in the daily life in the institution, makes up a chain of events and experiences which may motivate the patient to change his pattern of behavior gradually. When such a change is under way, it is common to observe that the inmate becomes demanding and acts in an infantile way as a defense against impulses or conflicts, or sometimes he becomes clinging in an attempt to attract attention and sympathy. Such reactions may be interpreted as a parallel to hypochondriac reactions of a more somatic kind.

Often the inmate realizes that development is under way but tries to hide it. It is not easy to accept change. Some inmates state clearly, "I am as I am and I don't believe you can change me." It is understandable that in these people defense mechanisms, as they are observed by the personnel who are with the inmates day after day, are of special importance. Such observations reported to the therapist

[24] D. H. Clark, "The Therapeutic Community—Concept, Practice and Future," *British Journal of Psychiatry,* 3 (October, 1965): p. 949.

enable him to notice what we called remedial regression and decide whether he should try to encourage it, slow it, or completely avoid it. The personnel in the ward act as supporters and the therapist as a catalyst helping the inmate to help himself, but it is sometimes not expedient or helpful for the inmate to obtain a deeper insight into the active mechanisms of his personality too quickly.[25] Sometimes he may consciously resent this, but the slow process, acting during a long period without any direct attack on the symptoms, seems to be effective, little by little. Much later, this process may give the inmate an understanding of important disturbances in his early relations with his parents and the later development of his role in relation to other people, as well as the influence his relations to the persons on whom he is most dependent has had, and will continue to have, on his life pattern.

In this situation it is especially necessary that the therapist's attitude be very flexible. If it is not, the inmate and the therapist will be dissatisfied with each other. This may result in the patient's viewing the therapist as unsympathetic and indifferent and the therapist's seeing the patient as difficult and unwilling to collaborate. In some phases of the therapeutic development, we may observe depressive reactions or hypochondriac-psychosomatic patterns as a substitute for formal acting-out and aggressive patterns. When this happens, the usual psychotherapeutical methods are easier to apply; but even in these cases, traditional formal psychotherapy is frequently impossible.

The therapist first meets the new arrival during the reception phase and, as early as the first day, discusses with him the basis on which he is detained in Herstedvester. During the coming weeks they discuss his pattern of behavior and his interhuman relations. The therapist works gradually to build up a chronological, systematic case history based on all the formal reports ever made about the inmate. Without this chronological arrangement, it is difficult to see important situations in their historical and psychological perspectives. Often these discussions show that the inmate has not been acquainted with the formal reports about him. Sometimes he has known of them but has not had a chance to take any position as to the correctness of these descriptions. Sometimes he did not even know they existed.

While formulating his life-story, he can elaborate on his own former statements, re-evaluate important factors in his personality

---

[25] Herluf Thomstad, "Psykoterapi ved psykosomatiske sykdommer," *Nordisk Medicin*, 63 (1960): 473–79.

development, and consider what he said in court and what was said about him. Little by little, occasions for controlling his point of view develop. The inmate's way of behaving during these interviews or his attempts to avoid explaining something may already give the therapist, and sometimes even the inmate, some insight into his patterns of reaction or his tendency to seek out conflict-producing situations.

Visiting psychotherapists have often asked me how we react when a patient begins to develop such an insight and what we do when he starts to recognize the undesirable consequences of his behavior. Each time I have had difficulty in explaining that the psychotherapists very often do nothing. It seems to me that usually in this period nothing special occurs in the therapist-patient relationship, and the therapist may not even realize that anything is happening, although something "new" often is occurring by means of contact established between the inmate and one of the personnel in the ward or workshop. These collaborators can see symptoms of insecurity—very small things to which they react on the spot, sometimes without even realizing that there is something new under way. In some cases there is so obviously something "new" that they inform the therapist. Sometimes the staff member will support the inmate, thus helping him through such an insecurity phase and sometimes drawing out the process; in other cases, the staff member complains that it is too difficult to continue to listen to the inmate's complaints or explanations about the same things, over and over again.

It is difficult to teach the ward officers how they should react in these complicated situations. It is still more difficult to coordinate the reactions of the staff members so that one taken into special confidence by an inmate does not react in a warm way and another in an entirely different way, perhaps coolly suggesting that the inmate see the therapist—the action he may least want to take.

The same thing happens in free society in therapeutical relations, but in Herstedvester we have a better opportunity to know what is going on outside the therapeutical contacts, and we may therefore see these reactions more clearly.

The therapists get most of their information about changes in the day-to-day patterns of their inmates' activities from the daybooks read at the daily conference and direct contact with the officers. Also important are the observations and activities of the lieutenants, who represent the primary communication between the ward and the workshop on the one side, and the therapist and other professional personnel on the other. These "interpreters," if really alert, can prove their great value by getting some sort of contact established between the inmate and the therapist at the right moment. Referral to the therapist does not mean that special therapeutic techniques have to be used in all cases. Sometimes it merely results in increased educational aid, together with ordinary human respect for the inmate as a person. This understanding may allow the development to continue at an acceptable speed and without too much risk of dangerous, suicidal reactions.

Emotion-Laden Moments

Therapeutic contact may develop through a conflict situation of the kind which in a prison would result in an official interrogation and disciplinary reaction. Sometimes the same thing happens in Herstedvester, but usually we try, in addition, to exploit such stress situations for treatment purposes. We must always remember that even if a detainee knows that the time he has to spend in the institution is limited, he does not know exactly how long it will be, and this puts him in an emotion-laden situation that is easily accentuated if something special or unexpected happens to him. Sometimes the officer on the spot may be able to interfere sufficiently early in the situation so that it does not grow to unacceptable proportions, but in other cases a disciplinary reaction is necessary. When this is handled in a therapeutic atmosphere, the inmate does not need to feel that our reactions are aggressive. It is possible for him to understand and accept the results of an analysis of what really happened. It can be accepted, as we all accept illness as being more or less inevitable, and it can usually also be accepted that we ought not to "misuse" illness in order to be taken out of circulation. I am not saying that actions requiring reactions are states of illness, but the mechanism responsible for their development is very similar to the development of psychogenic, more generally acceptable reactions which may really be just as objectionable. But in spite of this, because of the circumstances, we are forced to react differently to different situations, even when they have the same etiology.

Our psychotherapy aims at engaging the inmate in his own problems so that he sees them in a new light. Therefore we always try to utilize any opportunity to let him see himself from new angles. Time, by itself, puts things into perspective and is always of importance in psychotherapeutical work. It is not always right to hurry. Frequently, useful situations will first develop when the detainee of his own accord asks a specialist for help because he is no longer satisfied with the help he can get from the ordinary staff. When the machinery we have previously described is working, there is a great likelihood that this will happen in emotion-laden moments. In such cases he may be helped to experience "himself" in relation to his usual pattern of experience. It is like a sudden insight into deep personal affairs on the border between what is conscious and what is unconscious and is commonly experienced as a vague feeling brought to the fore not only during the situation but in the following hours or days. The importance of such an emotion-laden and therapeutically used moment for further therapeutical work is often easy to observe, especially when looking back, but it is also difficult to explain.

When I began my work at Herstedvester, using these emotion-laden moments was a practical necessity. I did not know the inmates, nor was I familiar with life in the institution; therefore I felt that it was necessary to be informed immediately when serious conflict situations arose.

The security cells were placed opposite my office at that time, and because a detainee had to be brought to one of these cells after a serious conflict, it was easy to talk with him immediately. Several sweating officers brought him to my office, and I let him in. Without anyone else present, I gave him an opportunity to continue talking about how irritated he was. My main problem was to get the man to sit down in a chair, just like my own, placed across from me at my writing table. While he was occupied in describing his own situation, I had plenty of time to refresh my memory from his chronological case history placed before me and to find in it situations of the same kind as the one which had resulted in the current conflict. When the detainee stopped his complaining and explaining for a moment, I could draw the earlier conflict into the discussion and relate it to the later one. This showed him that I was not only interested in solving the immediate problem but that I was also interested in the reasons for its development. Why did it not happen yesterday? Why not a week ago?

When, during a wedding, my attention was called to the fact that the church has always used emotional moments to put across certain ideas, I continued this work with increased interest and understanding. It was obvious that such discussions had a desensitizing effect on the inmate. If I could get him to recognize some sort of recurring pattern, it comforted him. This made it possible to construct some sort of perspective and later to restructure experiences and avoid the stereotyped pattern with which he usually reacted to difficulties.[26]

During the first years I was at Herstedvester, numerous serious conflict situations developed and I gained considerable experience in exploiting these moments. The resulting interviews regularly ended with the usual disciplinary reaction as neither staff nor inmates could accept such conflicts in the institution.

These situations soon became less common, but we learned to arrive at the same kind of results by exploiting less serious moments of the same type. Technically, the idea is to use the emotional tension and immediately involve the detainee in a discussion that makes him see his situation in a broader perspective before he has a chance to calm down.

Notes concerning our explanation of these moments are very meager in this period. It was a rather long time before I realized that these conversations—which I originally wanted for administrative reasons—were of utmost psychotherapeutical importance. I realized their value during later interviews when inmates mentioned "that day when you said this and that—you remember, when I was out of balance," and so forth.

The story of Ebbe will illustrate how minor, acute episodes may develop and be utilized. A sergeant telephoned me on behalf of Ebbe, a detainee whom he only knew superficially, but with whom he seemed to have acquired some contact and who expressed some confidence in him. He explained that Ebbe had been working for some time in the market garden section outside the walls but had become nervous and was now working in his cell. Ebbe's conflicts with his wife and three children were the essential reasons for his feelings of insecurity and emotional instability. He was a weak hypochondriac who had been in a special prison several times before and had attempted there to get special benefits by seeming very unhappy and thereby calling attention to himself. He now explained that he had become indebted to fellow detainees because his problems with his

[26] Karl Menninger, in his *The Vital Balance* (New York: Viking Press, 1963), called attention to Freud, who wrote his best works when he was in an irritated mood, and to Martin Luther, who was said to have declared that he never worked better than when he was inspired by anger: "When I am angry I can write, pray and preach well for then my whole temperament is quickened, my understanding sharpened and all mundane vexations and temptations depart."

wife had provoked him to smoke too much. He was afraid that she would leave him if she realized that she managed better with the children when he was interned than when he was at home. He had borrowed at very high interest from someone that he would not identify. The officer thought that perhaps he would explain that to me and that, in any case, it was necessary that he come to a therapeutic interview with me as his own therapist was on vacation. Therefore the sergeant asked me to call for Ebbe. I agreed, and he came a few moments later.

He explained his debt and asked that we help him pay it by letting him borrow from his saved capital. This is not allowed, according to our rules, so I refused and explained to him that if I let him do it, it would mean sanctioning illegal borrowing which must always be avoided. He was now in a difficult situation, and he began sweating. He said that he did not belong in detention and that his sentence was too severe. He thought he ought to have had an ordinary punishment but agreed that, because he had received an indeterminate sentence, he had to avoid a relapse. At this moment the sergeant phoned and told me that on his own initiative he had just searched Ebbe's cell. He had found writings of a childish character which gave the impression of being letters of departure saying that, if nothing worked, he would say good-bye to everything.

My interview continued with this new knowledge in the back-ground, and I pressed Ebbe to explain his recent emotional situation in more detail. He continued to discuss his wife's difficult situation. He knew very well that she herself would not go into debt in order to smoke more because of her problems. In relation to this, he said that he was like a fourteen-year-old boy who one moment wants to be a fireman, and the next, a furniture-maker. He did not think very far ahead. It was easy to get him to explain that he had been anxious, but he denied that we had any reason to believe that he had suicidal ideas. When I told him that our suspicions had a realistic basis, he became shocked. Then he suddenly explained that he had written some foolish things and called them teen-age ideas of the kind he had already mentioned, but he said that, considering his family as well as himself, he could not seriously think of carrying them out. Then the discussion turned to the reason for Ebbe's placement here and the necessity for him to find realistic solutions to small problems in order to learn to solve larger ones. At the end of our discussion he told me that his wife had said that her continuation of their marriage depended on his developing a more stable sense of economy.

No solution of his debt problem was arranged. After this interview we assumed that the risk of Ebbe's suicide was slight. The sergeant received a summary of our conversation and later said that he had been surprised to see how relaxed Ebbe had appeared after the interview. He made no suicide attempt, and he began to consult his therapist intensively.

Anamnestic Analysis

On the basis of experiences similar to the one with Ebbe, we arrived at a more systematic use of personal conflicts and formulated a treatment concept called anamnestic analysis, "a method aimed at the patient's emotional and intellectual reliving of earlier interpersonal conflicts on the basis of his attitude to interpersonal situations in the present."[27]

The expression "anamnestic analysis" was first used by C. G. Jung in 1931.[28] His concept was somewhat different from ours, since he used association tests and dream interpretations to bring unconscious factors into the consciousness. Using the method as we do, it is possible to get the detainee to recognize unsatisfactory personality patterns and notice how these reoccur in a peculiarly stereotyped way in many interpersonal situations. In the practical work we stress that the detainee who seems to progress in treatment must also demonstrate this progress in observably better relations to his surroundings and that he should appear more free and open in his daily life. Instead of relying only upon what occurs in individual interviews and on the detainee's own explanations, we can, by observing him in the wards and workshops, further control what actually happens in his interpersonal relations.

Anamnestic analysis has some similarity to character analysis, but it can more reasonably be called an analysis of development. We work by steadily circling around emotion-laden conditions that are not yet clearly recognized. Frequently emotion-laden situations develop during interviews and may be observed gradually and under control. Sometimes we try to get the inmate, between interviews with the therapist, to comment in letters to him about occurrences in the interviews and in his daily life. This gives us another chance to exploit the experience, combine it with observations of his inter-

[27] Erik Hoeck-Gradenwitz, "The Use of Anamnestic Analysis," *Bulletin de la Société International de Criminologie* (1960, 2° semestre):264–85.

[28] Carl G. Jung, *Seelenprobleme der Gegenwart,* 1st ed. (Zurich: Rascher, 1931).

personal relations, and use all kinds of material to support the social learning processes. The interview experiences are thus one link in the total chain aiming "to establish new attitudes and incorporate new knowledge."[29] In order to succeed, the therapist using anamnestic analysis must work in close contact with the other staff members so that he can form a many-sided impression of the detainee's life pattern and so that the detainee, himself, can recognize his "relatively enduring pattern of interpersonal situations."[30]

One of the results of anamnestic analysis has been the clear recognition that the majority of our people are handicapped and hurt primarily by their special way of perceiving and reacting to external situations. Most of the analyzed detainees have had great difficulties with parents, stepparents, sisters, brothers, people at school, and so forth. However, they have not been exposed to greater difficulties than many others have. It is as if these people have been especially sensitive, clinging to external difficulties, and are thus unable to make themselves free in new circumstances. Explaining why this is so is a complicated problem which is by no means solved. It is likely that genetic structure, somatic disorders at crucial times, and psychological experiences may be responsible and that the symptoms may be the same, regardless of the different etiology. These inmates are fixed in their relationship to other people and stereotyped in their reactions, which occur repeatedly in the same manner that they were released at the time of the original frustrations. Their emotional relationships to other people are insufficient. Frequently they have no confidence and are insecure, and this hampers their social learning processes and makes their perception of surroundings one-tracked. Because of these maladaptations and repeated disappointments, many of these persons develop a childish, egocentric pattern and react very immaturely.

I shall not discuss the maturity problems in detail here. We use Sullivan, Grant, and Grant's seven-step description of developmental aspects in daily work.[31] I should note that the inmate himself may also feel a subjective experience of regression. Hoeck–Gradenwitz

[29] Erik Hoeck-Gradenwitz, "The Use of Anamnestic Analysis," *Bulletin de la Société Internationale de Criminologie* (1960, 2ᵉ semestre):264–85.

[30] H. S. Sullivan, *Conceptions of Modern Psychiatry* (New York: W. W. Norton, 1953).

[31] Clyde Sullivan, Margaret Q. Grant, and J. Douglas Grant, "The Development of Interpersonal Maturity: Applications to Delinquency," *Psychiatry,* 20(1957):373.

described such a case in 1958.[32] At the age of ten, Hans lost his father, who was the only member of his family to whom he felt any attachment. His mother was hot-tempered and strict and often administered corporal punishment, although on the whole she was disinterested in him. As an adult, he was unable to free himself from the family in spite of the fact that he was ruthlessly exploited economically. He solved his conflict with his family (and during marriage, the conflict with his wife) by turning to crime. After each of several terms of imprisonment, he returned to his family. Later he said, "I have longed to find warmth and love in a home. Mother never told me stories or chatted with me, as I have read that other mothers do with their children. When I was released from prison, I found no joy in my homecoming. Each time I believed that it would be different; I hoped and yearned; and each time I came home it was the same flop. I wanted to please them and gain their love; they demanded more and more of me. I wanted to get away from it all and committed crimes. Then I was ashamed of myself and wanted to set things right. I was often happy at being arrested. Even though it was hell in prison, there was a kind of peace and quiet there."

We have observed different degrees of maturity (the levels of maturity obtainable—observed—in a given situation) in the same person in different situations. When our inmates get into difficulty they, like many other people, regress and are likely to react in the same way they have done in an earlier stage. One of the aims of this therapeutical method is to acquaint the inmate with his patterns of reactions, then to get him to realize the possibility of change, and sometimes to uncover the etiological process.

The results of anamnestic analysis are usually better with younger persons, twenty-five to thirty years old, than with the older, fifty- to sixty-year-old group. Often it takes a long time, sometimes several years, before their social learning processes have developed sufficiently so that their relapses really stop.

This story of a fairly characteristic case will illustrate the necessity for patience and for the integration of anamnestic analysis with the total psychotherapeutical apparatus of the total treatment system.

Karl was a housebreaker. Upon receiving his sixth sentence, he was sent to a mental hospital for observation. The Medico-Legal

[32] Erik Hoeck-Gradenwitz, "Maturity and Life Stages," *Acta Psychiatrica*, 33(1958):452–70.

Council agreed with the result of this observation and declared him to be "not fit for punishment." In the lower court he received a sentence of two years in prison; in the superior court this was changed to detention and he was admitted to Herstedvester in 1953.

It was soon obvious that Karl's childhood years had been considerably more frustrating than they had been described in the report from the mental hospital. His behavior could not be explained as the secondary, social consequences of his five previous prison terms.

He was born out of wedlock, and as a child, he lived with his grandparents. When he was in his teens, he went to live with his mother, who had married. He regarded his stepfather as a devil. Moving from his grandparents' home to that of his mother and stepfather was like going from paradise to hell. Later he was sent to institutions for juveniles, and he felt this was very unjust.

After he had spent fifteen months in Herstedvester, we obtained a series of realistic evaluations of his life pattern. Until then he had maintained a façade which was unapproachable. Contrary to what his wife (a foreigner of borderline intelligence, quite neurotic, and fourteen years older than Karl) said at the hospital where he had been observed, he claimed that his marriage was very satisfactory. His wife changed her story when he came into detention and agreed that their marriage was satisfactory. The social aide visited her home when a former workmate of the detainee happened to be present. He said he thought it was wrong for her to tell such stories because in reality Karl had been extremely hard to live with. She then stated that her first description of her hardships in the marriage were correct. She repeated this in an interview with the doctor at the institution and mentioned that Karl was explosive and often hit her. She did not want us to tell him about this interview. When he visited her home during a six-hour leave, she continued to try to present an idyllic picture of their marriage but he, himself, was more interested in his radio hobby than in her. On the fourth visit to his home, he broke out of his quiet role and became aggressive and irritable because he had not been able to get any clear answer from us about our view of his future. In his next interview with the doctor he said that he had behaved well in the institution. We agreed and said that we recognized this but that we still could not understand why he, a fully trained furniture-maker with a good earning capacity, had been living as a criminal. He lost his quiet mask and refused to discuss the matter further. He said he might run away either from his six-hour leave the following day or from the institution. The six-hour leave was postponed for a week, and the emotion-laden situation was further exploited in several discussions of his general situation. He became pacified and agreed that it was necessary to discuss his history in a series of interviews. As soon as these were under way, he again received his monthly leaves. During the next leave he met his guardian, who promised to file an application for parole with the court. After this short period of realistic interviews, we reported in our parole recommendation that Karl was a good worker who could obtain a well-paid job, but we also mentioned that we had not arrived at any really deep impression of the mechanics resulting in his crimes. On the other hand, he seemed to have obtained some understanding of his own problems and had developed a more friendly and understanding pattern in his collaboration with the institution. Furthermore, considering that he was a property criminal, we recommended parole in spite of the fact that we knew he would return to his wife and that her own behavior had not been irreproachable.

He was paroled, and after about a month he left home and asked for a separation from his wife. He moved to another place, and it was our impression that he was pacified and well-occupied. About half a year after parole, he began a new series of housebreakings which brought him back to Herstedvester. The defense lawyer protested his return and wanted a new mental observation, which his guardian and the institution did not think was necessary. Karl was angry that the guardian went against his wish and found a new guardian for whom he had great respect and confidence.

When he returned to the institution, he agreed that the return was just, and he wanted to be accepted immediately for group therapy. Here he described himself as just an "ordinary, dirty thief." Throughout his individual interviews his desire to live without any real contact with other people was discussed. It was a great advantage that he had a close emotional attachment to his guardian with whom we also had good cooperation. He also established good contact with the social section. From the ward observations we noted that the brawling and boasting behavior which had been dominant during his first session with us had disappeared.

He was paroled for the second time after a year and nine months, and this time the social section's contact with him was very close. After some months he became engaged. His divorce was not yet final and we did not try to hurry it. He worked for long hours, and

once he fainted on the street and was taken to the emergency section
of a hospital, but he left before the staff had finished examining him.
He earned a good deal of money, but he was not economical and
sometimes had to borrow money from the social section. He always
returned what he had borrowed.

Karl's relationship with his fiancée appeared very emotional in the
beginning, but this changed, little by little. His ambition to be independent in his work was curbed. After four years he moved away
from his fiancée but continued to keep in touch with his guardian.

A few months later Karl was apprehended for a very small theft at
work. He lost his job, but the police dismissed him before they contacted us or the guardian. He managed to get a new job and then told
the social section what had happened. We had been considering final
discharge for him but gave this up. The guardian explained that Karl
had been having difficulties for some time. Because the stolen goods
was only worth about 600 kroner ($100), and Karl had managed
without crime for four years, his case was closed with a warning that
he must keep the conditions of his parole. He felt that he had been
very foolish to "fall" again after having had such a long crime-free
period. Although he excused himself a little by saying that many
others steal from the shops where they work, he seemed to be solidly
balanced.

After this, our contact with him became sporadic. He found a new
girl friend and married without telling us, but in the following years
everything went well, and he was finally discharged after seven years.
During the next two years we had enough peripheral contact with
him to know that his social situation seems stable, and he has not
been criminal.

Hypnosis, Relaxation, and Narcosynthesis

At times we have had therapists who have tried hypnotic or
narcohypnotic methods. The results have not been successful enough
to warrant developing them into standard methods. Relaxation treatment of aggressive tendencies has been successfully carried out at
times for explosive inmates.[33] However, this treatment calls for
special abilities on the part of the psychotherapist and the relaxation
therapist, and we have not been able to systematize it so that it can
be used by most therapists.

[33] Jan Sachs, "Psykoterapeutisk behandling af eksplosive," *Nordisk Tidsskrift for Kriminalvidenskab,* 38(1950):218–24.

In order to make some basic observations about our narcoanalytic treatment, which we prefer to call "narcosynthesis," I will describe this program in a little more detail.

Narcosynthesis has been used in Herstedvester since the latter part of the 1940's. We already had the impression that so-called severe constitutional psychopaths were conflict-ridden and therefore we thought it worth while to see if a short-cut method could help us in treating them. It is well known that narcoanalysis should not be used in cases in which court decisions are pending because of the danger of self-incrimination and the necessity to protect the ordinary human rights of the inmates.

The case of Sven illustrates the use of narcosynthesis. His eighth sentence was four years for robbery and several housebreakings. During his imprisonment he developed a rather severe depressive reaction which required psychiatric treatment. He was transferred to Herstedvester for observation, and we found that some of his symptoms were caused by an attack by another criminal on Sven's sister. During his intensive treatment, aided by narcosynthesis, he explained that he was really not guilty of the robbery he was sentenced for but had severe guilt feelings concerning another robbery for which he was not sentenced. This confession placed us in a serious medicoethical conflict. His therapist and I advised him to bring the case before the court, but he did not want to do this because it might prolong his imprisonment. We found that his explanations were unsystematic and disconnected. We felt that we must not note this information in Sven's case history where it would be accessible to many people, so we kept it in a closed envelope as confidential medical information which, according to the law, must be kept secret.

During the narcosynthesis and related therapeutical contact Sven became relaxed, his acute psychiatric problem was solved, and he was transferred back to prison. Later he relapsed into new crime and was sentenced to one year of imprisonment. He relapsed once more and was sentenced to detention. We kept him for four years, then he managed outside for five. However, loyalty to a friend from the institution involved him in a small theft which brought him back to us. He was kept fourteen months and is now, after a little more than two years, balanced psychologically and has kept the sympathy of his family and friends, which he built up during his five years in free society.

There are other problems in normal prison work. Nearly all long-time inmates appear psychopathological; some encapsulate themselves, some are obsessive and think of wild inventions such as perpetual motion machines, and some are paranoid but have some understanding of the ridiculousness of their statements and cannot be compared with ordinary paranoids. Others have a gossip's interest in the institution which involves them completely and also furnishes the institution's walls with ears that misinterpret the tiny facts they collect. These curiosity-ridden prisoners develop stories, adapted to the other prisoners' expectations, that move through the prison like lightning, "explaining" what has happened in flagrantly wrong terms. All of this may disappear when they leave prison.

Having developed these mechanisms, the long-timers are ready to react in a way that deviates considerably from the ordinary. The mechanisms work as a shield, protecting them from difficulties and mistreatment, or, perhaps more correctly, what they experience as such, that may motivate them to self-pity.

If, suddenly and unexpectedly, we uncover such reactions and their backgrounds, it is easy to understand that aggressiveness and a feeling of being hurt by the therapist may result. A prisoner will feel over-sensitive if his shell that protects him against prison life is destroyed. In such cases the fear of not being able to manage through a long sentence, like any other serious anxiety, may result in the most unexpected reactions.

In Herstedvester, where the inmates theoretically can expect their periods of detention to bear some relation to the possibility of leading a crime-free life outside, the acceptability of narcosynthesis is fairly certain, but when the therapeutical machinery functions well the need for these short-cuts is not great. Intimate dependency on the therapist may develop in the inmate as a result of narcosynthesis, but we have not observed any type of continued aggressiveness or hostility against him. After we had some practical experiences, we found it reasonable to use narcosynthesis only where there seemed to be a clearly expressed need for fast assistance in actual difficulties.

The interview begins before the injection of the drug, continues during its influence, and through the waking phase so that the patient, half-awake, can remember what he has been telling us and we can immediately discuss with him what he said while he could not control what he was saying. Our technique is thus rather time-consuming, but, in order to build up the detainee's self-respect and his feeling of being the most important person in the construction of an acceptable way of life for himself, it is essential that he know exactly what he has said. Furthermore, the treatment is risky. Patients with latent aggressiveness may react very impulsively when their conscious controls are weakened and be of considerable danger to the therapist.

Our experiences with Erik illustrate these dangers. He was twenty-three when we began working with him. From the age of sixteen he participated in World War II on the German side. At first we did not know that, as a member of a what he called a Death Battalion, (Toteskopf Bataillon, a part of the SS Einsatsgruppen), he had taken part in severe cruelties against the Polish people. After having served some short sentences for service in the German army and for theft, he came into detention for housebreakings, thefts, and aggressive robbery. He was classified as self-assertive and morally deteriorated.

During detention, after some months of ordinary passiveness, Erik developed a period of depression, sleeplessness, and nightmares. He cried out in panic and seriously disturbed the peace of his ward. He could not explain why he suffered, but he found it strange that he now enjoyed other people's suffering instead of disliking it as he had as a child and during adolescence. He still clearly remembered the people he had killed and tortured in Poland. He knew that he might be dangerous in his nightly screaming phases, and he said that it had not been his fault that he had not committed more serious crimes than the ones for which he was sentenced. His emotional contact with others was not satisfactory. He freely admitted that during the war it had felt good to behave as he did and complained that there was something wrong in his not feeling any guilt now. He said he had really enjoyed being a soldier and that, after all, it was "only Poles who had suffered." This condition continued for about half a year. He became more and more troubled, was obviously suffering, and we supposed that he could be dangerous if his problems were not uncovered. Erik was eager to rid himself of his nightmares, so we attempted narcosynthesis.

During his first narcosynthetic treatment he suddenly jumped up from the couch while he was describing a battle. He screamed about serious attacks, especially against a little boy and a young woman, and threatened the doctor who at the last moment got help from others. The doctor, pale and shocked, came to see me shortly after the incident. I mistakenly did not take it very seriously for it seemed to me that it was too dramatic, and I wanted to see for myself what had happened. The therapist insisted that I should not be alone with Erik because he was still convinced that it could be dangerous. Unfortunately I did not believe this, but during the next narcosynthetic treatment the situation repeated itself, and the doctor and I, together, had great difficulty in managing this strong young man who thought of us as enemies. We put him in the isolation section and continued our interview there. During this and the following sessions he uncovered serious pubertal conflicts related to his mother. Later he observed her in situations that caused him to completely break his ties with her. Erik achieved definite relaxation from this treatment, but since his violence we have insisted that narcosynthesis be carried out only in the isolation section with the inmate tied down in bed. In this case, narcosynthesis, as such, did not lead to success.

In the following years, Erik attempted to escape, his nightmares reoccurred several times, and he lost confidence that anyone would do anything good for him. We were forced to repeat the narcosynthesis several times. Erik's limited intelligence and lack of stability made it very difficult to continue treatment over any length of time. One year later, when he was in an emotional mood around Christmas, we tried without any result to get him to go to church. Later we had the impression that the chemical effect of the drugs was pleasing him too much, and we tried a light hypnotic synthesis to which he was now receptive.

These treatments had an indirect effect on his future through the close contact he developed with one of the friendly, quiet officers who was on duty in the isolation section. After Erik had been in detention for three and a half years, this officer suggested to the therapist that perhaps he could get a good job for Erik if he were paroled. By then he had had several six-hour leaves, and he was less explosive than usual when he was with this officer. His obvious feelings of guilt increased when he read books concerning war. He re-established relations with his parents. He no longer mentioned his mother's earlier behavior and reported that his father's drinking was less serious. He was transferred to the open section and then paroled. The parole was certainly not peaceful, but we need not go through all of Erik's frequent conflicts during the following twelve years.

He married, and some months later an extremely serious drama of jealousy developed. Only the swift intervention of the friendly officer and the social aide kept it from resulting in homicide. At another time we had a telephone call from a small inn in the country where he had been heard to say that he was going to kill his unfaithful, former wife. Because he had to go several kilometers to reach her home, I had sufficient time to mobilize the local police, who picked him up. As nothing criminal had happened, the police and Erik, himself, asked me to take him back for a short time to cool off. He returned to the institution of his own free will on several other occasions when he felt that everything was going wrong. When he went on drinking sprees, he usually told the officer or the social aide about it. For many years he has not been sentenced for a new crime, although his finances have been unstable because of periodic severe misuse of alcohol.

Erik's case clearly illustrates another point. I have already said that narcosynthetic treatments solve only immediate problems and that long-range results require continuous close collaboration. Before his treatment, this unstable, insecure, and dull young man did not trust anyone in authority, although he did respect strong authoritarian behavior. Our willingness to help him and our respect for his own feeling of danger was important to him, and the narcosynthetic, short-range goals were valuable links in the chain of events which helped him. An unforeseen consequence was the fatherly way in which the officer he met in the isolation ward took charge of him. During the years, decisive interpersonal relations developed between these two men. The whole therapeutical apparatus of contact with the social aide, the officer, and the therapist has substantially assisted him in leading a crime-free life for more than seventeen years. However, although he is now more than forty years old, he has not succeeded in reaching the level of stability of an average citizen. I do not believe that we could have carried through a more thorough, individual therapy for Erik because his problems developed as a result of terrible experiences during a very sensitive period of his youth and his acts during the war were of a character that made it impossible to discuss them in a group. Our only way of helping him was to attempt to make these experiences seem far away.

Integration of All Activities

Bent's story illustrates the same type of integration of the whole treatment. A twenty-six-year-old property criminal, he was sentenced to Herstedvester for twenty-five housebreakings and three attempted housebreakings. While undergoing mental observation he had mentioned his fear that he would kill women, a fear which he said was related to a period when he lived with a sexually dominating woman who was some years older than himself. He was always attracted to women older than himself, and he could not get this particular woman out of his mind. During the mental observation he described his obsessional sexual ideas and talked vaguely about getting rid of them by killing some woman.

Bent was described as above normal intellectually, choleric, asthenic, and impulsive, partly because of difficult family relationships in his childhood and partly because of war experiences in the German army. He was supposed to be very dangerous and he seriously misused alcohol.

In Herstedvester he was tense and anxious but not very peculiar in behavior. He wanted to talk about what troubled him and stressed, as he had done during the mental observation, that "something must be done." During his first months in Herstedvester he was balanced and reasonable, but then he changed. He would not stay in the workshop, refused to be with "thieves and insane persons," was abusive, would not explain what troubled him, reacted aggressively, and sweated during interviews. He felt persecuted by the psychiatrist who had observed him. He said threateningly that he wanted treatment and wanted to go to the mental hospital, but his threats did not seem very sincere. He insisted that he heard voices and said that he was afraid that he would be psychotic like his grandmother. During this period I had some penetrating interviews with Bent about his life, and he regretted that he had been "foolish enough to tell about" his obsessions. Now he explained that he had had some of the obsessions for a very long time. He dreamed of falling, and sometimes he had a creepy feeling. When he was a boy he was afraid of the dark. He felt that his mother was very foolish, but he felt close to her. He had been severely punished by his father and he hated him and pilfered from him in revenge, but no one had ever tried to help him. He was often truant from school and at an early age came under children's care because of petty criminality. After escaping from a home for juveniles, he joined the German army and found the discipline to be more severe than in the juvenile home.

Bent escaped from the army after having been in a special punishment battalion, and he came to Copenhagen where he hid for some time before he was caught, court-martialed, and sentenced to death. The court-martial proceedings were so prolonged that his death sentence was not carried out. In a Danish court he received a short prison sentence for being a traitor. Later he was imprisoned again because of sexual relations with a thirteen-year-old girl.

He tried to escape from Herstedvester because he was bitter about what he felt was insufficient medical treatment. He still thought about killing a woman and also about joining the French Foreign Legion. He had no difficulty completing one month of isolation for attempted escape, but he still was silent, reserved, and had some paranoid ideas about not getting enough treatment "because he was a traitor."

Bent began to have further obsessions. Formerly he had felt compelled to count to five; now seven was his critical number. Some months later he was depressed, and because of his continuing feeling of pressure, we tried narcosynthetic interviews with him. He started talking about a bayonet charge on the Eastern front and about his wife, whom he had deserted in order to live with the previously mentioned aggressive woman. He spoke of his father in a derogatory way but did not show paranoid symptoms. During the third treatment he talked in detail about his childhood, his fear of darkness, his past punishments, and his revengeful stealing. In the German army he had asserted himself as much as possible before older soldiers. He had easy relationships with women and talked a great deal about them.

Bent now had great confidence in his therapist. After three weeks he told of suffering still more from memories of the war at the Eastern front. He could not sleep; he was hallucinating, had nightmares, and finally had to be treated in the infirmary. When an officer was attacked by a fellow inmate, Bent helped to take him to the isolation section. He became more and more depressed, suicidal, and anxious; finally he became so ill that we had to transfer him to a psychiatric hospital where he still suffered from depressive psychosis.

He wanted shock treatment but at first the doctors did not think it was indicated. For a time there was discussion about whether he should be transferred legally to the hospital, but that was decided against. Finally he received electroshock treatments, and he returned to Herstedvester in improved condition. At the hospital he became acquainted with a fellow patient, and he stayed in touch with him. Ten months after he returned from the hospital, he became aggressive again, nursed serious grievances, and refused to believe what we said. We had not lived up to his expectations, and he would not cooperate with us any more.

After a year Bent applied for a six-hour leave, which was not permitted. After some time he was allowed to work outside the walls.

For a time he became more open and positive, and he worked hard. We then recommended six-hour leaves.

In his therapeutical interviews he now freely mentioned his feeling of shame because of his relations with the thirteen-year-old girl and explained that at first he had denied the deed to the police because it was "as if it made it undone." He said he hated Herstedvester's atmosphere and the other inmates. "Half of them just have a homosexual interest in you and the other half are nuts," he said. He now felt that he was stable; he was not depressed, but he longed for freedom.

Bent was transferred to the open section, but three weeks later he had to be returned to the main institution. In a phone call just before midnight, I was informed that he had been on a six-hour leave which had seemed to be satisfactory, but during the evening he discussed escape several times. He was transferred to the infirmary, where he sneered at his fellow inmates, their psychopathic talk, and so forth. He told a woman psychiatrist, with whom he had previously been well satisfied, that women should not be employed in the institution. He also claimed that people had forced him to buy narcotics and that he would commit suicide if it were not unworthy to die in Herstedvester. He returned again to his paranoid idea that the observing psychiatrist had arranged for someone to spy on him during his stay in Herstedvester. He was depressed and angry, but his mention of hallucinations seemed very theatrical and was not convincing. Parole had been under discussion, but we advised against it.

A month later he was allowed again to go on six-hour leaves. This time he visited his family. His relationship to his father was excellent, and he seemed to be attached to his mother. He explained that he had given her a great deal of trouble and would now try to make up for it. However, the court followed our advice not to parole him at that time.

After two years and three months, his situation was much more balanced. He still insisted, but unconvincingly, that he had used narcotics. He seemed optimistic, had good self-control, and, because he really had a strong personality, we believed it was possible for him to maintain a life without new crime.

Although Bent's guardian had put his case before the court some months before we planned to advise parole, his development had been so good that we could not advise against it.

Two weeks before he was to be paroled, he explained to a new therapist that he was not so much opposed to individual homosexuals as to the institutional homosexuality which had troubled him because of the jealousy and sensationalism that developed. Then he explained that while he had been a young private in the German army he had been forced into sexual relations with a German officer; although he had been panic-stricken, he did not dare to resist. At that point he started talking about something else, and, because of his approaching parole, we did not dare to return to the subject.

Bent was paroled after two and a half years. We succeeded, with some difficulty, in finding a good job for him. A month later he was found unconscious on the street near Herstedvester, and the police picked him up. He refused to say anything to them but asked to talk with a doctor from Herstedvester. The doctor came with an officer who had taken special interest in Bent, took him to his home, and then placed him with a friend whom he had visited on six-hour leaves. He was not inebriated, and it was not clear whether he had taken narcotics. Because he had misused alcohol at times, he was put in touch with Alcoholics Anonymous and antabus treatment was begun. Everything went peacefully and happily for a while, then he had to enter a hospital because of inebriation and concussion of the brain.

It developed that Bent had married without telling the institution and had given his wife a very incomplete history of himself. At times he went to a mental hospital, and he was often inebriated, but he managed to keep a responsible job as a crane driver, although he complained that it was enervating.

In a Christmas greeting a few years after parole, he wrote to me and his social aide that he had a fresh view of what we had done for him at the institution, and he thanked us for what we had done. He went to his social aide and his therapist spontaneously several times for help with his marriage, but his wife left him.

Some days before this happened, he had asked for admission to a psychiatric unit, but they did not want to take him as an acute case. A few days later he discussed the possibility of working on a boat for a time, with a therapist who promised to help him get a berth. There was nothing special in his behavior at that time, but he committed suicide the following night.

It is regrettable that Bent would not accept ordinary psychotherapy during his parole period, but at that time he was so happy with the results already obtained from treatment that he was not at all interested in going further. He was probably aware that it would have been difficult to arrange because the therapist would have had to receive him in the evenings and this would have embarrassed him.

Drug Treatment

LSD (lysergic acid diethylamide) treatment developed a few years ago. This is an analytical treatment program, loosening the customary boundaries of consciousness for a short period. We tried it in a few cases, and also attempted synthesis, to reintegrate the patients' concepts of their own psychological development, but the treatment had no positive results and we gave it up.

Vanggaard has followed twenty-four patients treated in England and given a careful analysis of the results.[34] The five who were cured had been well adjusted in ordinary social and personal relations. They adhered to general norms with average conscientiousness, were reliable, and could tolerate disappointments. They also were able to establish and maintain close and stable relationships with other people. They were suffering from inhibitions and frustrations inherent in their conditions. The symptoms of each of these patients were delineated, homogeneous, and stable. None of them had abused alcohol or medicine. None of them had a markedly deviating personality or manifest perversions. In their habitual personalities, nothing was found which could arouse suspicion of a potential psychosis.

The characteristics of these patients are now commonly used as a basis for limiting this form of treatment. If these were ideal cases for LSD treatment, it is understandable that we had no especially good results. We work with a type of person whose personality is not strong and who does not easily tolerate a weakening of defense mechanisms with its resulting activation of latent conflicts. In our psychotherapy we try to "freeze" such conflicts, as only a few of our cases could face them openly. Our inmates basically hunger for interhuman sympathy but at the same time are afraid to receive it. Only slowly, and often only in new surroundings, do they dare to attempt to live a normal social life.

Some institutions and hospitals do not agree with our skeptical attitude about suddenly uncovering defense mechanisms, and they continue to use LSD treatment for persons with personality deviations. However, there was a case in Denmark when a conflict was activated

---

[34] Thorkil Vanggaard, "Om indikationer og kontraindikationer for LSD-behandling," *Nordisk Psykiatrisk Tidsskrift,* 19(1965):240–51.

in a female patient having ambulatory LSD treatment. One afternoon, after having received LSD in the morning, she killed her former lover.

In mental hospitals, treatment with many new psychopharmacological drugs has recently become very important. Troublesome, schizophrenic, manic, senile, hallucinatory, and paranoid states have been treated with great success. In hospitals a more peaceful climate has developed that encourages direct psychotherapy and useful occupations, as well as other attempts at re-socialization.

In treating behavior disorders which cannot be attributed to "disease" but which are immature reactions to surroundings, one ought to be reluctant to use drug treatment. Drugs may be of value for a short time, but they ought not to be used for combating disciplinary difficulties. The very unstable and aggressive person, often involved in conflicts he himself regrets, may be helped to overcome his aggressive tendencies and then to take part in group therapy. He may learn that other people do not always react as provocatively as he thought they did. This may start a positive development, but the administrator has to realize that drugs do not make the therapeutic work easier. Like therapists in hospitals, our therapist must spend more time on his patients when they want to collaborate than when they are isolated. Occupational therapy must be developed in order to make the most of the situation. If this is not done, no personality growth will result, and the patient may feel abandoned once more by authorities, just when he needed their help.[35]

We still use drugs only when symptoms are exceptionally serious and usually only for short periods while the inmate is in the institution or on parole. The most important result of drug treatment is the reduction of aggressive tendencies, but this, alone, cannot motivate parole. We must be certain that the patient will be able to avoid aggressiveness when he is without drugs.

In our sister institution, Horsens, it has appeared recently that antidepressant drugs of the Tofranil type have satisfactory effects on persons with characterological deviations such as sensitivity, emotional lability, and tendencies to paranoid misinterpretation. These observations have not yet been confirmed, but it is possible that

[35] Georg K. Stürup, "Les Nouvelles Chemothérapies en Psychiatrie: Leurs Possibilités d'Adaptation à Certains Délinquants," *Bulletin de la Société Internationale de Criminologie* (1957, 2ᵉ semestre):269–70.

drugs will be found that will help us in our therapeutical and re-social-izing efforts.[36]

Ødegård stressed that in our enthusiasm for innovations we must remember that the drug period has not brought about any revolution.[37] The percentage of discharges from mental hospitals has increased, but the proportion of readmissions is also high. To evaluate the influence of drugs on criminal behavior accurately, we would need to follow a series of case histories through many years, and the opportunity for this is not yet in sight.

Clinically, drugs may subdue explosive persons whose unpredic-tability makes the personnel insecure and causes the inmates them-selves to feel provoked. Through drug treatment a patient may be motivated to recognize his own part in a chain of situations and to realize that it would be desirable to ask for psychotherapeutic help to understand these relationships. In recent years the therapeutic climate in the institution has been more calm, and explosive cases have not been common.

In order to survey our use of psychopharmacological drugs, we analyzed the frequency of their use over a period of two months. Truxal and Largactil (chloropromazine preparations) were used in thirteen cases in November, 1964, and in twelve cases in November, 1965. Trilafon (Perphenazinum) was used in one case in each of the two months. Less potent drugs of a sedative type were used in eighteen other cases. Hypnotic drugs were not used in either of the two months.

Since the beginning of the 1950's, we have occasionally used a female hormone treatment (usually five to ten milligrams of estro-gen a week) in order to help some detainee suffering from a strong sexual drive. In 1949, Golla, Hodge, and Spence published a study of diminished sexual activity in men who have received estrogen

---

[36] The treatment in our two detention institutions is the same in principle, even though differences of a practical nature have developed. In Horsens the medical elements of treatment are stressed, whereas in Herstedvester we emphasize integration of a series of treatment elements that include psychiatric treatment. The staff at Horsens works, with the aid of drugs, to break the vicious circle of paranoid tendencies characterized by psychic instability which results in conflicts and defeats that further augment the difficulties. In Hersted-vester we also observe such vicious circles, but we believe that self-respect and personal responsibility are such basic elements that we should, as far as possible, avoid drug or other types of treatment that could be interpreted as some sort of "magic."

[37] Ørnulf Ødegård, "The Fate of Psychiatric Patients in Norway Before and After the Introduction of Drug Therapy," Neuropharmacology, 3(1964):565–71.

preparations.[38] In 1950, Bleuler and Zublin showed through experiments on animals that sexual hormones from the opposite sex had an
irregular effect on the sexual drive.[39] In some cases the drive was
higher; in others, lower. They gave testosterone proprionate to seventeen women, and, besides physical changes, they found an increase
in sexual drive and slightly euphorizing effects in mild depressive
states. In three men receiving large doses of female hormones, the
sexual drive became subdued.

In 1952, Hauser, Friedemann, and Baan used female hormones in
order to subdue male sexuality.[40] In 1959, in Herstedvester, Hoeck-
Gradenwitz used a conbination of estrogen treatment and psychotherapy with very fine results.[41]

It seems that supportive therapy, as well as more clarifying therapy,
can be carried through more easily when sexual problems are not
overwhelming. Some inmates feel so troubled by their sexual urges at
times that they become aggressive and provoke conflicts, and a short
period of estrogen treatment may be a great help in such cases.

GENERAL MEDICAL TREATMENT AND HEALTH PROBLEMS

When an inmate says he is ill, it is important that his illness be
accepted, but also that his whole situation and background be analyzed
so that symptoms of disease are not unnecessarily misused to allow
him to escape from a situation. This demand is idealistic. In practice,
some inmates having diseases with obvious hysterical overlayers or
clear simulations are removed to the infirmary. Although we may
risk allowing a patient to get away with a profitable simulation which
is dangerous to his personality development, we must treat his complaint as a "formal disease" if we are not absolutely sure that there
is not, behind the symptoms, a disease that demands somatic or

---

[38] F. L. Golla and R. Sessions Hodge, "Hormone Treatment of the Sexual
Offender," *Lancet*, 1(1941):1006.

[39] M. Bleuler and W. Zublin, "Zur Kenntnis der psychischen Wirkung von
Sexualhormonen in hohen Dosen," *Wiener Medizinische Wochenschrift*, 100
(1950):229.

[40] E. H. Hauser, "Psychische Wirkung von Sexualhormonen," *Schweizerische
Medizinische Wochenschrift*, 21(1952):566; A. Friedmann, "Beitrag zur Hormo-
nalen Kastration," *Beiträge zur Sexualforschung*, 2(1952):65; P. A. H. Baan,
"Zur Frage der Behandlung von Sittlichkeitsdelinquenten," *Beiträge zur Sexualforschung*, 2(1952):24.

[41] Erik Hoeck-Gradenwitz, "Diognosticering og behandling ud fra social-
psykologiske synspunkter," *Sociologiske Meddelelser* (1961), pp. 113–35.

psychosomatic treatment. This calls for very careful medical scrutiny, but we should never perform medically unnecessary special examinations, even if we risk an inmate's complaint that our medical treatment has not been thorough enough.

When a man reports illness, he may stay in his room for up to two days, but his door must be closed so that he is isolated. If he says that he has a headache, the result will be the same as if he simply does not want to work—he will spend the day in his room. He is not allowed to "recover" before the next day; he can not be ill in the morning but have a pleasant evening with his comrades on the same day. We prefer to let the inmates become bored enough by themselves so that they realize that they gain nothing of real value by being classified as ill. Furthermore, we argue that people who frequently fake illness have many difficulties in life in free society and that their dishonesty will influence our decisions about work outside the walls, work in free society, or even parole.

We give no sleeping drugs in the ordinary units and we seldom hear complaints about sleeplessness. If such complaints are made, we answer that most people sleep when they really need to and that experiments have shown that many people sleep more than they think they do. If a man insists that he needs a sleeping drug, we treat him as really sick and transfer him to the infirmary. Inmates seldom want this; a study of the number of patients at our infirmary during six months shows not a single case of this type.

The number of somatic diseases has been very small, probably because symptoms of disease are treated early. Each year all detainees and personnel are screened for tuberculosis.

Newcomers are usually reluctant to complain to the doctor, but people who have been here for some time are apt to go to the doctor for trivial somatic complaints. Perhaps insufficient motivation for work, caused by unsatisfactory workshops and low wages, plays a role in this development. However, many invented "diseases" must be recognized as attempts to make contact with "Section G," which houses the therapists and nurses. It is often obvious that the inmate's real need is to reach the therapist by talking to the nurses who then may "force upon him" further consultation with the doctor or preferably with his own therapist. This allows a detainee to avoid responsibility for calling on the therapist for psychological problems.

The ordinary requirement for admission to the infirmary is serious illness or a disease that has lasted more than two days. Sick pay is paid after three days of illness. Only a few private belongings are allowed in the infirmary.

An analysis of the forty-four admissions during the half-year between September 1, 1964, and April 1, 1965, shows that only ten inmates stayed in the unit more than ten days each. One of these was in the infirmary for almost the whole period because of a severe heart disease which had been present when he was sentenced to detention. He was a very difficult person, convicted of theft and fraud. After he had been with us for one and a half years, his somatic disease was so incapacitating that he had to be in a convalescent home after parole. A short time later his condition improved and he went to live with his family; he has now managed in a private home with limited assistance for more than two years, but he still needs to sleep in a special heart-bed.

Another patient suffered from colitis ulcerosa and a tendency to infantile, hysterical explosive reactions. We brought him into much better balance, and he was later able to work as an ordinary workman in the institution. He was paroled but committed new property crimes a few months later. He complained in court that he had received insufficient medical treatment, although it had been approved by a specialist who also had treated the patient in his hospital unit several times.

Eight of those admitted to the infirmary had mainly psychosomatic complaints. One was in the infirmary for one hundred and forty-five days. He could have been classified as a purely psychiatric case, as he was very paranoid; given a new psychiatric examination, he would probably have been classified as psychotic paranoiac. He could not be treated in a mental hospital because he escaped frequently and committed a new crime each time, until he was transferred to Herstedvester.

Five cases were in the infirmary for psychiatric conditions, one for almost the whole period, one for more than one hundred days, and three for less than a week each. One was a thirty-five-year-old, emotionally labile property criminal who had misused alcohol and who had developed a clear depressive reaction with short manic phases at times. He stayed at the infirmary because he seemed to be developing a manic-depressive psychosis, but this diagnosis was not yet evident enough to justify transferring him to the mental hospital.

Another was an aggressive, very sensitive Eskimo with periodic dysphoria and such severe impulsive reactions that he could not be handled in a general ward. After two years he developed a depressive reaction with paranoid ideas, and he threatened suicide. During an interview in the office of one of the psychologists, he grasped a rather blunt paper knife and pushed it six or seven centimeters into his abdomen, but he did not wound himself seriously. For a time after this he heard vague voices but had no clear hallucinations. A year later he had improved and received permission for six-hour leaves.

The third was a thirty-one-year-old sexual criminal, sensitive, without contact, paranoid, embittered, and aggressive; he had had a short paranoid psychotic period.

The last two were both word-blind. One, twenty-three years old, was aggressive, spineless, egocentric, daydreaming, and emotionally infantile; he developed depressive periods with paranoid ideas. He was seriously concerned because the father of a girl he had attacked, his observing psychiatrist, and I, myself, all had names beginning with the letter S. Although a schizophrenic episode occurred, he has maintained his balance reasonably well for a long time.

The other was thirty years old and had been cared for as a mental defective from the ages of twelve to twenty-five. After that, he was an alcoholic and was sentenced ten times for theft. He was very immature and was probably better suited to treatment in a hospital than in Herstedvester; however, the hospitals have a policy of not wanting to treat those who are not clearly psychotic, so we did not transfer him. We managed at the infirmary to get him through a short, depressive paranoid phase.

In the same half-year, two persons were in the infirmary after castration operations and one was there for sterilization. Six were transferred to the medical unit of the prison system, and twenty-three were treated in the local hospital—eleven for less than four days and twelve for six to thirty-five days. During this hospitalization several valuable friendships developed, and the detainees usually presented themselves in their best light.

ENDING THE DETENTION PERIOD

The longer an inmate stays in Herstedvester, the nearer we come to the time when the court must reconsider the security measures presently prescribed for him and decide what controls he will need in the future. As this decision is made by the court, we must give the court clear and adequate information about the inmate as a basis for its decision.

From the time the detainee arrives at the institution, the degree of security that he requires is an essential element in all considerations. Successful treatment is the best way to reduce the likelihood of his committing a new crime. When each detainee arrives, we consider whether his psychological imbalance makes placement in the infirmary necessary. Is he in danger of suicide? Is there (and this is true of only a few cases) such a threat of aggression that he must begin his detention period in the security section?

As I have said, newcomers usually go to the special reception unit and returning detainees to one of the general sections. In deciding in which ward the detainee should be placed it is not enough to evaluate his actual behavior problems, but we must also consider the other inmates in the unit.

Daily, mutual adaptation is basic to living together peacefully. As a result of discussions in the daily conferences, we make steplike changes in placement; each inmate progresses to units in which he has increasingly more freedom and greater responsibility that demand constantly improving self-discipline. The speed with which he progresses depends on the types, the intensity, and the severity of the crimes he has committed. In most cases it is a step toward parole when an inmate is allowed to work outside the walls, but in some cases other considerations may be more important. An agricultural worker with a light criminal record may be transferred relatively early to agricultural work which will teach him something useful for his future life in society.

In our work we find special handicaps in trying to determine what personality factors will be especially important in each inmate's future. In the beginning a detainee may tend to simulate symptoms. This may be a protest reaction against placement in detention, against authority in general, or against something else. In later phases, we may notice dissimulation such as that of paranoid ideas, a phenomenon which is both important and difficult to see through. The detainee's working capabilities must be evaluated as well as his ability to entertain himself. In some cases a detainee's working skills are adequate, but his inability to adjust to a general workshop may destroy his opportunities to keep jobs.

It is often suggested that it is a weakness in the structure of the institution that the superintendent cannot discharge a detainee in the same way that the superintendent of a mental hospital can. This is not true. The primary purpose of detention in either a mental hospital or a special institution is the protection of life and property. Because a criminal's sentence is given to protect the community, its imposition and continuation are matters to be handled by an observant and diligent court, and it is the duty of the institution to place before the court all observations which may be relevant to the court's decisions.

It would be extremely dangerous for the responsible superintendent, himself, to have such powers that he alone were responsible for the detention of the inmates, and it would not help the inmate's personal development if his adjustment to institutional life were based only on fear of such power. The superintendent has, and must have, considerable influence on those in power, but he should not be in a position to demand any specific change in the pattern of the inmate's behavior. He can, and should, appeal to the emotions and reasons of both the inmates and the authorities, thus giving his share of help and encouragement to the re-socialization of the detainees. In this way he shows that he regards the inmates as fellow human beings. He appeals to them and tries to manipulate and explain situations so that they are meaningful to them. When this is done, he must evaluate how much the inmates' behavior, and explanations of the behavior, are based on reality.

In considering parole, the superintendent must evaluate the danger from the inmate's criminality and predict his probable reactions to living in free society. The superintendent must also ask himself if this is a well-known criminal who has committed a widely publicized crime such as homicide or arson. If so, we probably must let several years pass, usually not less than five or six, before the case is forgotten by the public, and the court will grant parole.

Sometimes a journalist sees it as his mission in life to keep alive the memory of an inmate's crime. In such cases the need to respect the newspaper's idea of public opinion is not of prime importance, but the detainee's ability to withstand condemnation directed against him personally is vital. The way he is received in his new surroundings is important and may influence the likelihood of his calling for help from Herstedvester. Usually the inclination to call for assistance is less in parolees who are still acting-out and greater in those suffering from insecurity and inferiority feelings; therefore, the latter group are in less danger of provoking new conflicts with society.

I must carefully consider practical questions such as the inmate's ability to evaluate the risks involved in conflict situations and his ability to avoid them. Will he be able to realize soon enough that he needs our help? Will he be able to master opposition and seek our assistance, even at the risk of being considered a sissy?

In our parole recommendation to the court we attempt to integrate all of these elements with our over-all evaluation of the probability of new crime and our psychiatric knowledge of the inmate's probable future.

It is regrettable that this kind of psychiatric knowledge is still so limited. We do not possess a sufficiently systematic, scientific analysis of our experiences, although one could be made by examining criminal case studies.

Sometimes we have to express doubt about an inmate's future, and, if his former crime has been serious, his chance for parole is thereby lessened. This may mean that he will have to stay with us in spite of good behavior in the institution. If he is once again designated as dangerous by the court, this may influence later evaluations and develop into a self-fulfilling prophecy. In such cases we seldom get an opportunity to learn if our evaluations were wrong.

One of the main motives for the establishment of Herstedvester was that we should not be able to discharge a man after some fixed period as "untreatable," just because the time had passed. He continues to be a treatment problem for us. Even though a "cure" cannot always be achieved, we can sometimes reduce the risk of his causing inconvenience and danger to society enough so that he can be released. The time comes when we, as well as the court, feel that we cannot keep an inmate any longer, and we have never had reason to regret such a decision. In some cases we probably could have arrived at that conclusion a little earlier.

To prepare a detainee for parole, we try to make him realize that a crime-free life outside the institution will not be easy. Sometimes it will be more difficult than his life was before, and it will often be more difficult than life in detention. This means that the parolee must be able to stand strain. Therefore it is important that he have an adequate feeling of self-respect and believe that the new difficulties he has to face and the work he has to do are worth while. It is also important to discuss with the inmate how his possible life pattern looks from our angle and to do this in such a way that staff members do not antagonize him and become afraid to express themselves. The therapist must tell the inmate the results, but not the words, of evaluations from the workshops and the ward. However, he should not interpret all the reported reactions solely as an expression of the man's psychopathology. The inmate must have an opportunity to give his point of view, and reasonable explanations should never be dismissed. Treatment programs must always be tentative and flexible.

Making our parole recommendation for the court requires extracting and coordinating information from a long series of observations and critically evaluating the importance of these observations to the inmate's future life. Only a therapist who is involved in the daily life of the institution can carry through a truly realistic evaluation of all this information. In this endeavor it is especially obvious that we, although we are therapists and doctors for the patient, must represent society. Actually, this has seldom reduced our chances to influence an inmate's attitudes. We know the critical situations he may meet, and he knows that we know them. Although he does not always say so, it is a comfort to him that he can get our help when he gets into difficulty. If staff members have given him support at times, he will be willing, in this late period of detention and during parole, to call for their help again when it is needed. At the same time it is important to free the detainee of any strong feeling of dependency and avoid his feeling that he can monopolize the therapist's time.

We have established a variety of transitional arrangements as a preparation for parole. In recent years Herstedvester, itself, is being used as a sort of halfway house by allowing detainees to continue to live there while working outside in society. However, the most important of these methods is placement in Kastanienborg.

Kastanienborg

As early as 1943 it was obvious that Herstedvester needed its own reception home, located not too far away. It could house newly paroled inmates who were looking for work and people who had been out on parole but had lost their jobs. The prison system had some reception homes, but they were not well suited to our purposes and were too far away.

We needed some way to help a paroled person who had gotten into difficulties which he could not solve himself but which did not warrant his being taken back into the institution. His problems might be so great that it would be dangerous to leave him to his own devices. Such cases must be handled with the greatest care; it hurts a parolee to be taken out of free society, and we must explain clearly and fully to him

The open section of the Herstedvester Detention Centre
at Kastanienborg, Denmark.

why this is done. If he does not realize the necessity of the action, it
may be more harmful than helpful. Having a reception home near the
institution would make it easier for the man to accept coming back
and for us to help them re-evaluate their situations and make plans
for reintegration into society.

A plan for our own reception home was carefully worked out, but
during the war years we were overcrowded and the plan had to be
changed to getting a farm where we could place people preparing to
leave the institution. This would also give the sexual criminals who had
been castrated a place to stay while they accommodated themselves
to their new situations. In the spring of 1944, an officer told me that
a farm in Avedöre, between Herstedvester and Copenhagen, had been
vacated the night before. The farm belonged to the Defense Ministry
and they had no use for it since the Danish Resistance Movement had
removed military equipment hidden there. The farm was suitable for

us, even though it was located in the middle of the village, and we succeeded in getting the Ministry of Justice to buy it from the Ministry of Defense. During the summer furnishings were planned, with padded chairs to make a more cozy atmosphere than is usual in public homes. In an article in Herstedvester's newspaper in June, 1944, the inmates were told that being transferred to the open section indicated the staff's confidence in them, and that, if they did not live up to this trust, they would immediately be returned to Herstedvester.

On October 17, 1944, this open section, which was still called, roughly translated, a "walking out home," began operation. Four detainees and two employees drove to the farm every day and started cleaning it up. Although the house was not finished, it was occupied on November 4, 1944. Ten detainees, including those who had worked there for a fortnight, were transferred to it. They and the three employees lived in very primitive conditions.

In the main building of the farm there is now a flat for the local director and his wife, and upstairs there are rooms for detainees. Other rooms in other farm buildings are used by inmates; there is space for nineteen detainees in Kastanienborg and for another nineteen at a neighboring farm.

We have never set up special regulations for Kastanienborg. We stress that everyone should attempt to find a way of living acceptable to himself, to other inmates, and to society. No inmate may move outside the boundaries of the institution without being escorted by a staff member, but everyone has free access to the whole area within the farm. Inmates may receive visitors on the farm and in the sitting rooms but not in their own rooms. The personnel and detainees still eat togther in the main dining room. The market gardening instructors supervise the work and demonstrate how it ought to be done, and often they work at the heads of their groups.

No special control of visits has been attempted, and abuse of this freedom has seldom occurred. Many family groups come to sit and drink coffee with their own relatives as well as their friends among the other inmates.

Because of the war and our rapidly changed plans, the residents of the village were not well oriented as to the use we were going to make of the farm. However, the staff succeeded very well in establishing good relations with them. It was fortunate that we could help neighbors when they acutely needed more workers. It also helped when the neighbors saw that the farm was kept neat by the detainees and used in a commercially sensible way. The village residents even wanted to participate in our holiday celebrations, and it was hard to keep the detainees somewhat separated from the guests.

Some years later we bought an adjoining farm. We made two relatively independent groups, but all of the detainees still eat together in the main dining hall. Some small houses on the outskirts of our area have been bought for homes for some of the staff.

The personnel have been satisfied at Kastanienborg, and the director and several of the staff have stayed since it opened. One of the staff assists the social section in preparing inmates for parole, helps the director in coordinating the daily work, and is a group counselor.

The men watch television, but other spare time activities interest only a few people. The heavy work in the open air usually tires them, and in the summer most inmates want to stay outdoors as long as possible in the evenings. On Sundays they may attend the local church or walk in the surrounding area in an escorted group. Once a week a group of inmates may attend the local cinema, and they appreciate this opportunity to participate in ordinary life.

Even though the atmosphere usually seems quiet, it is clear from group discussions that difficulties in living together frequently develop. Rumors start very easily in such a small group, and the detainees themselves relate this to their need for sensation. When they have an opportunity, they like to color their daily existence. Jealousy of paroled comrades is common.

Other troubles arise from living with former inmates who are received as guests for a short period. The detainees feel irritated that the guests can leave when they want to. The guests, on the other hand, blame the detainees for the difficulties they meet. The inmates ask teasing questions such as, "Why do you really want to come here? You have your freedom." Others are reminded by a guest's arrival in the unit that life outside is not as easy as they believe, and so they start criticizing him. Most of the guests have been grateful for the help they have obtained by coming back and realize that they must endure unpleasant remarks.

A great proportion of the inmates at Kastanienborg are awaiting court decisions on their applications for parole. This is a tense period that may result in emotional instability and anxiety or in reactions that put them back in the main institution. It is as if they want to put the responsibility for eventual return to detention on the fact that, in spite of all efforts, preparation for parole was not as thorough as they expected.

As the length of detention has declined considerably in recent years, it has become difficult to find enough detainees who have permission for six-hour leaves to fill Kastanienborg. To compensate for this, we have frequently obtained permission to place at Kastanienborg other people who do not present any special risk. However, as can be seen from the number of escapes, five or six detainees fail each year to live up to the confidence shown in them.

During 1965, thirty-six detainees were transferred to Kastanienborg; twenty-seven were paroled directly from Kastanienborg, some after only three months, most after about six months, and three after a stay of up to one year and seven months.

One of the first detainees continued to stay at Kastanienborg as a guest. He was the oldest in the early group. He had been sentenced for ten cases of indecency against boys and girls, and it was his second sentence for sexual crimes. He had been in the institution for several years but did not want castration. He had caused no difficulty, but he had absolutely no initiative. At Kastanienborg he became a stable, useful handy man and he did almost the work of an employee. In the free atmosphere of Kastanienborg he displayed no sexual interests, even when he met children, and he was paroled quite soon. We were unable to find him a suitable job, and he decided to stay on. He was not very well physically, although he could take trips to visit his family in Jutland, and he had obtained permission to go outside the section without an escort. He lived in this way for about a year, then he died from a cerebral hemorrhage.

Since then, many others have lived as guests in Kastanienborg. Most of them have been on their own for some time and then had trouble. In 1965, there were thirty-eight guests in Kastanienborg, and thirty-six of them left the same year. Twelve stayed for only a few days, nine for five to ten days, and the longest stay was ninety-nine days. To these were added eight who came directly from jails and were placed in the open section with the agreement of the court.

The variety of the work at Kastanienborg gives new perspectives to the personnel, but it also causes instability in their daily life which may accentuate the inmates' unrest, which is inherent in this latter period of detention. For several years coordination of the officers' work has been especially difficult. In order to give the employees working conditions which are as satisfactory as possible, they now work for two consecutive days, sleeping in the open section as night watchmen. After that they are free for two days, and once every four weeks they have three free days. This distribution of working hours has satisfied the personnel, but it has made it more difficult to guarantee continuity in the work and in contacts with detainees.

Working in Free Society

In 1948 we first allowed a detainee to work outside the institution in order to finish his training as a furniture-maker. We found that it would help him to work for some time in a private workshop and that he also needed to attend classes at the local technical school. We obtained permission to let him attend the school, three or four kilometers away from the institution (he went on his bicycle), and also to let him work for a time with a private furniture-maker.

During the following fifteen years, fifty-four inmates worked in free society in preparation for parole. One tried it twice. A number of cases who had returned to Herstedvester were placed in private work for a time before their releases in order to facilitate their transition to free society. At Kastanienborg, we have had several detainees working for neighbors.

There are four reasons for letting a detainee work outside: (1) to improve his technical skills or other abilities; (2) to give finishing touches to a skilled worker's training or retrain a previously skilled worker; (3) to train for semiskilled work by evaluating an inmate's technical skill and retraining him in another occupation—for example, retraining a salesman as a factory worker; (4) to give social therapy; and to stabilize an inmate in his work in ordinary workshops, and to help him toward an easier transition to free life.

These motives would justify outside work in many more cases, but security problems limit the early use of such freedom, and many of our detainees cannot stand the stress of returning regularly on their own to the closed institution. It is important that a man not work outside for too long a period. Such work should start at a time when it seems possible that we can file a parole request before the court in a few months. As it takes two or three months to get a case through the court, the period of outside work may cover less than half a year.

Unfortunately it may be difficult to arrange outside work for the group of detainees who need it most. The best workers do not need special retraining, at least no more than we can give in our own workshops, but a few may need some finishing touches to their earlier training. Groups (2), (3), and especially (4) may present considerably greater occupational problems, and we have carefully selected detainees to work outside who, before detention, have had the worst difficulties in keeping their jobs and getting along with other workers. We usually feel that these difficulties have been substantially lessened while the inmates have worked outside.

One must realize that detainees who work outside meet several special difficulties that they would not find if they were paroled. The employer knows that they live in the institution, but usually fellow workers do not, and probably should not, at least not until the detainee himself feels like telling them. The fact that they are not allowed to go out at night or to go for a beer at noon may make fellow workers very curious. Other difficulties develop when an inmate is tempted to risk forbidden activities such as visiting his wife or fiancée, drinking, and so forth, and leaves work under the false pretense of being ill. Or he may establish a friendship with one of the girls in the workshop and find it difficult to return promptly to the institution after work.

If the detainee does not steadily abide by the rules, he will lose his right to work outside. Our strictness, which we believe to be necessary, may sometimes provoke a detainee to escape if he has put himself into a difficult situation and cannot see that he will be still worse off if he runs away. In a few cases the strain of working outside has been so great that detainees have developed clear hysterical reactions, sometimes even accompanied by hysterical fits.

Further stress may develop through pressure from fellow detainees who want those doing outside work to telephone messages to their friends or smuggle goods in or out. This has made it necessary to place those doing outside work in a special section where they can stay mostly isolated from the rest of the detainees.

When working outside, an inmate pays one-third of what he earns, a maximum of twelve kroner a day, for room and board in the institution.

The results of working outside are difficult to evaluate in figures, but the case of Lars can be cited to show the personal benefits. Lars was thirty-eight years old and had a long history of property crimes, mostly fraud. He was paroled after two years at Herstedvester, was arrested one month later and returned for a further year and a half in detention. Paroled again, he managed without crime for seven months and was then returned for fraud and stayed two years. After his third parole, he worked as a salesman (which was not very suitable work for him) for a year; then he committed new frauds and was returned to detention for the fourth time.

Lars's ambition had always been to earn money quickly, but during his last stay with us he seemed to learn that this was foolish. He said that his ambitions were now much more reasonable and that he would not need to earn big money; he would try to earn what he needed for normal living by doing general factory work. We thought it was reasonable to give him a chance to try such work before parole, as he had never before been in a factory.

When Lars was forty-seven years old, he started to work in a factory outside the institution. Four months later, in 1961, he was paroled. He continued to work in the factory for three months after parole, then had various jobs and again started to work as a salesman. He married and has now lived without crime for about five years. His ambitions did not remain modest, but his seven months of stable work in the factory probably helped him to develop a more realistic view of his capabilities so that he has not tried to earn big money quickly, as he did before.

The main conclusion of an evaluation of working outside by G. Ømark[42] is that the result of the experiment is positive but that it is necessary to be very careful in choosing detainees to work outside and to be equally careful in discussing the risks with each man, avoiding any type of pressure upon him to make him accept this burden. A detainee may, through such an experience, convince himself that his feeling of insecurity about working in a new workshop does not mean that he has to leave it, and having to stay in one workshop may give him an opportunity to feel at home in such a place for the first time. The result is better for group (1) than for the three other groups, as one would expect, but, of the whole group, about half have succeeded outside for some years after the period of outside work has ended. This is not to say that they managed better than they would have if they had not been allowed to work outside, but clinically the result is so satisfactory that the opportunity to do so must be preserved and, if possible, enlarged, in spite of the difficulties.

Without doubt the inconveniences could be reduced if those doing outside work could live in a little unit outside the walls. We could

[42] G. Ømark, *Om Udearbejde* (Mimeographed, Herstedvester, 1964).

keep the necessary control of the group, and at the same time the detainees would avoid some of the stress of returning daily through the gate of the institution.

Social Service

The inmate's contact with the social aide is best established if the aide participates in the treatment from the beginning of the detention period. This is possible because the whole period of treatment inside and outside is one entity under the same direction.

Frequently a newcomer says that he probably will need no social assistance. In such cases it is best to answer very kindly that the help we can give him is limited, that we are thankful for all the things he can do for himself, and that we try not to hamper anyone by interfering in personal relations, but that if he should, in spite of his expectations, need to discuss such matters, we will try to assist him.

The help needed during the parole period is just as varied as that needed during detention. In cases where our treatment has been of a more palliative character, that is, where we have not attempted to solve many of the detainee's personal problems, transition difficulties are usually limited. This is especially true if the detention period has been reasonably short, two years or less. If our psychiatric treatment has succeeded and the detainee has experienced essential changes in his view of himself and his relationships to his family and former friends, the situation may be more difficult for the social worker. The detainee's new surroundings have to be carefully screened, and it is important to discuss and clarify the possible results of his plans. Many collaborators, especially the social aide, must participate in these discussions with him. The social aide will have to integrate his special knowledge with the special psychological experiences of the therapist and realize that he may end up treating not only the detainee, but also his whole family.

Although the social section is usually overworked, we have found it necessary to do everything possible to establish, and continue, contact between inmates in the institution and the social aides. This means we cannot relieve the social aides of duties such as supervising the use of saved money, buying clothes, and so forth, even though they could be handled by other collaborators.

For a time we tried concentrating these internal problems on some social assistants inside the institution, and at the time that the inmate could expect to be paroled, we transferred him to a social assistant specializing in outpatient work. We found that, although this gave us better opportunities to decide which aides would be best suited to outpatient work with a particular inmate, it also caused many difficulties. It is not easy for a social aide to help the inmate in the institution in such a way that a successor can be well prepared.

Because of the development of the therapeutical programs, the administrative section became so crowded that it was necessary to move the social section to a building just outside the walls. This made the section more accessible to the paroled people, who prefer to avoid passing through the gate when they visit the social aide, an advantage that counterbalances some of the disadvantages of distance from the institution.

It should be remembered that one of the main goals of the social assistant during the detention period is to help the detainee acquire an attitude which will make it possible for him to carry out his plans for his own future. The best basis for collaboration during the parole period is reached when he does not want help constantly but does contact the aide sufficiently early if he sees difficulties coming.

Parole Recommendation

Our evaluations of an inmate have to be embodied in an official recommendation for the court's use when parole is requested. The content of this is first discussed in a "pre-meeting" (see page 42) in which all the employees who have been closely involved with this detainee participate. His therapist then drafts a recommendation which is discussed at the weekly staff meeting. As long as emphasis was placed on the traditional concern with the seriousness of a crime as decisive in determining the length of a criminal's internment, there was no stimulation to make clinical analysis of observations during his detention period. In our recommendation we now try to be aware of the importance of the detainee's crime and also to summarize every relevant observation concerning his ability to approach varied situations. Because small situations are usually managed in the same manner as large ones, the way a detainee meets situations which arise during his detention seems to us to be of considerable importance in evaluating what methods he will use for managing difficulties outside. We consider whether the detainee is inclined to return to his old surroundings where the risk of new crime is great and whether he is able to avoid dangerous stress situations. In conclusion, we outline the factors which we think are most important in the particular inmate's case.

A guardian frequently files a parole application with the court at a time when it is too early for us to give any positive recommendations. In some cases this may result in a long, troublesome period of anxious instability for the detainee while the case is pending in court.

Johan's experiences illustrate this. Time and again we carefully explained to him that his optimism was ridiculous and we refused to support his parole. In a recommendation when he was thirty-two years old, we mentioned that Johan was very likely to commit new frauds, the same crimes that he had committed before, and that we believed that a longer stay in the institution might help him to acquire a more realistic view of his problems. His defense attorney advised the guardian to withdraw the application, and then, in accordance with a very unsatisfactory practice, it was re-entered after five months. At that time I could only say that in these few months, while he had been anxious to get a new hearing of his case, there had been no change in our evaluation of his ability to live without committing crime. I added that the optimistic point of view in my first recommendation could probably not be sustained in the future, and I still advised against parole. Again the case was withdrawn, but Johan did not attain the peace that he needed to reach a true understanding of his over-optimism.

Four months later a new recommendation was requested. In this I stressed the relatively small danger connected with his type of crime, and I no longer advised against trying to adapt Johan to society. I also mentioned that he had probably mellowed some, that he was a healthy, stable worker, and that he was very easy to get along with if he did not meet obstacles. He was paroled, left his original job, obtained a new one, and then gave it up in order to become a salesman.

He got into trouble at the age of thirty-five and was returned to Herstedvester. Eight months later parole was requested again. We objected, and the case was withdrawn, but it was filed again after four months. In my recommendation this time, I said that Johan's excess optimism was still evident and the judge decided that he should wait some months longer to see if he could earn a better recommendation. Although Johan planned to obtain a higher technical education, his parole was discouraged. Eleven months later we again had to describe his self-assertive, unfounded optimism, and we still could not advocate parole.

Johan was now in the open section at Kastanienborg, and he was very clever as a skilled worker. For a time he worked with one of the neighbors and, partly because of this, he was paroled in spite of our cautious advice. He was now thirty-eight years old. He continued to work for the neighbor for a time after his parole, but this collaboration ended after a severe conflict that resulted from establishing a partnership with his employer. Seven months later he was involved in a new fraud and was returned to Herstedvester. Because of his technical skills, he could work outside the walls at his trade.

After a year and four months, Johan's guardian called for a new recommendation for parole, and again we could only advise against it. Five months later another recommendation stressed his technical skill as well as the continuing risk that he would again try fraudulent business enterprises to get easy and fast money.

Neither the low court nor the superior court would allow Johan's parole, and this subdued him somewhat. He became embittered and verbally aggressive, saying that he could expect support from no one, now, and that our recommendations were built on loose assertions. During the following years, Johan relapsed after each of a series of paroles, and it is our impression that the steadily repeated parole requests resulted in continued stimulation of his aggressive attitude and kept him from developing a realistic and useful point of view.

Disability Pension

Some years ago the formal conditions for receiving disability pensions—worthy behavior, not having had a prison sentence, having led a decent life, and so forth—were abolished, and now we can obtain disability pensions for our inmates. As the structure of modern society calls increasingly for stable personality rather than physical strength, personality defects become a more and more important handicap in the competition for employment. Full employment in Denmark makes it possible to place a rather large proportion of these insufficiently equipped persons in normal industry, but there are some whose personalities are so deviant that they cannot keep jobs. The kinds of work which formerly gave these people a reasonable chance to earn a normal income no longer exist.

We have had state insurance in Denmark since a law was passed on May 6, 1921. The first law said that a disability pension should be paid when the insured is no longer able to acquire more than one-third of what is earned by the same kind of work by a physically and psychologically healthy person with equal training. The insured's abilities and strength are considered, as well as what can be expected of him in view of his training and former occupation. Since the criteria were changed in 1950, a special Disability Insurance Court has more freedom to decide whether the disabled person's ability is substantially diminished, but the basis for decision is still whether or not he can earn one-third of a normal wage. In 1964 further changes were introduced, especially in the size of the pensions that are paid.

Until ten years ago there was great reluctance to give pensions for incapacitation from neurosis or psychopathy. It was found that medical evidence in these cases is not sufficient to cover the socially incapacitating state that is characteristic of most nervous diseases. Furthermore, there is an important emotional reaction to these diseases.

The law has no clause stating the acceptable cause of the economic disability necessary for obtaining a pension, and psychopathy may thus be considered a disease by the Disability Insurance Court.

Hermann suggested that a psychopathological person may be called incapacitated if his characterological development is so insufficient that, in spite of normal teaching, prolonged medical treatment, and attempts at adaptation to normal economic life, he still cannot maintain an acceptable social life and support himself and his family.[43] As an example, Hermann said that a spineless psychopath who is not adapted socially by his fortieth year probably never will be and that it is not rational to make him scrape through on welfare payments, just because his symptoms are of a special kind. Furthermore, he said that some psychopaths are neither contrasocial nor asocial, but hypersocial.

In 1966, about forty of our former detainees had pensions. It is our impression that this support has succeeded in making these people regard themselves as "respectable citizens," living on their pensions just as other incapacitated persons do, and this has made existence considerably easier for them.

In a few cases we have had to administer this money for former detainees. This is necessary for an alcoholic tramp with low intelligence who has a strong deformation of his back (sinistro-convex kyphoscoliosis). He frequently hides in our open section where, with

[43] Knud Hermann, "Neuroser og Psykopati som Invaliditetsårsag," *Nordisk Medicin,* 58(1957):1597.

the help of his own money, which we keep for him, he is re-established for a period.

Another man has obtained a disability pension for mixed somatic and psychiatric reasons. He was first sentenced for arson at the age of twenty-one and was sent to detention. He has borderline intelligence, near the normal level. He grew up in a gloomy, poor home and is very immature and dependent—a daydreamer with emotional moods. He tried six times to commit suicide. The latest attempt, just before detention, resulted in a permanent nervous lesion and some paralysis of the left leg that produced a physical handicap. He walks with his foot in a brace, but manages by himself now, after years of detention, with a disability pension.

The Parole Situation

While his request for parole is pending in court, a detainee has the right to uncensored correspondence with his defense lawyer, as soon as such a lawyer is assigned to him by the court.

He may also participate in group discussions in which parole problems are discussed. The standard conditions for parole are carefully stated: when a detainee is paroled, he may leave the institution when he has suitable work and lodging; he must not break any laws; he must submit to Herstedvester's supervision; he may not change occupation or lodging without previous permission from his supervisor. If he loses his job or does not carry out his supervisor's instructions, he may be placed in a reception home or some other suitable institution. To these conditions may be added special directions that concern treatment for alcoholism or require an immediate turn to the institution if he gets into difficulties. If he is returned directly to Herstedvester, the court's agreement will be sought within six days.[44]

When the court's decision about parole is made, the institution receives a telephone call reporting the result. This practice was introduced after some defense lawyers succeeded in sending results to detainees in uncensored letters before the institution had obtained such information. This occasionally caused trouble because a denial of parole may result in serious reactions by an inmate, such as escaping from a six-hour leave.

After the telephone call, the social aide starts to prepare the practical implimentation of the decision, but, until the possibility of an

[44] See Appendix E for some special conditions for parole.

appeal by the prosecution is finally settled, no decisive steps can be taken. Sometimes the local representative of the prosecution has said immediately that an appeal would not be lodged, but even in such cases we have been surprised by appeals from higher prosecuting authorities. We now always wait until we have the decision in writing, before we announce it formally to the detainee. We also do this because there may be nuances in the special conditions laid down by the court that we must state absolutely correctly to the inmate. There must be time for practical arrangements about his finances, his private belongings that are deposited with us, and the returning of equipment that we have issued to him. A day or two usually pass before these practical arrangements are finished.

It takes some time to arrange for satisfactory employment for parolees, even though jobs have been easily available in recent years with full employment throughout the country. If a detainee has been working in free society, the job problem is usually solved by his continuing to work where he has been. Occasionally a parolee must be escorted on visits to prospective employers. Usually he speaks alone with the employer because it might debase him if his future fellow workers should see that he is escorted. Usually it is best to prepare the way by telephone calls, especially if we must inform an employer that the applicant has committed a serious crime. If an escort has carried out preparatory work during six-hour leaves, he will continue to work as the contact man during the parole period. With his knowledge of the parolee's family relationships, this may be especially useful.

There is often difficulty in arranging for satisfactory lodging. Our last decision is how much money the detainee will need during his first few weeks on parole. Some want to have all of their saved capital, but experience has taught us that we must be prepared for the parolee to change jobs and need to make a new start. It is important for him to have enough funds to make a second start comfortably and do it with his own, saved money. This decision, of course, is related to his former economic behavior, and, if he is an alcoholic, we are very careful not to give him much money until we see how he manages his alcohol problem.

During this emotion-loaded planning of practical arrangements for parole and the reading and signing of the parole conditions, we can stress the necessity for maintaining close contact with the institution.[45]

[45] Further instructions are given to him in a printed folder which is translated in Appendix F in this book.

In spite of all our preparation, the detainee usually believes that the social aide will now interfere in all his private relations. The social assistant needs to emphasize again that we will try to help him to avoid new crime but that we cannot control his daily behavior.

Once more we need to discuss the practical problems of the parolee's future contacts with Herstedvester. Social assistance with practical matters consumes less time now than it did in the first years of the institution. Then it was always a problem to find jobs and sufficient clothing and to make other quite elementary arrangements for parolees. Now most of the social aide's time is used to assist them with interhuman problems and to talk with their relatives.

INTEGRATION INTO A SOCIAL SETTING

The process of integration into society cannot be schematicized. It is an individual process, and only a few of the problems which arise can be illustrated. Still, more than in any of the other sections of this book, we must abstain from abstraction and principles and base our description on examples. Even if good contact is established between the social aide and the inmate when he leaves the institution, many situations develop which were not expected. The parolee comes under new influences, and, just as it took a long time before we really obtained a clear insight into his real problems, now we have to contend with the problems of his family and friends. It takes a long time for an inmate, and for us, to understand these realities, and sometimes this does not happen until he has relapsed and returned to Herstedvester. Only then, he realizes the necessity of obtaining help sufficiently early in a parole period.

If he has been interned for a long time, small problems, such as how to behave in a restaurant, will make him feel insecure. He may not like to admit these problems; nor would most of us. We all want to be grown-up people who unquestionably can manage such activities. The parolee meets most of these difficulties alone, and he has to find his own solutions. Sometimes when he is troubled, he is lucky enough to be able to contact his social aide immediately and get some relief from talking with somebody he knows and trusts.

The social aide has to take his position on the spot. Sometimes he may take a temporary stand on a complicated problem if there is no time to discuss it with a colleague or a therapist. The aide will not be able to avoid nonverbal communication of his own reactions, so it is useless to try to disguise them. They may be useful bases for further analyses of what can actually be done. Sometimes he may be forced to react authoritatively; if so, he must try to arrange for a new meeting with the parolee and discuss the problem again after he has talked about the situation with the therapists or thought the problems through alone.

We must realize that we cannot control the situations a parolee meets as adequately as those he encountered as an inmate. We can discuss his plans critically and point out pitfalls in his arguments and in what he thinks is realistic. We may even show him that his plans will not work, but we have to be very careful not to tell him more than "perhaps it would work better if you sought a solution in this or that direction." He must have full responsibility for his own life, and he should not feel that we are forcing ourselves and our ideas upon him. We are his helpers, not his masters. The social aide may be called a "supervisor," but this word must not be taken too seriously. The social aide is the parolee's professional friend, a stable person who is involved in his life and especially concerned that he avoid any new crime. The aide receives confidences but does not share his own problems with the detainee. In many cases it is necessary not to be too active, and sometimes even to be clearly passive for a time, until the parolee himself requests our active support.

I have asked several parolees who have managed to live a normal social life about what they felt was important in the help they received. Some answered that their social aides "had only to be there." Further analysis shows that these people have frequently turned to their social aides for assistance in dramatic situations and have obtained human assistance of a kind which did not have a professional touch, even though it was based on the social aides' professional knowledge. Important advice to a social aide is to stick to his professional knowledge but act in such a way that the parolee is not aware of his professionalism.

At the same time, he must try to recognize a dangerous, developing situation early enough to stop it. Such a dangerous development is often detected intuitively, and we have to accept this as a condition of our work, although it may be especially burdensome for the social aide or the therapist. Intuitive impressions cannot be used as a basis for limiting a person's individual freedom, and only seldom will there be enough facts to carry out security arrangements before a criminal act is actually performed. In most cases we have to call the detainee's attention to what we sense as being risky and base further measures on the interhuman contact which we develop with him. I have tried many times to get social aides who have many years of practical experience to describe the cases in which they carefully avoid tackling problems too directly and the ones in which they invite parolees to call for actual assistance. No one has yet been able to see any clear pattern for these decisions.

Very often a parolee needs to talk with his social aide simply because he feels lonely or needs to confide in someone with whom there is no need to hide his criminal background. Loneliness is, of course, a very common element in life, and we must be careful not to encourage the parolee's feeling of being worse off than other people. Often we must explain to him that we all know and feel the basic loneliness of man. This is not intended to minimize the special loneliness of the chronic criminal who has been institutionalized for a long time and who does not even trust his relatives.

Knud was a lonely one. For eighteen years he had been considered a mental defective and a more or less hopeless case. About twenty years ago he came into detention because of arson, and he was very aggressive. Although he was not very bright, he also was not a mental defective. He was, however, naïve and hot-tempered. He was paroled for the third time at the age of about sixty. During this parole period, he established contact with a middle-class widow of his own age who had previously been the guardian for one of his younger comrades in detention. At Kastanienborg, these three had often drunk coffee together. For a time she corresponded intensively and emotionally with this younger man, and when he was paroled, he moved in with her. However, after a short time he found a girl friend of his own age and left the widow.

Now she began to correspond with Knud, who had also been paroled. He visited her several times, and after some months they became engaged. Although they never married, he wore a wedding ring. Knud visited his family for the first time in many years but he did not tell them about his "great experience." It was very important for him that the social aide was willing to read his fiancée's letters from beginning to end and to listen to his whole love story. He needed someone with whom he could share his "great experience" but he did not trust his family for that.

Sometimes a detainee's family need someone to talk to as much as the detainee does. For a long time, the mother of an inmate telephoned every morning to the social aide at about seven o'clock to discuss her situation, and sometimes she mentioned that she was thinking of suicide. For several years she had lived with an older friend of her son whom she had met at Kastanienborg. He found her difficult and moved away, but he still visited her and sometimes helped her when she was in a desperate mood. Her son's problems were much easier for the social aide to handle than hers.

Often problems with families appear after a man is paroled, but, although we have been aware of this danger, we believe that the detainee is aware that he cannot manage the burden of their problems. Ludwig was the victim of such a situation.

During Ludwig's detention period, we worked hard to get him to realize that the problems of his weakly endowed, grown-up son were too difficult for him to handle. He had agreed that his own problems were more than enough to manage and decided to live alone. However, the day he left the institution he sent his son some of the money he was to use until he received his first pay check so that the son could visit him. The son came, but his visit did not end, and the father tried to make a good home for him. Ludwig could not understand that his son was probably a mental defective and was unable to go out and sell the drawings that his father produced in his spare time. The son went to bed weeping, had pains here and there, and then his father had to take care of him and could not go to work. He lost his job, got a new job, and so the story repeated itself five times.

For a long time we did not know what caused these unexpected difficulties, but when we found out, we had to try to solve the son's problems. We arranged for the reinstatement of his public insurance, which had not been kept up, and obtained public assistance for him, even though he was uncooperative. Finally Ludwig was able to keep a job.

Relation to Women

Some inmates start daydreaming about women during the later period of detention, and a few react with impotence when they are first released. Some are terrified by this, but we can usually explain to them easily that the difficulty will disappear if they will wait a short time and concentrate on developing an adequate social background so that they can meet women they can respect. The central problem for these men is their feeling of inferiority because of "what she would say if she knew who I really was." Some of them need continuous support for some time to develop their self-respect.

Other chronic criminals take a haughty attitude toward women. For instance an older, completely disillusioned swindler, said, during the discussion of an extemporaneous play, "None of the women we meet are strong." In this play, a situation was presented in which a parolee stole a girl from a man who was still in the institution. We saw how the paroled swindler used half-truthful statements. In spite of the elegant presentation he used, some of his audience opposed him, saying that the seduction was morally very wrong. Others remarked bitterly that the girl ought to have chosen better the second time. The man who played the role of the seducer, who was himself thoroughly experienced in this field, spoke of the vanity behind the Don Juan role he had created. He said that he had not planned the seduction at the beginning, but, when he started with a friendly greeting, he began to feel that he would be a "real man." And then "you suddenly feel that you need to hurry, the situation runs away from you, you ought to say 'stop,' but the emotion has caught you." His viewpoint was criticized again, and his conquest of the girl was called a very deliberate grasp for security. In this and other discussions, we developed the feeling that we must be very careful about standardizing our evaluations of these relationships. The potentials of the men we investigate are important, but so are those of the women they meet and with whom they may live.

Socioeconomic Situation in Relation to Work

In their work, our inmates run into widely different situations. Some parolees get very good jobs and keep them for years, but most of them exchange their first job for others, and others again, before they settle down at last or get into trouble. Between jobs, parolees often have to be received as guests at Kastanienborg. Some people do not recognize their own deficient earning capacities, and, even though we have tried for years in the institution to convince them that they need some economic assistance in order to live a decent life, their pride makes it impossible for some of them to accept such advice. It may even make it difficult for us to give this advice too directly. In some cases we have sent parolees to ordinary sheltered workshops run by the state. Sometimes one of our men will listen to what the professional advisers in these workshops say, then accept a disability pension and feel satisfied with a small extra income from additional jobs which they can manage competently.

Alcohol Problems

A large proportion, in recent years up to 50 per cent, of our parolees have some type of problem with the use of alcohol. This is partly because they frequent small bars where they meet and talk with people whom they do not meet again, at least not on an intimate level. Here they begin to drink too much in order to counteract their feelings of insecurity. They spend too much money and develop an unstable, irregular way of life which hampers their re-socialization. However, an acute situation, such as a drinking spree, may sometimes be of great value. If the man receives genuine help from the institution in such a situation, he may establish a stable relationship with his social aide and break the vicious circle of spending and drinking too much.

Our lack of easily accessible facilities for continued outpatient therapy prevents sufficient use of antabus treatment. Rather often it is obvious that a parolee ought to come regularly for continued therapy, but his work may make it practically impossible to do this. Placing a fisherman in a factory might make continued treatment possible, but such a man may refuse to work in a factory and insist on sailing, even if he and the staff agree that this may lead to his misusing alcohol again.

Sometimes the parolee's home situation is very different from what we expect. For example, Magnus moved in with his mother, and she treated him like a baby. In order to manage his problem, he established contact with a girl older than himself. A jealousy conflict developed, and he started drinking in accordance with his old pattern of spineless, hyperthymic behavior. He also tried to conquer his inferiority feeling by extravagant spending.

When Magnus came to Herstedvester the second time, he felt as if freed from a burden and worked happily again in the furniture shop, although he was dysphoric, querulous, and very dissatisfied with himself. In active psychotherapy he became more realistic and less sensitive, and he was paroled again. His drinking pattern reappeared, but in his great need for companionship he was lucky to find sincere sympathy in a very independent and mature woman.

In spite of strong protests from her family, Magnus married her and he became very stable and was finally discharged after three years. Both worked and they had no children. Magnus was very happy in his new group of friends, but remained very perfectionistic. Eight years after his parole, his wife called upon me because he was having a new period of dysphoria. They had kept in touch with the social aide, but she had left Herstedvester long ago and had referred them to me to obtain help with his alcohol problems which were becoming severe again. He was badly upset every time he got drunk, blamed himself afterwards, and became depressed. In long interviews with Magnus and his wife, we discussed his sensitivity and perfectionism carefully, but for a time he continued to have these difficulties. He gave in to any severe opposition but gained control over his emotional dysphoria with help from his wife. He attempted no new crime. The case of Magnus shows that it is quite possible for an alcholic, chronic criminal to be re-socialized and cured of crime without first stopping his use of alcohol.

After an experimental treatment of criminal alcoholics, Hansen and Teilman reported, ". . . our investigation indicates a probability that comprehensive, continuous and intimate social-psychiatric treatment, with disulfaram [antabus] as an adjuvant, is suited to reduce criminal recidivism in psychologically abnormal hypercriminal alcoholics."[46] They treated a small group, including thirty detainees, in the years 1949 to 1951.

In 1965 I made a new, follow-up study of the thirty cases from Herstedvester.[47] Seven were sexual criminals, and, because most of them had been castrated, they managed well enough to be of no interest in this connection.

Nine of the other twenty-three cases relapsed and have been readmitted to Herstedvester or have received a prison sentence. Only three of the nine developed lasting criminality.

Six are now dead: three committed suicide, one became psychotic and died in a hospital, and two others continued their alcoholism until they died of it. We have followed twenty of these men for a reasonable length of time; eleven of them have remained crime-free for over ten years, one for eight, two for seven, two for five, and three for four years. Only one has not been able to maintain a crime-free life, and he is still in Herstedvester; he drank heavily each time he was paroled. At the end of their last detention period, three were over fifty years old, ten in their forties, five in their thirties, and two in their twenties. But only one of the eleven who remained free of crime for over ten

---

[46] Alois Hansen and K. Teilman, "Treatment of Criminal Alcoholics," *Quarterly Journal of Studies in Alcohol*, 15(1954):246–87.

[47] Presented in a lecture in Prague in 1966; published as "Attempts at Treating Chronic Criminal Alcoholics," *Selected Papers Presented at the 12th International Institute on the Prevention and Treatment of Alcoholism*, 2:73.

years also controlled his use of alcohol. Two of the eleven reduced their alcohol intake considerably over a few years and then stopped their misuse of it.

A large majority of our group gave up crime but continued to misuse alcohol. As a general rule, it appears that they have solved the main problem of continued criminality that made life a burden for them but that they have not had enough stamina to fight their alcohol problems as well. It seems that the misuse of alcohol is based on a different sort of personality problem than crime is.

Psychosomatic Symptoms

It is our impression that psychosomatic symptoms are more common during parole than during detention in the institution. The most frequent symptoms are heart neuroses, gastric symptoms, and simple fatigue due to stress. Sometimes these symptoms develop even though a detainee has been maintaining stable social relationships such as a new marriage or a steady job. Heart symptoms seem rather common when there are fundamental changes in one's life pattern. Usually we react to these heart symptoms by complimenting the parolees on their good behavior and telling them that we are happy that, instead of using their old defense mechanisms, they have found new ways to cope with stress symptoms. The heart symptoms help us to feel sure that these parolees are no longer criminal risks. This form of "flattering support" often has a calming effect. The parolee feels understood and respected, and he often starts to explain further about his sincere hope that a new life is dawning for him.

It is a little more difficult to manage simple fatigue symptoms. Often a detailed analysis shows that the detainee really is physically overworked. These chronic property criminals, often physically and psychologically strong, have great difficulty in understanding that it takes time to gain social respect. They are very impatient and want to regain their social positions quickly. Therefore they accept overtime work in order to earn more, perhaps to pay off large debts that their families have been forced to incur during their detention. Unpaid taxes and debts to the state for maintenance of children—mostly illegitimate—cause severe problems.

Out-Patient Psychotherapy

We seldom succeed in attempts at systematic outpatient psychotherapy. Usually we have to be satisfied with supportive therapy, and we must realize that about half of a therapist's time will be wasted by unkept appointments. That is true even in cases where we suppose that contact with the parolee is excellent. When these people do keep their appointments, the therapist often receives a very realistic impression of the troublesome life they lead.

Collaboration between social aides and therapists can be difficult to administer. Both parties need to be careful not to establish themselves as authorities outside their own specialties. Usually the social aide should feel responsible for the case. The coordination ought to be carried out in the outpatient phase by the social aide and in the internal phase by the therapist.

Some of our difficulties in establishing systematic psychotherapy are clearly related to our geographical location, thirteen kilometers from the center of Copenhagen. As long ago as May, 1946, I officially suggested the establishment of an outpatient psychotherapeutical clinic for sexual criminals. I felt that it was wrong that some of our sexual criminals had not received any psychotherapy before they were sent to detention. No solution to this problem was found.

In 1951 an arrangement was made to pay private psychotherapists, but few of these are available, especially for our cases. The difficulties of keeping appointments ended these experiments. In one case, a former detainee was returned to our supervision after he had been finally discharged for many years; in 1948 and 1950 we tried unsuccessfully to establish outpatient therapy for him. No one could pay his expenses for transportation, and his loss of income because treatment had to be carried out during ordinary working hours was also a handicap.

Short Readmissions

We also attempted other methods to re-establish our whole treatment machinery for parolees. We tried to get a man to return freely to the institution so that we could re-establish psychotherapeutical contact for a short time as well as put his economic and social affairs in order.

The idea for this experiment came from an older property criminal who had been placed in family care during his parole. One day he appeared at the gate and asked how many bicycles he had to steal in order to be readmitted. He could not manage by himself any longer, but he would not go to an ordinary hospital. I discussed him with a representative of the Ministry of Justice by telephone, and, a little reluctantly, he granted permission to take the old man back, if he confirmed in writing that it was his own wish and if we would let him go when he wanted to leave. It was a great help for this old man. He got a new start this time, as he did several other times after that. We repeated this kind of readmission a number of times with other inmates.

In 1952 the question of readmission was raised more officially. It was then supposed to be evident that in cases of petty criminal acts, if no action was taken, the re-socialization would suffer; the same was supposed to be true if a criminal was returned by the court to Herstedvester for a new, rather long period of detention. A short jail sentence would be of no re-socializing value, but, if we could receive him for a short period in the institution immediately after he admitted his guilt, we would have a better opportunity to analyze the background of his new crimes and to help him. The courts accepted this line of thought, and now we frequently include in the conditions for parole a possibility for the institution to take the parolee back, "if circumstances make this necessary." These "circumstances" include the commission of new small crimes, breaking other parole conditions, becoming emotionally unstable, or drinking excessively. Now it is always stated that such a direct readmission to Herstedvester shall be reported to the man's guardian and to the prosecution so that the prosecution can secure the subsequent approval of the court. Many persons have come back for short periods, and then, without further formalities, re-established themselves in society, sometimes in a new lodging and usually in a new job, sometimes directly from the main institution and sometimes after a period of weeks in Kastanienborg.

Examples

The social aide's work with parolees, as it is carried out in our institution, is to some degree office work, but this is the smallest part of the work. The social aide, male or female, must get involved in actual situations where difficulties are developing or are already full-blown. He has to handle people who are sometimes afraid of seeking help. Much of his work is of a personal kind which cannot easily be taught in theory but must be learned in practice. He frequently works outside the institution, in cafés or in parolees' homes. Some of the married social aides have opened their homes to parolees who visit them and their families.

I will illustrate some practical situations which aides have dealt with, some satisfactorily and some not.

Max was an old man who had committed nearly every kind of crime and had inflicted a variety of mean tricks on his family and acquaintances.

In his late forties, and again in his fifties, he had been in detention. The social aide had been in contact with him since his first parole period. We had to abstain from any moral evaluation when observing him and listening to what he said. Very few people escaped his slander, but once an acquaintanceship was well established between him and the aide, he maintained a correct and sometimes friendly attitude. He often mentioned that he knew so much about his relatives that he could get them into serious trouble with the law, and apparently he had really done so. During his second parole he frequently mentioned his attempts to catch a rich woman—he was not particular about her looks. He advertised in the newspaper and many women naïvely replied. Without shame he discussed all that the women had confided to him, showed their letters and photographs, and described his visits with them.

Max was a clever repairman, and, when he was employed in wealthy homes, he told the housewives about his poverty, praised their charity, and thus influenced them to give him expensive and usable clothing. He showed the aide these things and was very proud of his abilities. When he had enough for himself, he sold the goods to secondhand dealers or acquaintances.

At one time Max was attacked by an acquaintance who hit him in the head with an iron and inflicted a severe cranial fracture. The motive for the attack was never clearly established, but a homosexual attack by himself or some financial disagreement between the two was suspected. On another occasion he was deeply offended by the police, who guessed that he had stolen some laundry in the district where he lived. Because they knew how difficult Max could be, they discussed their suspicions with his social aide and arranged to call on him when the social aide was making an unscheduled, professional visit. The police came, and Max was very friendly until he heard why they had come. To suspect him, who had been such a clever criminal, of something so simple as stealing laundry was degrading to him. In the end, the police apologized, and Max often told of the episode later.

For many years Max had sought a son living in one of the large towns but had not found him. He asked for help, and the social aide located the son and visited him. After some thought, the son explained that his father had hurt him very much during his childhood, had tormented his mother, and had refused to see him when, as a young man, he had tried to visit him in prison. The son himself had a criminal record, but for years he had been building up a solid way of life with a wife and children. He considered very carefully whether he should undertake the care of his old father. He decided that he did not want his father to know where he lived or anything about him because he was afraid that the father would destroy the good life that he had with his family. He himself had tried to obtain information about his father and had sent him gifts, but he never learned anything good about him. We did not inform Max that we had found his son.

Peter's case was different. He was a very aggressive man who had had a long series of conflicts with his environment and served several long sentences. When he was fifty-one years old, he was sentenced to detention, and for a long time he felt that he had been mistreated. He had behaved so aggressively against one judge that his case had been transferred to another court. This offense had influenced his last sentence. He did not trust anyone, but after spending some time at Herstedvester, he reacted sensibly and was never aggressive.

Peter was paroled after one and one-half years. We considered him to be more threatening and noisy than seriously dangerous. His contact with the social aide was well established, and, although he kept his uncompromising attitude, we were able to influence his behavior. The aide visited him frequently, and, after some time on parole, he started to talk freely about his earlier life. He could be very ironic about himself, and, when he visited the social aide's family, he was entertaining and amusing.

Peter insisted on returning to the town where he had lived all his life, and, even though he took a new name, he had a very difficult time. Many years after he came back, a local newspaper published an interview with a person who told how Peter once had been arrested. He was described as a very dangerous man and his photograph was in the newspaper. The article and the picture hurt him very deeply, and his old hatred for society and authorities nearly overwhelmed him. Instead of taking action himself, he came to the social aide, who talked him out of his plans to attack the editor of the newspaper. He remained unhappy, but the discussion persuaded him that inferior people exist outside the sphere of convicts. In other situations when he felt provoked, he came for discussions and wondered how other people could treat him badly, even though he really tried to behave better than he had before.

After eleven years, he was finally discharged. He has stayed in touch with the social aide and is now a respected citizen. He is happily married and has lived in the same town for many years.

In Peter's case there was a good emotional bond between the parolee and the social aide. However, we are not always successful in this way, and sometimes parole ends with a new crime or suicide.

The suicides give rise to very serious discussions in our groups as to whether or not they could have been avoided. Usually, like suicides within the institution, it seems unlikely that we could have prevented them.

Paul was one we wondered about. He was a thief and house-breaker who came into detention at the age of thirty-eight. He came from a harmonious but poor home, got along reasonably well in childhood with his sisters and brothers, but left his family in order to become an artist. He did not succeed and started a criminal career and a very unstable way of life. He was self-assertive and quarrelsome, and he easily developed paranoid feelings that injustices were being done to him. Behind this superficial pattern we found deep insecurity. Paul felt that he was only respected in a group of former criminals, but he evidently really wanted to try once more to be accepted socially.

After two and one-half years Paul was paroled. A few months later he committed suicide in a hotel. He was tired of his life and disappointed that he had wasted his abilities, and he still could not find his place in society.

He described these feelings in a letter he sent to the social aide the evening before he died, and he told the aide what he was going to do and where he could be found.

He also wrote, "When you receive this letter I will not be in this world. It may look like a flight—and maybe it is—but don't believe that it is anything rash—it is an idea I have had for a long time—but after my last visit in Herstedvester, it took form. . . ."

He had been in the social office some days before this and wanted us to recommend him for a job for which he was qualified. We tried to help him, but the prospective employer did not want to appoint a former detainee, even if we believed him to be suitable. Paul did not mention these problems in the letter, but he sent greetings to everyone he knew and to the people in the institution who had treated him kindly. Then he added, "I phoned yesterday to Mr. _____ and said that I couldn't come as I had obtained another and more secure job. He didn't know what sort of security I thought of, but—it was the long sleep—now let me not be dramatic but talk practically about what will happen." The letter then told what he was planning to do, and continued, "Forgive me the trouble I am making for you, but it cannot be otherwise. I do not dare to continue. May I dare to take this last trip. I know I will have to go through a crisis tonight but I have gotten some alcohol as well as drugs. It may look ugly but nothing can be done about it. I have to succeed. Help my mother all that you can. P.S. I have paid for the room. My money is under my pillow."

As soon as Paul's letter arrived, we telephoned the hotel. He was dead but still warm. The police were there when the social aide arrived. They found another letter written during the night, between 9:35 in the evening and 4:05 in the morning. The letter showed his deep fears.

"9:35. I am full of fear. I write in order to pacify myself. I have been drinking. I hope I'm not such a coward that I don't dare to carry out what I have planned, but my heart is banging. I feel I need more alcohol in order to be courageous enough. We are so small— meaning me. Even though this has been planned several days and in some way it has been a fear and a comfort—'my soul be fresh and happy'—so he says in the broadcast now. 'Let God help you,' he continues. Maybe it is a warning. I'll just see what program it is—I can't stand it. I close."

Several more entries followed, then one at 12:38 in the morning. "It is funny, I am still not drunk—I am indifferent—I have now two beers and a quarter of a bottle of port left—I take it now. Then— I plan to take the pills [Bromisoval] mixed with water—they are already like porridge and then the Hypnophen [a barbiturate preparation]—and then I hope it is soon over."

Then he wondered whether he should try to stretch out the time and told about someone laughing in another room. After he took the drugs, he went to the toilet.

"1:50. It is said that when dying, one can hold neither water nor feces—that must be inconvenient for people who find the body. . . .

"3:16. I have just taken the key from the door in order to avoid the question of compensation if they should have to break it. Oh, so much I would write—but time is short now—I am tired. I am afraid of thinking too much. . . . If I can, I will continue to write—I will let the lamp burn but—Remember mother—Thank you for everything good."

There were some more notes and then, at 4:05, he mentioned that he felt drunk. "I can't see what I write. I hope it can. . . ." The writing ended and Paul obviously lost consciousness.

Return after Parole

When a detainee is paroled, it means that the court has decided to use a security measure that is less severe than placement in a special institution. Section 70 of the Criminal Code gives all the alternatives one could wish. Only the court can change the security measures. Theoretically they may do it whenever the conditions for parole are broken, but usually a parolee is returned to detention only if he has committed one or more new crimes.

We ourselves are reluctant to advise revocation of parole if only minor problems have arisen. Our principal reason is that confronting negative behavior with a negative reaction seldom gives positive results. It is much more convenient to take a parolee directly back for a short time. This is easier for the detainee, because he can accept it as a protective device which will end as soon as the aim is accomplished.

The attitude of the prosecution differs somewhat in various parts of the country; some prosecutors prefer to ask the court for a short imprisonment for petty offenses, and sometimes we agree that a fine would be a reasonable punishment. In very exceptional cases, a short prison sentence is used; this is, and should be, a rare occasion, but what to do in such situations can never be decided theoretically. The parolee's social situation, the length of time he has spent without committing a crime, the possibilities for continuing outpatient treatment, and the risk to society must be evaluated before his parole can be revoked.

Alf's case illustrates this. He was a chronic thief with good vocational abilities. He had not been especially interested in psychiatric assistance, but in the wards it had been possible to get him to control his domination of comrades, and he had participated in group therapy. We suggested parole, and the court agreed. After one year Alf married a girl who already had two small children. For a time he tried to control his misuse of alcohol. His wife's frigidity was a burden, and after five years, he moved in with a girl friend. A few months later he was arrested for receiving two stolen radios. Why this crime happened at that time is not clear, but during the five years of his parole we had learned that he became very dissatisfied with himself when he did not completely succeed in living up to the expectation of his relatives, of the authorities, or of himself. He had gone on a drinking spree, as he had done several times before.

We avoided revocation of Alf's parole, and started treating him again for alcoholism. He returned to his wife for a time, but the pattern was repeated once more. This time he stole cigarettes from the ship where he worked. Although they were worth only about $3.00 it was difficult to avoid severe legal action. We suggested giving Alf one more warning; the Medico-Legal Council did not agree with our suggestion, but the court did.

Alf then went to live with his girl friend, who guided him very well. With her support, he came through another difficult period some time later. A theft had been committed at his place of work, and there was a police investigation. This is usually a difficult situation for our men, but Alf held up through this incident, and has not misused alcohol or committed a crime for more than three years.

In Gunnar's case, our attitude was to suggest his return to detention. When this happened, he was in his thirties—a superficial, somewhat blunted man, a homosexual-pedophiliac who was difficult to communicate with. He had been in detention for about five years. He felt that castration was unnecessary and thought that his misuse of alcohol, which had been present in his whole family, was the main reason for his pedophiliac behavior. When he was paroled, he did not let his family know, but he secured a good job and was well satisfied with his life. He used some of his savings for nice personal effects and a small motor bike. A little more than a month after his parole, he met a former detainee who was on parole from our sister institution at Jutland. Together they committed a housebreaking arranged by Gunnar's companion, who was a professional housebreaker. They were caught on the spot, so no theft was accomplished. When it was proven that the men were trying to steal drilling machines, which were all they could take from the place, I thought we should return him to Herstedvester. I suggested that he stay for a short period that would make it possible for us to make him realize that contact with former detainees is just as dangerous for him as contact with his family. The lower court decided that this was too severe a punishment, but the superior court followed our suggestion, and he was returned. A few months later Gunnar was transferred to Kastanienborg. A little later we suggested to the court that he be paroled again, and he was. He accepted our whole reaction as reasonable.

We have often seen that a second stay in Herstedvester may be much easier for an inmate than the first, but in some cases inferiority feelings may become stronger.

Final Discharge

A detainee's final discharge is granted only by the court. Usually we do not recommend final discharge until after about four successful years on parole. Sometimes this period is extended considerably, usually because the detainee himself is afraid of losing legitimate contact with the institution. Time after time, parolees stress that as long as they officially belong to our caseload (there are now about 350 on parole), they have a right to ask our advice and help. They know very well that they will always get our help, even after they are finally discharged, but they are less likely to ask for it then.

The number of people who are finally paroled has very little practical meaning when we evaluate the results of treatment. Here we must rely on our knowledge and clinical experience and hope that at some time it will be possible to evaluate a greater proportion of the cases we have followed for many years.

Chapter III

HOW WE LIVE TOGETHER

LIFE IN HERSTEDVESTER

Clemmer has described prison life in *The Prison Community,*[1] and Sykes has given us a modern American study in *The Society of Captives.*[2] These important works have had a great influence on the general concept of "life" in correctional institutions in general. Therefore it should be of some importance to describe how we in Herstedvester live together in our smaller society of captives. We have already described this from an institutional angle, emphasizing our purposes and how we hope to accomplish them. But how does this life look if we try to see it from other angles?

No systematic, sociological investigation has been carried out in Herstedvester, but I think that, having lived in its society for many years, I can offer my own, unique point of view as just as truthful as the observations of an outsider. Any kind of research will change the object studied, no matter how and by whom the research is conducted. The dream of any researcher that he can remain objective is an illusion. Some who work with the underdogs look at the institution from below and end with a one-sided view.[3] Other outsiders become involved during one period with the staff, and during another with the inmates, and constantly reproach themselves for not being impersonal and objective.[4] Usually the investigators' brief engage-

---

[1] Donald Clemmer, *The Prison Community* (New York: Holt, Rinehart and Winston, 1949).

[2] Gresham M. Sykes, *The Society of Captives* (Princeton: Princeton University Press, 1958).

[3] Erving Goffman, *Asylums* (New York: Doubleday, 1961).

[4] Yngvar Løchen, *Idealer og realiteter i et psykiatrisk sykehus* (Oslo: Universitetsforlaget, 1965).

ments are difficult, and give them a feeling of insecurity, of not belonging, or of being outcasts. Such attitudes, combined with the brevity of observation, make it difficult to note and evaluate long-range values and developing attitudes. These arise over the years from continuous changes which take place in the interpersonal rela-sionships in a therapeutic and flexible institution.

An independent observer, on the other hand, has the same advan-tage as an evaluating psychiatric observer who sees a patient for a short period in a special situation. The picture he sees is simple, logical, and uncomplicated, and therefore description and generaliza-tion are easy.

A close observer, who has known the inmates and employees of the institution for many years, obtains a varied, rich, and detailed picture of interpersonal reactions, but it is not possible to describe this richness in simple terms. It is clear that the descriptions of prisons given in books like Clemmer's and Sykes's from America, and Morris' from England,[5] do not indicate what we observe in a small institution like Herstedvester which is broken up into many small units.

The classic, scholarly analyses of large, maximum-security prisons are an impressive warning to us. We often forget that a prison is a place where many good citizens have spent, or will spend, a part of their lives. Almost all the prisoners we have now will be our free, fellow citizens again. The frequency of real criminality for men in Denmark is not less than 12 per cent. (The risk for property crime is about 10 per cent and for aggressive crime about 2 per cent in provincial towns and a little less in the capital. The risk for sexual crime is about 1½ per cent in the towns.[6]) This means that 12 per cent of the young men over the age of fifteen in a town will serve prison sentences before they are sixty years old—a high percentage.

To my mind, the big security institutions are inhuman machines that frustrate the good intentions of inmates and staff alike. I hasten to add, however, that in these institutions many members of both groups do have good intentions, and, even though many of their efforts fail, some succeed in spite of the handicaps.

Sociologists have stressed the informal aspects of life in an institu-tion. A psychiatrist may stress the important role of the individual

[5] Terence Morris and Pauline Morris, *Pentonville, A Sociological Study of an English Prison* (London: Routledge and Kegan Paul, 1963).

[6] Karl O. Christiansen, Lise Møller, and Arne Nielsen, "Kriminalitetsrisikoen i Danmark før og efter krigen," *Nordisk Tidsskrift for Kriminalvidenskab* (1960):300–313.

qualities of inmates and employees in this way of life. Here life is
bursting with contrasts that become understandable and easier to
tolerate when it is made clear to their victims that we all live in a
series of almost insoluble dilemmas. Attempts to protect the rights
of individuals, especially the weak ones—including offenders who have
no political influence—against the strong ones, call for uniformity in
modern society. They also lead to our humanitarian efforts to help
every criminal to become an ordinary, free citizen like anyone else
instead of being hidden away because the general public do not wish
to see him again. There is a conflict between the demand for justice
and equality and the equally important demand for the fullest
possible rehabilitation of every individual. Formal and traditional
rights must be weighed against the vaguely defined but equally essential needs to help inmates in their efforts to live decent lives based on
self-respect.

Life in an institution is likely to make an inmate dependent on
others. He becomes childish because we take away, and indeed must
take away from him, responsibility for solving the demands of day-to-
day living. In Herstedvester we try to counteract these destructive
consequences of institutional life. However, the close contact forced
upon inmates and staff limits permissible dissimilarities in our interactions. These dissimilarities might be interpreted by personnel and
inmates alike as unfairness in treatment, and this would make life
more difficult for both groups.

If uniformity is stressed, one is tempted to use didactic postulates.
One must then limit intimate contact between inmates and employees
and also, to some extent, between different categories of employees.
This limitation reduces the self-confidence of staff members and
inmates, increases mutual anxiety, and tempts everyone to "seek
escape in stupidity," which allows the toughest and most self-assertive
people to dominate.

Therapeutic thinking calls for a treatment which tends to make
life more difficult for both inmates and staff. Democratic principles
may increase the self-confidence of the individual and counteract
mutual anxieties, but democracy also calls for a larger and better
educated staff and creates more strenuous living conditions for individual staff members as well as individual inmates. It will, however,
facilitate the inmate's later adjustment to free society.

Although our democratic form of administration encourages
inmates' self-confidence and ability to withstand disappointments and
defeats, it also carries the risk that in the beginning only a few will be

able to stand the strain. Therefore it is necessary in a security institution to let democratic methods develop slowly and to make compromises in the beginning.

Institutional life tends to generate a pretense of adjustment. The inmates partake of privileges that are given openly and gradually to all. False adjustment here makes adjustment to free society more difficult, and it may help to stigmatize the inmates in their own eyes and in the eyes of free citizens. Nevertheless, the personnel have to recognize and reward the inmates who control their habits of aggressive and oppositional behavior and try to act in a reasonable way. They must also recognize and reward an inmate's disassociation from those who try to be indifferent. Recognizing a positive attitude and well-balanced self-confidence is, however, a difficult task. It is the therapist's daily problem to decide what is real and what is pretended in an inmate's behavior. Experience has shown that frequently an inmate develops a real adjustment after a period of pretending to act as if he were seeking contact with the therapist. Uncertainty as to how to react to this kind of pretense places a strain on the therapist, and he may develop protest reactions such as a pessimistic, critical attitude.

The better an institution is arranged, the better one living there can know everyone, not just his equals, and the easier it is for the staff to observe problems and to find acceptable compromises. Small dimensions have a value in themselves. The visibility of what goes on in a little institution makes it possible for people to understand one another and encourages a feeling of confidence to develop within the whole.

In our small institution, we really live together, and I will now describe some of the more general patterns of reactions typical of the various components of our group.

THE GENERAL ORGANIZATION OF HERSTEDVESTER

Our community consists of inmates, ward officers, a porter, a mail clerk, the superintendent, a truck driver, office girls, social aides, nurses, teachers, psychologists, psychiatrists, etc. The system of fellowship is regulated by certain norms as to what is, or is not, allowed within the strongly secured institution, Herstedvester, and the open section, Kastanienborg.

We are often too categorical in our observation and classification of such an environment. Every section of such a community has a face of its own, but the expression changes constantly. In the fifteen sections of Herstedvester, we have gathered the most peculiar chronic criminals and the most eccentric (though not insane) dangerous criminals in Denmark. These form the nucleus of the groups in our living units, workshops, and open section. In addition to these there are the staff members, who are not necessarily selected as being especially suitable, but who are interested in working with human beings and in exercising their ingenuity in trying to help them.

The characteristic mark of an ordinary prison community is that important events throughout the day are seen in relation to security problems. In Herstedvester we have a wall, and in Kastanienborg there are rules, to give a prisoner a certain amount of protection against curious strangers and to limit any temptation to escape. While living in our open institution and working outside the walls, an inmate's security lies in the strict observance of the rules. The two factors—wall and rules—have a strong influence on the people who are subject to security measures, as well as on those who have to maintain them. The inmates' happiness, as well as the degree of their hatred of the authorities, is partially rooted in these circumstances but is not the absolute result of them.

It is important to the local culture in Herstedvester that our primary purpose, re-socialization, be clearly understood. We like to emphasize that our attention is aimed at treating individuals. However, we encounter some inmates in whom security problems are so dominant that we have to be satisfied for a long period with attempting simply to limit their injuries caused by the security system. Some cases can be placed in one of these two categories for a long time, but in certain other cases the treatment aim is dominant during some periods and the security aim at other times. Both aims must always be kept in mind. This double purpose complicates the lives of all members of the small community. In addition, the immediate, practical demands of housing, feeding, and employing the inmates are always present in an institution.

For many years in Herstedvester we have maintained that the supposed conflict between security and treatment does not exist. This idea derives from a general attitude of Danish psychiatrists that they have a dual duty to the mentally ill patients in a hospital. They must treat psychiatric patients individually and give them the greatest possible freedom while, at the same time, they must constantly guard against danger, both for the patient himself and for others.

As early as 1910, it was recognized that treatment is most important in hospitals; yet they have always received dangerous, mentally ill criminals. The hospitals also have noncriminal patients who are dangerous but unable to admit their illness. To protect the patients and society, hospitals must prevent these patients from committing dangerous acts. This has been pointed out in laws concerning the mentally ill and also in a note written by the medical superintendents of the hospitals in answer to a complaint about the lack of attention given to the problem.

In accordance with a royal decree of 1940,[7] security comes first in a detention institution such as Herstedvester. However, Danish psychiatric authorities have always agreed that security and treatment must be weighed against each other in each individual case and that the best security for society lies in rehabilitation. The interpretation of these viewpoints has, of course, brought about public discussion, as well as official debate on an administrative level. Because the temptation to run away from difficulties, instead of trying to work out realistic solutions to them, characterizes a great number of our inmates, we must have security methods that hold them. Practically all inmates will, sooner or later, admit that our security is reasonable, even though they do not always accept it. They find it especially difficult to admit the fairness of prolonged use of maximum security. However, even the most extreme control problems result in interpersonal relationships which may be used to influence the offender.

In the more theoretical studies, it is often said that a treatment institution is oriented toward dealing with any situation in a way that is adequate for the individual inmate. In practice, however, it is also necessary to consider the whole institution and to make it clear to the inmate that we have this double consideration in mind. This may cause some tension, but we must accept this if we are to keep realities under control.

We have, rightly or wrongly, inherited problems from the traditional interpretation of the law that requires setting a reasonable length of time for custody in each sentence. The main concern ought to be risk of the criminal's committing a new crime. The conflict between these two points of view causes tension, but it is the court that decides finally whether security measures are to be changed.

Indefinite sentences themselves cause problems. If the personnel feel that the indeterminate time is a serious and unjust strain on the inmates, this will cause trouble for the inmates. They will at once perceive the staff's feeling and react according to the rules of double

7 See Appendix A.

expectation so that they will suffer. The situation is reversed if, as in our case, all the more experienced staff look upon the indeterminate time factor as a positive stimulation. This strongly motivates a majority of our inmates to seek help, not only when this is convenient and immediately satisfying, but also during times when many of their former life patterns have to be replaced by new ones that do not seem to offer immediate satisfaction. In addition, few staff members, and no inmates, can disregard the fact that a limited criminal record will require a short internment. On the other hand, if an inmate has a serious criminal record, we do not feel free to suggest his parole to the court very early, even though his re-socialization might be encouraged by such a move. Our motive is not punishment, but we cannot ignore public opinion if we release a man too early. This may place such a heavy strain on him that he will commit a new crime that will endanger him and society and destroy the citizens' trust in the way we manage our responsibilities.

The accomplishment of our purpose is based on the interaction of the inmates and different groups of personnel as controlled by the rules. These, as they are given in the royal decree of 1940, are firm and limiting, and they draw us toward traditional practice. The working conditions are, as already suggested, indirectly influenced by the ordinary layman's expectations and, in certain instances, by unco-ordinated praise and attacks from the usually unenlightened press.

For many sensitive people, publicity about crimes committed by themselves or by family members is really a severe punishment. Public discussion, dominated at one moment by the concept of the "terrible criminal" and at another by the concept of the "unhappy" or "ill-treated criminal," is the surest source of the feeling of general degradation that is considered by many convicts to be their most terrible punishment. Such publicity is probably unavoidable.

Among the inmate's nearest relatives, there seldom is a noticeable tendency to discriminate against him, but he often thinks there is for a long time. Later the "lost son's" feeling of degradation may decrease, but it is easily revived if he discovers that some vocation that was possible before the crime is now closed to him. Even though some members of our society have become a little more tolerant, their tolerance still does not go very deep.

In my survey of the Herstedvester community and its functions, I will start by looking at the inmates, then at the personnel, beginning with the uniformed staff members, who spend the most time in direct contact with the inmates, and continuing with the teachers, therapists, and social aides. Finally I shall comment on how I, myself, view the superintendent's role.

THE INMATES

The best way I know to describe the attitudes of the inmates of Herstedvester is to summarize a study done in January, 1962. This was based on a questionnaire by Stanton Wheeler and his colleagues as part of a larger, Scandinavian project.

The date chosen for the investigation was unfortunate, because an inmate had been killed the month before and the police had revealed that the murderer was his ward officer. The officer had become sexually dependent on this exceptionally asocial person, who used the situation to obtain special privileges and smuggled alcohol. The officer had for years been loyal to Herstedvester and was caught in a severe conflict, afraid all the time of the certain exposure of his relationship with the inmate which would lead to the loss of his position. So he slipped a very poisonous insecticide, parathion, into the smuggled alcohol he gave the inmate.

I openly discussed the incident in the Hut and told the inmates the actual circumstances as soon as I knew them. This prevented rumors and the inmates were not strongly affected when the institution was strongly attacked in the newspapers.

Order was maintained in the institution during and after the police investigation. There was no increase in the number of disciplinary cases.

On the day that Stanton Wheeler submitted his questionnaire, 155 out of our 182 inmates participated and 141 (85.2 per cent) gave useful answers. The participants had a median current age of thirty-three years and admitted, themselves, that they had been in difficulties from an early age. Seventy-four per cent had been in homes for child care, and 14 per cent had been in youth prisons. Seventy-seven per cent had served one or more ordinary sentences, and 17 per cent had been in the "work house."[8] Approximately half of them had been in a detention institution or in "security detention"[9] before. Only 7 per cent were married. Seventy-five per cent were living

[8] A special open prison for those sentenced to one to five years.
[9] "Security detention" is a special institution for the more dangerous criminals who are not sentenced in accordance with Sections 16 or 17 of the Criminal Code. The minimum time there is four years, the maximum time, twenty years.

in Copenhagen when they received their latest sentences, and 70 per cent did not have any education beyond elementary school.

Complaints about the strain of an indefinite sentence are often voiced during the detention period, and they were heard by the interviewers who ran the investigation. We do not know whether these would have occurred as often, if the publicity about the inmate's death had not been current. Such complaints are usually a kind of protection in times of stress. Taken too seriously, they are often exaggerated and become an unnecessary annoyance to the inmates.

Actually, the inmates are quite able to judge what is a reasonable time to be kept in the detention institution. It is the job of the personnel, especially of the therapists, to keep their dreams and speculations about parole dates at a realistic level. If the staff can unanimously and systematically point out the advantages and disadvantages of an inmate's plan, a constructive task is given to him, and his indeterminate sentence becomes more than an empty time of waiting for an unknown future. In such cases the indeterminate time may develop into a good tool for motivating the inmate to change. If there is no teamwork and the atmosphere in the institution is pessimistic, the indefinite time to be spent there is not a useful tool but quite the opposite, a heavy and useless burden.

In the inmates' answers to the questionnaire, only 4 per cent did not say when they expected their cases to be brought before the court. Of the others, 21 per cent estimated stays of three months; 22 per cent, three to six months; 16 per cent, six to twelve months; 10 per cent, twelve to eighteen months; 6 per cent, eighteen to twenty-four months; and 10 per cent, two to three years. Only 5 per cent expected to stay three to five years; and 6 per cent, more than five years. These are quite realistic expectations, though many of these estimates are at the lower limit of what will turn out to be true. Such optimism is not to be regretted, even if it sometimes causes disappointments. Here again, disappointments can be worked with rationally from a therapeutical standpoint. The question is whether or not the advantages of inteterminate sentences compensate for the disadvantages. The advantages outweigh the disadvantages in most of our cases, but this may not be true at times when the inmates are being encouraged in their self-pity by outside authorities or by influential members of the staff.

Only 19 per cent of the inmates felt that they were justly sentenced considering what they had done; 68 per cent felt that they were unjustly sentenced, and 11 per cent did not know how they felt. These figures are not radically different from those collected in the nearby State Prison where 22 per cent of the prisoners felt that they had been justly sentenced. We will not conclude from this that conviction is unjust in all these cases, and the inmates' regard for the fairness of the court will not change the practice of the courts. One can understand their subjective feelings if one imagines himself in an inmate's situation and tries to see things from his point of view.

Most inmates assumed that the court psychiatrist had the greatest influence on their sentences. Because all are sentenced in accordance with Section 17 and are found to be unfit for punishment, this may be an understandable supposition. But it is astonishing to find how many of them thought that other participants were most influential; 16 per cent gave this credit to the judge, 10 per cent to the police, 8 per cent to the prosecutor, 3 per cent to the psychologist, and 0.7 per cent to the defense attorney. In fact, only one inmate believed that the defense attorney had the greatest influence.

When questioned about daily life in Herstedvester, a great proportion of the inmates (42 per cent) thought the psychiatrist had the greatest influence; 17 per cent thought it was the officer; and 18 per cent said it was the administrator. A considerably smaller group said that a teacher, psychologist, priest, or social aide was the most important influence.

When asked with whom they would discuss a personal problem, the answers became completely different. Only 13 per cent chose the psychiatrist, 17 per cent the psychologist, 18 per cent the officer, and 11 per cent the social aide, while a smaller number chose other employees. One-third of our inmates were quite satisfied with the contact they had with the officers, another third wished to have less contact, and the last third wished to have more. This even distribution corresponds very well with the fact that only half of the inmates would have liked to see the number of rules reduced, and only one-fourth felt that the personnel seldom overlooked small violations of the regulations.

On the other hand, there was greater dissatisfaction with the contact with therapists—77 per cent thought it could be better. Whether this response indicates that these inmates are frustrated by a need for clearer understanding of their personal problems is not definite. As already mentioned, most of these men are rather primitive and many are not very intelligent. Even though they may learn to state their problems, it is necessary for them to learn to solve their own trifling difficulties in a more simple way than they are accustomed to. Many of their conversations with therapists are sought only for vague reasons and are perhaps stimulated by the notion of making good impressions or following some whim of fashion. If the therapist does not take a strong stand, such interviews lead to eternal hairsplitting of small problems which have already been thoroughly discussed. Taking such a firm stand may be uncomfortable, but it may force the inmate to attempt to solve his own small problems. The conversations are apparently satisfying to the inmates, in most cases. About 40 per cent of the inmates had the impression that they get straight answers to questions that they pose to the personnel and in the therapeutic group meetings.

The inmates also said that the personnel understand their viewpoints to a reasonable extent. Sixty per cent believed that this is the case with the officers, while 50 per cent thought that the therapeutic personnel are more understanding. This difference, which is not statistically valid, seems more logical when one considers that inmates have closer daily contact with the officers. The fact that 22 per cent of the inmates questioned had been in the institution less than half a year must also be taken into consideration.

It appears that the inmates have a relatively clear impression of the democratic management we try to maintain. Forty-seven per cent said that the officers have much to say about the inmates in the institution, but 74 per cent said the same for the therapeutic personnel. Only 18 (13 per cent) said that these two groups do not decide anything. When we compare this with other investigated institutions, the result is very satisfactory.

The classic query as to whether we are able to treat inmates who do not regard what we are doing for them as treatment is irrelevant, considering our treatment concept. We must remember that this concept is just as blurred to the subject of the experiment as it is to the rest of us. The problem is not what words we use, or which conversations we work through, but whether we can successfully use individualized pressure to make an inmate move toward rehabilitation. If human interactions, both verbal and nonverbal, cannot be used systematically, and we do not succeed in motivating the inmate, we may as well save our efforts.

Those who were questioned stated that the personnel, as well as the inmates, exert general pressure. The personnel direct their pressure toward developing a positive attitude toward inmates. Two-thirds of the inmates sometimes felt this pressure, but only half sometimes felt pushed to work harder than they wished or were influenced to keep away from inmates who appeared to be in conflict with the personnel.

The distribution of the results is similar in the matter of being pressured by other inmates, either to keep at a distance from the personnel and to work less or to support fellow inmates in conflicts with the staff.

The inmates felt that they were being helped only to a certain extent, but there are about three times as many in Herstedvester that feel they are being helped (30 per cent) than in the State Prison (11 per cent). In Herstedvester, 46 per cent of the inmates claimed that they were being hurt as opposed to 53 per cent in the State Prison. These figures are to be taken with the greatest reservation.

To a number of more detailed questions, more inmates answered positively than negatively. Fifty-seven per cent said that they had obtained better insight into their problems during the time they had to think these over, and 29 per cent stated that they had been helped by the personnel to a better understanding of themselves. This feeling of being helped must be compared to a feeling of being fairly treated in the institution, and here we get a different point of view. Only 29 per cent of the inmates felt that they are treated fairly, as compared to 69 per cent in the State Prison. Even this means that they feel more fairly treated by Herstedvester than by the courts (see page 148).

This presents a serious problem. To what extent should we attempt to further the inmate's awareness of being justly treated, and to what extent should we aim at rehabilitation in spite of his temporary feeling of lack of justice? Which should be most important? In spite of this uncertainty, satisfactory development seems to occur during the inmate's stay in the institution.

This development is demonstrated by the fact that about 60 per cent of those who had been in the institution less than six months felt that they had been injured by their stay, but this feeling appeared in only 42 per cent of the group that had been in the institution for more than six months. This seems like a good development curve, one which reverses in state prisons, but is like the one in youth prisons where it is on a lower level, changing from a little over 40 per cent to 25 per cent.

Older inmates, discussing the figures from the questionnaires and their own impressions of the institution, frequently smile and confess that at first they saw the future in a gloomy perspective but that their opinions changed. One of the frequent recidivists expressed it this way: "When I was waiting for my sentence last time, I yearned very much for Herstedvester." He read and reread our letter that said that we were disappointed about his new trouble and that we would have to try once more. He had gone through a long period without criminality during the time we had known each other. The fact that we "who knew him so well" dared to be optimistic "helped him over serious thoughts of making an end to it all."

This man was a petty criminal who let himself drift along on his impulses and, like so many others, was unable to explain why he had been without criminality for many years, then relapsed.

Another former inmate differed and, after a series of attempts to evade the question, said very frankly, "It really is as if there is a veil over the entire period in Herstedvester. In spite of attempts to try to recall it, it all becomes pale and unreal. I guess I had a kind of wound that now has healed. I only see the scar." This man had spent nine years of his life in Herstedvester and now, after seven years away from the institution, is a solid citizen and family man who has established a very respectable, middle-class position for himself.

Evasion is a problem in questioning inmates. Another difficulty is their tendency to adjust memories to the present situation (retroactive categorization).[10] If I point out an inmate's distortions, which I am aware of because I was present during the earlier situations, he may apologetically smile, indicating that the distortion was not made on purpose. However, I may not always know the background and be able to compare statements, but an outsider could never have such an opportunity.

I have often tried to find out what kind of help people received in the institution, but individual incidents are seldom pointed out as being especially important. Frequently an inmate mentions that an ordinary officer, very likely one who has escorted him on leaves, has contributed to the recovery of his self-respect. He could "turn to the officer for a chat," but he seldom recognized that this had a moderating influence on the tension that was annoying him when it took place.

Any individual interview must be related to the actual interviewing situation. Previous knowledge of the events of the inmate's criminal period is a great advantage when evaluating the result of the conversation. This advantage may be so great that it compensates for the risk of tendentious conclusions. The answers to the questionnaires

[10] Franz From, *Om oplevelsen af andres adfaerd* (Copenhagen: Nyt Nordisk Forlag, 1953), p. 106.

made it clear that our imprisoned people look quite differently upon the society which confines them, upon the professional people with whom they associate in the institution, and upon their fellow sufferers. They react to the difficulties of their existence in the institution more outspokenly and more strikingly, as the difficulties become greater. When the inmates' difficulties are great, it is easier to find common traits in them. It is important to try to do this and to try to advance a hypothesis of how a given group of persons will experience such a special role as that of an inmate, but it should be remembered that the more outspoken the reactions, and the shorter the period of observation, the easier it will be to see a unified picture. From the point of view of nonparticipants, it is easier to see the negative sides of any organization, including Herstedvester, and more difficult to find out to what extent the organization (at times even through the "negatively" experienced elements) fulfills useful purposes.

As one takes part in countless discussions with inmates in the institution, at the beginning of or during the detention period, during the nervous period before and after release, or at chance meetings on the street or in Tivoli, one obtains a much more varied picture of the men. At the same time, it becomes more difficult to advance a correct hypothesis of how each inmate will react. His personality elements show through to a certain degree, but different elements appear in different situations. We know little of these unique situations in advance. We know that certain situational patterns occur more frequently than others, but the next situation may be the unexpected or unusual one. To this difficulty in understanding the inmate's point of view we must add the fact that observing a situation ourselves does not suffice. We are able to see it only from the outside and do not acquire a subjective experience of the situation surrounding the act. We have to guess at the influence of double expectation on the inmate's perception of a situation and what he thinks will happen.

If an inmate's feeling of being divergent is confirmed, as it often is following a sentence, especially to detention, his attitude will change. Almost any chronic criminal, shortly after he is sentenced, is ready to try to start a normal life again, but at other times he is just as likely to want to give up as soon as difficulties appear.

The lack of realism in the different attitudes of the inmates can be illustrated. About a year ago, the following letter from a former inmate to the editor appeared in one of the largest newspapers in the country without causing any comment:

May I be allowed to make a proposition that means a lot to me and maybe to others of the same standing—make a prison reform which permits prisoners to let themselves be used as "guinea pigs." This would not only be of importance to medical research, but would also mean a great deal for the re-education of the prisoners. It is true that when someone other than a hardened criminal goes to prison he loses much besides his liberty. He loses his ego and his self-respect. Worst of all is the feeling that he is unable to do anything to prove that there is still something good in him. We prisoners are forgotten by society, but many of us would do anything to rehabiliate ourselves and regain our own and our families' self-respect. The world outside the walls ought to give us this chance.

This letter was signed with the full name of the writer (I will call him Mogens) and his cell number in the Copenhagen jail, and it clearly shows that, in spite of many similar experiences, he was suffering from his arrest. He did not think of himself as a "hardened criminal," even though he had appeared in court many times. The first two times, he was put under continued supervision of the authority for juveniles; this was followed by long stays in juvenile institutions and five sentences to detention in Herstedvester. He did not think that his attitude toward normal work had been proven to be unstable.

Soon after his last parole, I met him by chance on the street. He stopped me, proved to be in a very good mood, and claimed to have promised himself that he would use the chance he now had to get something really worthwhile out of life. He meant that he had the best possibilities he could wish for, under the circumstances. I got the impression that Mogens sincerely wanted to try to make a better life for himself. However, the very next day he failed to appear at his job but showed up a couple of days later. He did not come for his antabus treatment at Herstedvester and we felt obliged to arrange for him to receive it elsewhere. Subsequently he disappeared and was searched for but he had enough time to commit larceny before he was arrested. After his arrest, he wrote to the therapist who had worked with him, "I have received much help and support from you in one way or another. I have always been willing to cooperate, but, nevertheless, I have become less and less capable of taking care of myself. I have spent over ten years here. During countless conversations we have discussed my problems, but alcohol gets its grip on me anyway, every time I am paroled. It is the anxiety of living, or, rather, the anxiety of not being adequate in life outside the walls, that gets me down." The day he committed the larceny, he was a "complete psychic wreck." He wrote, "My decision to create a reason for a charge was not a result of mature consideration but came spontaneously. In my condition of depression and intoxication, I believed that perhaps this would arouse the authorities and draw their attention to what was really my problem, namely, alcoholism."

It was difficult for Mogens to find an opportunity to acquire any self-respect under the conditions in which he lived. A vicious circle started by drinking had overwhelmed him, and therefore he talked about what others should do and shrank from trying to solve his own common, everyday problems.

When Mogens returned to us, I talked to him again. This time he wondered why we had designated him as spineless, but he admitted the accuracy of the description. Then he wanted to know what elements of his personality had been inherited, what ones had been acquired, and which ones were more important. We explained to him that both influences had played their part. He is usually happy and plays a good deal of poker. He tends to blame his failures on his environment, but eventually admits that he has been acting as if he were fourteen years old. Actually he is worse off than an average fourteen-year-old who has social experiences and support from a family.

When we send him on his way the next time, we will, as before, try to keep in close contact with him and attempt to prevent his misuse of alcohol. At times he is interested in our attempts to treat his alcoholism, but at other times he rejects them. He is still unstable as far as work is concerned.

In 1947 I participated in a panel discussion with Julius, a sixty-year-old former inmate who had been in almost constant conflict with the law from the age of 17, usually as a swindler. He had also been an active pedophiliac homosexual since his mid-thirties and had at times been described as a very dangerous criminal.

Julius pointed out that, as a rule, the most prominent trait in psychopaths is their optimism. "They think there is nothing they cannot do and no situation in life, no matter how sad, that will not be followed by a total change for the better. If you talk to them about low income or poor opportunities, they are likely to say that they are positive that they will get money and a pleasant job, anyway. They expect everything to be ready for them when they again go out into the world." He added with a certain irony, "especially swindlers." He wrongly believed, just as so many others like him do, that swindlers

are the largest group of property criminals in the detention institution. He said, "They often believe that life has the best things waiting
for them." He respected the importance of reality as it is stressed in
Herstedvester. However, he regretted that it still was under the
jurisdiction of the prison authority, even though he was "not blind
to the fact that the future temples for human justice would be institutions of exactly this character but without an indefinite term of
punishment. It is difficult for us to bridge the gap between nervous
strain from the indeterminate sentence and the fact that we know
that it will help us."

Both of the chronic criminals I have described are intelligent.
Mogens is still young, but Julius was an old man when he left
Herstedvester. Julius, however, committed a small fraud six years
later. During the years between this incident and his death, he
remained in touch with the staff member who had taken special care
of him.

Mogens still has an uncertain future. Depending on how he sees his
particular situation and the role he plays at the moment, at times he
will act "censorious"[11] and, at other times, thankful and content. In
this respect he does not differ from the staff. We also are likely to
evaluate the inmates on the basis of the roles they and we happen to
be playing at a given moment. The very fact of admitting that he is a
prisoner modifies the inmate's experience of himself, and, in the detention institution, this is marked by a rapid oscillation in moods, the
development of which even those who live within the institution do
not recognize until it has reached a certain size.

As a part of a battle to regain his self-respect, the inmate sometimes makes very complicated plans. For example, an inmate who
planned to go to a folk high school wrote:

> I think it is quite clear that it is more difficult for me to get started
> each time I have been in detention, and it is equally certain that it is
> even more difficult for us to convince anybody here of our honest
> intentions and have them believe that it is of any use for us to take
> responsibility ourselves. I, of course, have many faults and probably,
> as a fourth-time man, have been given up as lost. This is the way I feel
> sometimes, but nevertheless I hang on and seek new ways. One of
> them is this high school idea of mine which originated one and a half
> years ago. It started with some study circle programs concerned with
> young peoples' spare time occupations. Here I got an insight into life

[11] Thomas Mathiesen, *The Defences of the Weak* (London: Tavistock, 1965),
pp. 150–93.

in high schools and into how human beings could gather in a varied group, discuss some event, and at the same time act naturally towards one another. This is what I miss a great deal. Of course, I can be like everybody else in a folk high school, just as I am like everybody else in quite different circles. Among thieves, prostitutes, and pimps, there is also a mutual fusion. I "belong to the circle" and feel that "it is nice," and then, just as soon as I am among others who never have been imprisoned, I lose the feeling of security. I do not know if you can imagine my thoughts. It is not easy to put it right, but my ideas and plans of going to a high school are in order to become more secure and balanced in relation to all situations.

We tried energetically, but unsuccessfully, to fulfill his wish, especially because he saw this as his only chance. Not until nine months later did the court agree to parole him. He then became involved with a quiet, sensible young lady who knew his problems, and he forgot about folk high school. They now live together in a provincial town in Denmark where he is not known, and, for the time being, it seems to be working all right. His letters to the social aide and therapist indicate that he has found a normal group of friends.

We have to evaluate the isolated statements that appear in individual and group conversations with the greatest care. Presumably, the group conversations are the most important. In a well-knit group like that in the Hut, we can count on the inmates' offering as much help as they are able to in understanding their problems.

In March, 1965, we had a group discussion about their reactions to being placed in Herstedvester, stressing their personal experiences. To start, I referred to the fact that when a man is placed in detention for the first time, he is likely to have an optimistic outlook on life for the first few months—an outlook that is reflected in letters and conversations. This stage is then replaced by a confused phase, a period of skepticism and bitterness along with a certain aggressiveness toward the institution and a sort of uncertainty and bewilderment. This in turn is replaced by a hopeful, relaxed phase that is upset just before parole when a final, anxious phase appears.

These phases were recognized by everyone as being correct. The initial optimistic period was thought to be a reaction to the frequently long custody in the Copenhagen jail and the fact that, during the first months, the inmate was repeatedly called for conversation with someone who showed a positive interest in his condition and thus satisfied his need for human contacts. A few of the inmates pointed out that it may take one or two years to work one's way out of the second phase. The disappointed phase was explained as a reaction to the prosecutor's and judge's "rosy stories that you are going to a place where you can cook your own meals and where there are physicians who will take care of you." They had been told, moreover, that this was "certainly not punishment." After arrival, however, they discovered Herstedvester's locked doors and heavy security measures, and their attitude changed.

In the discussion it was brought up several times that conditions needed improving, and there was strong criticism of the security measures. The inmates complained that we did not trust the wall and felt that there was not enough liberty inside it. When we moved from such general statements to specific, existing conditions, the discussants expressed satisfaction with their own circumstances in the Hut. Nevertheless, they often visited friends in other sections with whom they shared mutual interests such as stamps and music. They also did this because they, fifteen to seventeen men almost constantly together, felt a need to do something different.

An outstanding fact was that there was never, at any time, any trace of an aggressive attack against the personnel. This confirmed my idea that the personnel are not looked upon as a concept or symbol of the institution, but as a group of individuals with whom most inmates are able to get along. We frequently find that the detention period passes peacefully for an inmate who had severe adjustment difficulties in other institutions. When, during parole or later, we ask him why, he often answers that he was treated like an adult in Herstedvester. It is hardly this simple, but it does mean that, even though we limit his liberty and often do not agree with him or have to refuse to comply with his wishes, our willingness to explain what we do gives him the impression that he is being looked upon as "a human being." Also of great importance is the inmate's personal contact with the staff members who are permanently connected with the same section or workshop. Frequent changes of staff in wards or workshops would soon result in stereotyping the inmates' attitudes toward employees and weaken the individualization of treatment.

Prison architecture is also important. Herstedvester is a small institution with a decent garden and with houses that do not look like fortresses. Although they are far from charming, they provide better living conditions than a traditional prison has. As for prison architecture and administration, Lombroso has not lived in vain. The prisoners in ordinary prisons are looked upon as being potentially dangerous, and security has attracted the greatest part of the architects' interest. They have not considered that unnecessarily uncomfortable living conditions in ordinary prisons have an important influence on the behavior of the prisoners. As this fact is being recognized, understanding is developing that it is wrong to impute to the prisoners the sole responsibility for all their reactions. We have mutual responsibility for all the situations we create. In an esthetically ugly building where there is formal discipline and little cooperation between prisoners and personnel, special traits develop that mark both parties. When such personality patterns of prisoners and prison personnel are publicly described, the ordinary citizen lowers his opinions of both groups.

A former inmate of Herstedvester who had some literary success was provoked by a television debate on the problem of punishment. He wrote the following for a newspaper in March, 1964,[12] under the title "Return to Life":

> I myself made the mistake—I say it and mean it—of writing a book that was going to tell those outside a little about us behind the iron curtains. I was filled with a pure idealism, and I sincerely wished to succeed in rehabilitating myself and to give my friends a fair chance to teach people out there that we really were exactly like them, with the same longings, the same dreams, the same regrets, and the same ambitions. The book was well received; I was interviewed quite a few times. . . . You may say that we lawbreakers also are shortsighted! Yes, of course we are. We are made of the same blood as the rest of you out there in the community and think just as you do. Only we have the advantage that we, little by little, may learn, with the lash on our own backs, that condemnation is wrong, that everything has a background, and that you have to know before you start not to condemn but to judge the immediate situation. . . . We who break the law know quite well that we have sinned and that we will have to pay for it. Not a single one of us would dream that you should not arrest us. . . . Why should you not do that? No, we have to go through our punishment, and then, while we serve it, we have to try to find a little bit of ourselves and our personality. We are not at all at odds with prison authorities; there are just a very few prison officials whom we do not greet with a smile when we meet them as free citizens. No, our punishment is the terrible feeling of loneliness and anxiety about our past being discovered. We know very well that, if somebody traces our past, we are game being hunted by bloodhounds. These people are not 80 per cent of the population but the 20 per cent that are insufficient themselves and who, until now, have been lucky enough to escape the

[12] Quoted from the manuscript.

arm of the law. It is these people who live under great strain with
themselves (and they really should know just how similar in psyche
they are in their insufficiency to the majority of law breakers), and
therefore their mouths water when they find out that here is an offender
who is weaker than themselves . . . and they think, "Well, we are going
to grind him under our heels."

That loneliness is a constant element in the criminal world is clearly
proven by the regularity with which it is presented in the extemporaneous theater and by the enthusiasm with which inmates discuss
it.

An inmate gave this description of an extemporaneous play that
was presented in 1954:

> In the play a parolee's loneliness is shown and how, regardless of
> good living and work conditions and his good intentions, he nevertheless
> collapses. It is clearly demonstrated how inner insufficiencies maneuver
> him into conflict with his surroundings and how those same insufficien-
> cies, time after time, hinder him from grasping the helping hand ex-
> tended to him from outside.

> We see the parolee, accompanied by the welfare worker, arrive at his
> new room where the landlord, who does not know of his past, receives
> him kindly. He then meets a woman to whom he very soon tells the
> truth. Because he brags at work in order to cover his past, his colleagues
> discover that there is something wrong. When they become aware that
> he is a former convict, they become indignant at his lies but are still
> willing to accept him if he stops lying. He does not stop, however, as
> his feeling of inferiority still tortures him. Then his landlord discovers
> his past, and their relationship becomes cool. He neglects saying
> anything about these failures to the welfare officer who, he surmises,
> will only think he is in the wrong. His relationship with his girl friend
> becomes difficult as her parents continue to speak of the necessity of
> his finding a home before their planned marriage. She won't live with
> him without being married and so they break up.

In the last three scenes the disintegration of his situation is shown
and commented upon in this way:

> He now sinks deeper and deeper into his loneliness. He goes on with
> his work, but he has lost interest in it. What he does, he does mechan-
> ically because he knows his job, but he doesn't enjoy it. Consciously he
> supports the barrier between himself and his colleagues. He only meets
> his landlord when he pays his rent or by chance in the hall. He refuses
> to accept their kindness as it seems odd to him. In his relations with
> women he returns to his old habits of having a casual date when he
> needs to, but avoids any firm relationship. His spare time is no longer

something to be enjoyed but is full of loneliness. He tries to read, but after ten pages any book bores him and he throws it aside. He sees a great number of movies, but after he leaves the cinema he is unable to describe what he has seen. He walks up and down the street without noticing where he is going.

He drinks, but not excessively. He wants to get drunk but is simply unable to stay long enough in one place. His thoughts begin to wander. In Herstedvester there was the intimacy of friendship. One did not have to be alone. And if one was alone it was because he wanted to be alone, because there were plenty of available activities with which to fill the time. Time was never a torment. He thought this way because he had forgotten or did not wish to remember all that had then embittered the slowness of the hours. Behind this embellished picture, the wish to return to Herstedvester grew and became vague and unrealistic, but urgent. The thought of death as a relief also arose, but was rejected as being cowardly and unworthy. However, the curiosity to see what the next moment would bring is no longer so much the reason for refusal of the suicide thought. This is what is dangerous."[13]

Protest Reactions

What the former inmates say about life in Herstedvester is often pleasant but does not cover everything. Another way to get an impression of the life of the inmates is to review their protest reactions—suicides, automutilations, and escapes. Other disciplinary problems and our reactions to them mark the hours of despair and unrest. Such periods are unavoidable, and it is not likely that giving inmates opportunities to complain orally or in writing can substantially reduce their acting-out. For several years we have kept a careful account of these reactions.

Suicides. Suicide, the most regrettable and severe protest reaction, has been rare. If we include a suicide in 1935, shortly before the group was moved to the new institution, there have been eight during the thirty-one years of the institution's existence. There was one in each of the years 1935, 1940, 1941, 1942, 1945, and 1951, and there were two in 1962.

The 1935 case committed suicide three weeks after he was placed in detention at the age of thirty-three. He was considered an aggressive brute with hysterical emotional reactions. He had previously been sentenced for theft and housebreaking and placed in a special prison. There he had also been considered hysterical and emotionally

[13] The author of this was paroled for the third time after this was written, and he is still free.

reactive. Then he was sentenced for arson. He had not pleaded guilty and although he had not at any time clearly denied his guilt, he was angry to have been sentenced on the evidence which had been produced in court. He had difficulty in getting along with the other detainees, and he worked alone in his own cell because they would not work with him. During the few weeks he was in the institution, he was polite and easygoing except for resenting the physician whose description of his stay in special prison had been read in court. In a sudden depressed mood, he hung himself.

The 1940 case was sentenced for homosexual pedophilia of a recidivating type. He asked for castration, withdrew his application, and reapplied again one month later. The operation was performed in September, 1939, and he was given permission to go on a six-hour leave in December of the same year. In January, 1940, it was discovered that he wrote love letters to a fellow detainee and in one of these he described the excellent effects of his operation: "I now have such a wonderful peace of mind. I am no longer restless or jealous when I see you with other people. . . . If I should have to consider the operation again, I would say 'yes.'" Then he explained that he would now consider himself as a brother of the fellow detainee; he would always support him, work for him, and so forth. The day after this letter was found, he complained of nervousness and vague dyspeptic symptoms. He was left alone for ten or fifteen minutes, and during this time he hung himself in his cell.

The 1941 case had been sentenced for attempted homicide. From the time he was thirteen years old, whenever his sexual drive was not satisfied, he wanted to hurt other people. He thought about hitting people with a stone which he carried in a stocking, but at the decisive moment he stopped. He believed that he was the reincarnation of Jesus, that Jesus had taken all the world's wickedness with him, and that he himself would now have to go through several lives in order to rid himself of the guilt. He insisted that he had fought his aggressive tendencies in "four bad three-year periods and four good four-month periods"—thirteen years altogether. His fiancée had broken their engagement, and he had suffered much from that. Then he attempted to kill a six-year-old girl by strangling her and stabbing her several times with a knife. He said he was surprised when he "felt the wickedness rise in him." Previously he had committed robberies but said it was "too uncomfortable" to explain the details. He was psychiatrically observed in a mental hospital and found not to be psychotic.

During daily life in Herstedvester he had an air of insecurity. At the same time he wanted sympathy and managed to obtain several privileges. He said that he had amnesia about his crime, but this is doubtful. He denied that his criminal acts had any sexual character. He started to complain that he was not understood and had insufficient opportunity to study, but he stopped talking about Jesus. He worked well at copying books into Braille for the blind, and this achievement satisfied him. When his fiancée told him in a letter that she might marry another man, he reacted very strongly, and he hanged himself the next night.

The 1942 case was forty-two years old and had a long criminal record with eighteen formal sentences, mostly for theft and housebreaking but some for aggression. He was difficult to handle while serving his last, rather long sentence, and, shortly after he arrived at Herstedvester, he was aggressive against other inmates. He was very explosive at times, but between outbreaks he was peaceful. Once he attempted a sexual attack on the matron and tried to touch her genitals, but he was embarrassed when he had done it. After a time his behavior became demented and uninhibited, he was much more blunt, and he had hypochondriac complaints with no psychotic or neurological symptoms. One day he asked permission to sleep in a security cell because he "wasn't sure of himself." This was granted. He returned, seemingly satisfied, to his unit the following morning, and during the day he committed suicide by hanging himself.

The 1945 case was thirty-eight years old and had had a long series of sentences for theft. Once he had been in detention for indecency against small girls. During parole he lived as a tramp. He was returned to Herstedvester in order to prevent new crime, and this time he was morose. During his first stay in detention, when he was thirty-three years old, he had swallowed a thumbtack "by mistake," and, several times after he was returned to Herstedvester, he swallowed foreign bodies. Once he barricaded his cell door, and another time he attempted to strangle himself by tying one end of his undershirt around his neck and the other to the window. We did not think this was a real suicide attempt. Sometimes he refused to eat, and sometimes he ate foreign bodies. When he was thirty-six years old, he escaped. At that time our cells were crowded with two detainees in each. The inmate was soon returned, repeated his explosive actions, then rubbed indelible ink in his eyes in order to be put into the infirmary, near the nurse on whom he relied for support. Six months after his escape he asked to see me, and, instead of calling him to the office, I met him in his ward. He resented this, and an hour later he told the staff that he had swallowed a safety pin. He had no symptoms. Three days later he was transferred to a hospital because he said that he had swallowed some razor blades, and he now complained of pains in his chest. With a laryngoscope, a safety pin was located in the upper part of his esophagus. He died five days later at the hospital because of a mediastinal infection.

The 1951 suicide was fifty years old and had been sentenced for housebreaking. He had borderline intelligence and was stubborn with emotional moods. After some years his emotional instability was reduced, but he remained a scheming person. After he tried to set fire to the Hut, we transferred him to our psychiatric observation ward. Here he was disheartened and became embittered when, after this attempted arson, he was not allowed to move back to the Hut. He felt that he was being teased by his comrades. We transferred him again to the security section, and then moved him back to the infirmary when we supposed he was pacified. He hung himself the following night.

The first suicide in 1962 was thirty-four years old and had been sentenced three times for attempted robbery and theft. This was his third time in detention for theft and housebreaking. During his last period of detention he stressed that he did not like supervision. He felt that he should be allowed to do whatever suited him and that no one should interfere in his private life. In spite of this, he participated with interest in individual as well as group therapy. In the beginning he was stubborn, but after some time he became much less demanding and more natural in manner although he still had some emotional moods.

When we sent a recommendation to the court after two years, we said he was too dangerous to be paroled. He had had great difficulty in adapting himself to normal workshop conditions, and we suggested that it would be better if he were allowed to work outside the institution before parole so that he could learn to discuss work problems with us. He was dissatisfied with this recommendation and got his guardian to withdraw his request for parole. He continued to be eager in his contact with the therapist, believing that she was personally interested in him, and he wanted her to have pity on him. Six weeks after our unfavorable recommendation, he hanged himself.

The second suicide in 1962 was an intelligent, twenty-six-year-old man, sentenced for killing a twelve-year-old girl without sexual assault. His mother died when he was six months old, and he was educated by her family. Then he was placed with his father, who had remarried, but he had trouble with his stepmother and ran away several times. He worked as an apprentice in a machine shop for a year and a half. When he was sixteen years old, he had a serious conflict with his stepmother. He broke into an empty vacation house, stole a rifle, and fired it. He was reprimanded by the court for this and sent home. He continued to be very unhappy and tried to buy sleeping tablets in order to commit suicide, but the druggist gave him only headache tablets. He left a farewell letter when he next left home, and the next morning he broke into an empty vacation house, found a pistol and amused himself with some shooting, got angry, and wandered around aimlessly. Then he met a woman and shot at her, hoping she would lose her handbag. He missed her, and she ran. Once more he tried to shoot at her, but the gun did not work, so he hit her with the pistol butt. After he was arrested, he was examined by a medical officer who found him spineless and emotionally childish.

He was placed in a juvenile home. Because of his impulsiveness, which was not in accordance with his usual correct behavior, the doctor of the juvenile home suggested a special psychiatric examination. The boy ran away several times and then was transferred to a mental hospital for observation. Here he recognized his irresponsibility and admitted his thefts, but he had no guilt feelings. He was found to be pliable and fit for punishment. Probation and placement with a family were suggested. He was put on probation and placed with an aunt with whom he was happy. Four weeks later he went for a walk, seemingly in a good mood. Late in the day his mood changed, he became restless, and he bought some beers and a few strong drinks. Then he killed the twelve-year-old girl in a park by stabbing her several times with a knife.

After he confessed, he explained that for several years he had had difficulties controlling himself. He was afraid that he would be aggressive again against women. On the day of the murder he had thought that he might kill another human being, and he wondered who it would be. He met some boys and rode on their sleds. Then he met the girl. She refused to let him use her sled, and he went out of his senses. He did not remember how he had stabbed her. Afterward he walked around planning suicide, but he gave this up.

At that time we did not know that he had also been aggressive in the juvenile home but had escaped discovery because he had only helped to smuggle in a piece of lead which was later used by two others to hit a staff member. How long he had been thinking about killing someone is uncertain.

He was sent to the mental hospital again for observation, and it appeared that at the time of the murder he had been in an emotional storm with aggressive, and probably unconscious, sexual elements. His statement that he had no memory of the murder may be correct. He was thought to be very dangerous and was sent to detention.

When he arrived at Herstedvester at the age of eighteen, he said that his attempted robbery resulted from his aggressive feelings against his stepmother. He felt that it was wrong to stay with his mother's sister because, although he liked her, he had started hating women because of his stepmother. He was childish and once attempted suicide by plunging a piece of wire into his stomach, but nothing serious happened. One year later he was still reckless and afraid that he "would explode again." No schizophrenic symptoms were discovered. After sixteen months, during a routine physical examination, fresh superficial cuts in the skin were found that he said he had made two weeks before in another suicide attempt.

He became an apprentice funiture-maker in our shop, and after four and one-half years he was moved to the Hut where he participated energetically in group meetings and received permission for a single, six-hour leave. After five and one-half years, he was disappointed that we would not recommend training him as a radio operator. We believed that his personality structure would not be sufficient for the type of responsible job he might one day obtain. When he had been in detention for about six years, his behavior became rather peculiar, but he worked well in the workshop.

When a visiting psychiatrist had an opportunity to talk with him, he raised the question of beginning schizophrenia because of the boy's emotional behavior during the conversation. Sometimes he was unstable, and he broke off his technical school work. During conversation he sometimes started to weep. He was afraid that he would never be accepted in the normal world, and he was embittered that he was no longer as happy and carefree as in the beginning.

In his unit everyone had the impression that he had not changed and that he was still immature. His guardian had tried to put his case before the court for parole, but we could not recommend it. After seven years he began to cooperate a little more and was more emotional, but he still had little contact with the personnel or other detainees. After seven years and four months, he committed suicide. A few days before this his aunt had visited him, and he had given her a little note saying, "Thank you for everything," but, no one had paid much attention to this.

He killed himself in the bathroom of the unit. After taking a bath, he had arranged himself, lying on the floor dressed in clean undershirt, and shot himself in the heart. For a gun he used a piece of pipe; for ammunition, a bit of lead; and for gunpowder, percussion caps from firecrackers which we had packed in one of the workshops for a short period. He exploded his homemade ammunition with a piece of cotton and a cigarette lighter.

The first three of these eight suicides happened during the early years of the institution's history. One may think that the fourth case should have been kept longer in the sick ward, but he was not much more peculiar in behavior than several others, and he did not really belong in the sick group. The deaths of the last five were absolutely unexpected. I have known all these men personally. In many other cases we have suspected suicidal intentions and acted accordingly, but there was no reason to expect suicide in any of these cases.

Automutilation. In the beginning it was rather common for inmates to swallow foreign bodies, especially sharp pointed objects or razor blades, sometimes wrapped in paper. As a rule they swallowed several foreign bodies at one time. At the end of November, 1943, there was an epidemic of eating foreign bodies, and during one month there were seven cases, three of whom had made arrangements to be together in the hospital. We thought it necessary to try to stop this kind of acting-out and established a psychiatric indication for non-operation, as opposed to a possible surgical indication for operation. Surgical intervention may be a little more complicated after possible perforation of the intestinal tract, but we decided to place the patients who said they had swallowed iron and razor blades in isolation near the sick unit and watch them. They were carefully observed so that signs of perforation could be discovered as soon as they appeared.

This system limited the inmates' immediate gains from these hysterical reactions. When isolated, they were forced to try to cooperate; loss of face becomes less important to them, and it was easier to compel them to face realistically the problems that had caused them to swallow the foreign bodies. This procedure has been so effective that we have seldom seen such a phenomenon; in the four years from 1962 to 1965, only two inmates have eaten foreign bodies.[14]

Very seldom has an operation been necessary, because foreign bodies usually pass through the intestinal tract without doing damage. In cases where symptoms of perforation were unclear, the inmate was hospitalized in a surgical ward.

In one case an inmate's esophagus was perforated by a safety pin, and he died. (This was the 1945 suicide case.) Recently the most common automutilations have been slashing or puncturing the arms with nails. Once a very primitive man plunged a paper knife into his stomach during a conversation with one of the psychologists, but he did not cause any intestinal damage. One put indelible ink in his eyes, and some have tried to intoxicate themselves by taking nicotine from boiled tobacco. Some have taken drugs that they managed to collect in spite of the fact that the staff give most drugs in solution to prevent this. None of these incidents were followed by severe or lasting inconveniences. All were caused by momentary emotional reactions or were protest reactions.

Escape. The least frequent protest reaction is escape, but it is a most serious disciplinary offense. If we include attempts, escapes vary between five and twenty-two a year. The twenty-two escapes recorded in 1962 were related to our increased attempts to allow inmates to work outside the institution. For this we selected primarily the insecure people who were unaccustomed to a stable work situation and who needed the experience of working outside.

During the twenty-one years from 1935 through 1965, twenty-five persons escaped from the main institution. The other escapees were such good risks that we were justified in giving them greater freedom; thirty-one escaped from work groups outside the walls and forty-seven from the open section at Kastanienborg. Twenty-eight escaped in other ways such as during travel from one place to another or when working outside.

In 1966 Freitag and Kjerulf analyzed the escapes during the years 1953 through 1958.[15] In this period there were fifty-one escapes or

[14] Jan Sachs (*Nordisk Medicin,* 35[1947]:1789) has analyzed nineteen cases. Together they have swallowed foreign bodies fifty-two times. Thirty-five times these men swallowed more than one foreign body, seventeen times only one object. Eleven persons swallowed foreign bodies several times, and one of these persons did it eight times. Three of the eight who only did this once in Herstedvester had done it previously. They were all self-assertive, hysterical, explosive and very emotional.

[15] P. Freitag and L. Kjerulff, "Undvigelser fra forvaringsanstalten i Herstedvester 1953–1958" (Mimeographed, Herstedvester, 1966).

attempted escapes (committed by forty-nine persons), and forty-seven of these were examined. Four case records were unavailable at the time. Most of these inmates were not dangerous at the time of escape, and only one escaped from maximum security.

Of the forty-seven escapes studied, four were uncompleted attempts. One man escaped from the main institution, nine from six-hour leaves, five from work outside the wall, twenty-five from the open section at Kastanienborg, three from work in free society, and one while traveling.

The time they stayed out was short; fifteen were free for less than twenty-four hours, and only nine were free more than twenty days.

Only one escapee committed a serious crime during his escape. This was Kaj, a very sad, periodically psychotic, middle-aged detainee who has been confined almost continuously since he was sixteen years old. First he was in an institution for juveniles, then stayed a short time in an ordinary prison, spent seventeen years in a mental hospital, and finally came to Herstedvester. About twice a year he is psychotic for a short time, and in between these psychotic periods he is clearly schizoid. In his psychotic phases, especially when he was younger, he has been very aggressive, attacking people, destroying property, and setting fire to forests. In detention, he has also hurt himself and committed arson in his cell. His psychotic, restless phases have been fewer in recent years.

We, as well as the Attorney General, have been troubled by Kaj's long period in detention. At one time the Attorney General raised the question of bringing his case before the courts so that they could decide about continued detention. We did not dare to recommend parole at this point, but we felt obliged to place him in the open section. After five days he escaped, set fire to a house, and turned himself directly over to the police, telling them what he had done. We supposed that his motivation was fear of being paroled. In the ten years since then, Kaj has been relatively unchanged, but with increasing age, he has become more subdued.

Eleven other escapees committed minor crimes typical of their escape situations.

Most of the escapees have been young; forty-three were between the ages of twenty and forty-four; of these, only 19 per cent committed any crime during the time they were free. None of the older detainees who escaped could manage without committing crime. The longer the escape, the greater was the risk that the escapee would be in a situation where he could not support himself without committing crime. Nine of the fourteen who had been on their own for more than ten days committed crimes.

Escape seems to be a little more common among thieves than among other types of criminals. Several of our cases had previously escaped from some other institution. Three to five escapes seem not to destroy the possibility of a man's leading a crime-free life later.

If we relate parole success to the number of escapes from Hersted-vester, we find that 64 per cent of the twenty-five who escaped once are re-socialized. Until the summer of 1965, 20 per cent of the group who escaped twice, and none of the group who escaped more than three times, have returned to society for a reasonable period of time. It seems safe to say, therefore, that a single escape from our institution is not important for the future re-socialization, but several escapes are part of a more fixed, asocial pattern of behavior.

Sudden impulse is the most commonly mentioned motive for escape. In some cases an escape seems to have been related to dis-appointment about parole or to the strain of a pending parole case. In eight cases the inmates wanted to visit their wives or fiancées to see how they were living, four returned to their mothers, and twenty did not state any goal.

Treatment of the escape problem is extremely difficult, but we have attacked it very openly at Herstedvester. In 1951 I answered a detainee's question about our reactions to it in our institutional news-paper somewhat as follows:

Formerly, disciplinary reactions to escape were fixed. For the first escape, an inmate was placed in isolation for three months, and, for the second, six months. Disciplinary reactions now vary from six to eight weeks in isolation. There has been much discussion in the therapeutic groups about the value of punishment as an element of treatment. The isolation period may be of considerable importance in helping some people to find their way. In other cases it is not so, but, in a society as small as ours, it is necessary to consider the treatment of the whole group as well as the treatment of the single inmate. Generally, members of the staff assume that we must use direct, severe, disciplinary measures in cases of serious violations of institu-tional rules. Such violations have often been supported by other inmates who were more loyal to a comrade than to the whole group. For a time we tried to avoid a specific pattern of punishments for escape, but many staff members got the impression that the detainees did not understand this and looked upon it as an invitation for them to be reckless. This could encourage further limitation by the Ministry of our right to handle our security problems as we think best. The authorities had tightened controls in 1942, and we wanted to avoid having the central administration continue this way. I pointed out at the end of this article that ordinary citizens follow attempted escapes with great interest.

Other Protest Reactions. The most common offense, refusal to work, is a passive protest against the way of life. This was on the rise in the years 1961–1963 and then fell conspicuously. Probably individual refusals to work bear some relation to the number of persons who are called ill. (See Figure 3.) Sometimes there is doubt about

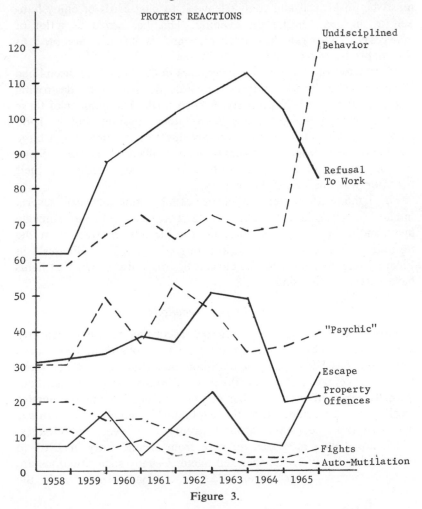

Figure 3.

naming an inmate's behavior psychic illness, general psychic imbalance, or simply refusal to work without any dominant changes in his psychic situation. In reality, these are artificial definitions that have to be made, and physicians interpret them differently. For the individual inmate, it does not matter much how the refusal to work is defined. Sometimes we cannot classify dysphoric behavior as refusal to work, and we have found it necessary to react in more or less the same way to both types of behavior. A person who refuses to work is isolated and confined to his own room until the following morning. The same is true if he is excused because of illness. He must stay in his cell and cannot leave it to play cards or enjoy him-
,self in any way during the evening. This has saved us a lot of unnecessary and valueless decisions and is usually accepted as reasonable by the inmates.

More active offensive behavior appears in the form of undisciplined behavior, impertinence, rudeness towards the personnel, destroying institutional or personal property, and so forth. The number of these reactions during the years has been rather constant, but in 1965 there was a distinct increase, probably due to our employing a large number of very young and inexperienced officers that year. Some inmates have acted in such a way that we could see clearly that their behavior was due to psychic causes.

For fights and property offenses, collaboration between several inmates is necessary. It takes at least two to fight, to smuggle merchandise in or out, sell merchandise illegally, or steal from the institution. These three types are termed "property offenses" in Figure 3 and are shown in one curve. Figure 3 also shows that fights have become fewer since 1958.

Disciplinary Reactions

Protest reactions can be evaluated according to what measures are used to enforce discipline. (See Figure 4.) Isolation in the inmate's own room has been the most common punishment, used not more than once every second or third day. Many small offenses are formally "charged" and no other action is taken. For others, inmates receive only a warning from the captain. The number of warnings has been rather constant, around twenty-six a year, but charges, which are a little more severe, rose from around forty in 1961 to about eighty in 1963, and then fell again. Usually such situations are valuable occasions for therapeutic intervention. Placement in the isolation section is our most severe disciplinary reaction, and its use has been relatively constant.

Our isolation section has only six cells. Five have wash basins with water regulated from the outside; none have toilets. In each cell, the bed is bolted to the floor, windows are made of unbreakable glass, and the table and chair can be moved. When a new inmate is received, he is not allowed to have a table and chair. All six cells face south and have a good view of the institution.

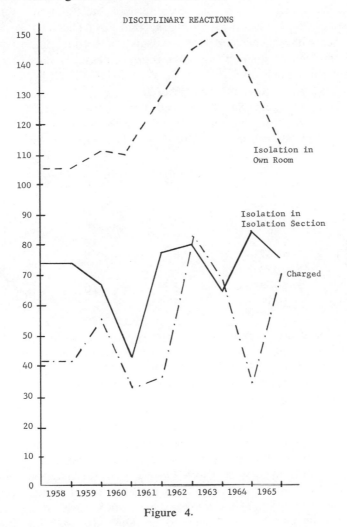

Figure 4.

Cell number six is partially soundproof. In front there is a small entrance room in order to keep noise from the isolation room from penetrating into the general ward. This cell can also be used on the orders of the man in charge of institutional security at any moment, usually the captain or a lieutenant, or in an emergency when the ward staff find it necessary. In practice, there is seldom time to obtain consent from a superior employee before using this cell. The bed in cell number six has a belt with fingerless gloves and a foot fastening. When a prisoner has been secured, the situation is reported by telephone to the doctor in charge that day. The man in charge, together with the personnel of the isolation section, has to handle such an acute situation and all security measures must be used. Because using cell six is difficult for the personnel, and because these rules are stiff, it has not been misused.

When the doctor in charge and the staff think it is safe, the security devices may be removed; this usually happens within a few hours. That this cell is seldom used may be seen from the following table:

	Number of Inmates	Number of Uses of Cell Six
1959	7	9
1960	4	14
1961	12	16
1962	8	9
1963	6	7
1964	5	10
1965	6	7

Disciplinary use in recent years has been even more limited than indicated by the figures because some men returned directly from parole were placed in cell six to sober up. In these cases only the belt was used, and only if necessary.

Complaints

Inmates have a right to complain in uncensored letters to the Minister of Justice. He gets the institution's explanation of the situation and answers the letter. Once a year the inmates can complain verbally to a representative of the Ministry of Justice when he visits the institution. If the inmate is not satisfied with the Minister's decision, he may then complain to the Ombudsman, who, after an investigation, makes the final decision on the legitimacy of the complaint.

An analysis of complaints to the Minister of Justice and the Ombudsman in 1958 shows that nineteen persons sent complaints to the Minister of Justice, seven sent open letters, and six made verbal complaints during the Ministry's inspection of the institution. Of the six inmates who made verbal complaints, five had been in the institution for only four to twelve months and thus were in the "confused" phase. The other one had been in the institution for a longer time and complained of having been in isolation. All felt much relieved by being able to talk to the higher official, and none of them reacted when, after examination of the institution's relevant information, their complaints were not accepted.

Only one of these inmates had been in detention for as long as two and one-half years, and he had been transferred from our sister institution in Horsens. He had a constructive criticism of the ration and quality of tea. Inmates had repeatedly given this complaint to me, and I had passed them on to the administrator without result. This new investigation led to an improvement of the tea. This inmate also complained about the amount of wages, a reasonable point that was much discussed at that time and one that he wanted to bring to the attention of the central administration.

The open letters complained of not being able to be examined by the physician, of being put in isolation, of not being allowed to send money home, that the Ministry of Justice does not take the initiative in placing inmates in the open section—but leaves that responsibility with the institution, and that the parole procedure is not satisfactory. Many of these complaints derived from momentary annoyances and lacked a general view of all the complications of each situation. They were really meant as petitions to the superintendent. The Ministry of Justice was unable to do anything in any of these instances.

Two of the nineteen persons who complained in uncensored letters were "big complainers." One of them was manic and wrote ten complaints. He had become manic several times before, and each time he got into such a state that he started to complain bitterly about hip trouble that, under normal circumstances, never bothered him. Then, in his manic phase, he went on to complain of everything. He is presently in a mental hospital.

Another inmate mailed twenty-one complaints as part of a campaign headed by himself, supported by a lawyer, and stimulated by a disgruntled former staff member. The excitement which he created rubbed off on some of the other inmates and caused an especially difficult year.

Three other inmates were responsible for five, four, and three complaints apiece, and fourteen mailed one complaint each. These were about letters retained by the authorities as being absolutely unsuitable for delivery (confirmed by the Ministry of Justice), refusal of the right to appear personally in a divorce case, and not permitting money to be sent home. A sensitive homosexual felt haunted by fellow inmates, a couple of inmates complained about being isolated (one had been isolated because of the risk of tuberculosis infection), and a man who had been in detention for a long time complained of the medical treatment. None of these complaints received support in the Ministry of Justice.

A few complaints concerned the staff's treatment of the inmates, and we especially noted one which was so detailed that we were able to make a minute investigation. It concerned a man who was looked upon as being extremely dangerous because he had committed several murders. The personnel had been informed that special security measures had to be taken, and this necessarily caused difficulties in the daily routine. No matter how carefully the personnel carry out this task, there is no way to prevent the inmate from being annoyed by it. The hearings on this man's complaint showed that there really was some rigidity in the relationship between two staff members. Their attention had to be drawn to this, but they were told that they had to continue to be careful and not slacken their attention to security, even if the inmate's behavior was satisfactory in his daily routine. It seemed that the two staff members involved had allowed their irritation to pass on to the inmate. He was not really hurt and has not had any conflict with staff members since then.

Also in 1958, the Ombudsman received four complaints about medical treatment (one of these was from the manic) and two about isolation and discipline. These complaints were also dismissed. Four inmates addressed purely legal questions to the Ombudsman concerning their cases, and these had to be dismissed, simply because of their nature. In one case, there was a complaint about a delayed letter. It turned out that there had been an unfortunate mistake that could be explained to the inmate.

THE UNIFORMED STAFF

In an institution like Herstedvester, the duties of the uniformed staff constitute the backbone of the everyday work. The quality of this group determines how they will influence the inmates and how the staff members themselves will conduct their work.

When the institution was founded, the staff was acquired mainly from other prisons while some accompanied the inmates who were transferred from the temporary section. The few who were directly hired by the institution were first trained for a short period at the State Prison in Vridslöselille. Most of this training was in security procedures.

In 1942 the uniformed staff numbered 75; in 1966 they had increased to 199. This increase resulted from a considerable enlargement of their responsibilities. The uniformed staff has taken over escorting inmates on six-hour leaves, and they must supervise each floor of the houses, each having two independent sections for 10 or 15 men. The workshops have been greatly expanded, and this required the hiring of a considerable number of workshop leaders. The establishment of the open sections, the Hut and Kastanienborg, created an additional demand for men, and the uniformed staff now has to assist in the organization of school and leisure activities. It is important that the work week has been shortened to forty-four hours, and the personnel have longer holidays than in the past.

In 1942, 64 per cent of the personnel came to Herstedvester from other institutions; after 1942, recruitment from other institutions decreased. Now only 28 per cent of Herstedvester's personnel come from other institutions. However, many of the staff members who had served at other institutions still remain with us. The majority of the personnel transferring to us have served in other institutions for only short periods, the average being one and one-half years, but one served elsewhere for twenty-two years.

Most of the personnel are skilled workmen. A survey of the previous occupations of the present uniformed personnel shows:

Farmers and gardeners 37
Unskilled workers including drivers 30
Carpenters, masons, and funiture-makers 17
Smiths, mechanics, and electricians 9
Food trades (bakers, cooks, butchers) 12
Commercial or office workers 19
Sailors and fishermen 6
Printers, graphic artists, and bookbinders 4
Public service, including male nurses, social aides, mailmen,
    and so forth. 23
Barbers 2

Approximately two-thirds of those referred to above have been in prison service from ten to forty years. Twenty-one men have served less than half a year, and twenty-two have served from six months to two years. The majority of our staff is more than forty-five years old; twenty-five are between twenty-one and twenty-four, and twenty-three are between twenty-five and twenty-nine years old.

The youngest people in this group have a special handicap when they have to manage a therapeutically accentuated contact with some of the older inmates. Because of this, it would be advantageous if the minimum age for such service were twenty-five and if there were a longer practical and theoretical training period before a staff member's actual service began. If these changes are not made before long, the newly expanded training program for male nurses' aides in Denmark will drain off the well-qualified men that we need.

A course of instruction of approximately thirty hours does exist at the institution, and the employees, after some service, attend the Prison Department's Central School for three months and take a hospital course on the mentally ill for a two-month period. Supplementary courses by psychiatrists and psychologists have also been offered. Even so, a significant number of the uniformed personnel have not yet had the opportunity to participate in any such special training, and none of them have had any type of formal psychological or sociological education. However, during their employment they frequently attend group discussions with therapists or other supervisory staff. Because the cases discussed are those with which they are personally acquainted, these meetings have a great educational value.

Our pay scales are the same as civil service rates. An officer receives about 22,000 kroner ($3100) yearly, a senior officer about 24,000 kroner ($3400), and a lieutenant about 25,000 kroner ($3500). A work instructor at the lowest wage level receives only 23,000 kroner ($3300), and a senior work instructor in the highest wage level is paid 32,000 kroner ($4500). All of these are beginning wages which increase according to seniority and are (in 1966) adjusted according to the cost of living. For comparison, I can add that the beginning wages for a psychologist are 31,000 kroner ($4400); for an assistant physician, 36,000 kroner ($5100); and for the superintendent, 69,700 kroner ($10,000).

The uniformed personnel still feel some aftereffects of earlier authoritarian conditions in Denmark. Difference in social standing is now less important. This was felt not only in society as a whole, but, for some of the older ones, in earlier service at other institutions. As mentioned previously, in Herstedvester we have attempted to imbue the uniformed staff with democratic ideals and a treatment-oriented attitude toward the inmates. We have succeeded to some degree in changing the attitudes of those who previously worked in regular prisons. Many of the uniformed men are now personally involved in their jobs but do not always feel that they receive sufficient support from the supervisory staff. They often show a significant hypersensitivity and, at times, a tendency to give up their therapeutic efforts, even though we have tried faithfully to praise the contributions the personnel make to the treatment process in discussions with both personnel and inmates. Some colleagues think we have been overdoing this.

It may be necessary to find more effective ways to curb this hypersensitivity and promote mutual understanding between the different levels of employees. During the last few years, the captain and the administrator have run the Wednesday meetings with this in mind.

Our knowledge of the employees' impressions of the institution is gathered primarily from our common life in the institution as observed over a span of many years. I must admit, however, that although I honestly try to see things from the personnel's point of view, it is difficult to do so.

One basic factor that we must take into account when dealing with the interpersonal difficulties of both inmates and staff is that all men need to feel that they are of value. We have tried to satisfy this need by conducting seminars on institutional problems for the personnel. Reports from these provide clear insight into their viewpoints. But reports cannot illustrate the tensions and pressures that are often present while the discussion is occurring. Therefore the seminars that I have conducted have increased my own insight greatly. It has become evident that the ordinary, uneducated staff member is unable to obtain the needed self-respect by himself. Not only children need understanding and love; we all need them through our lives and we must achieve a certain amount of recognition in order to retain our self-respect. If we do not receive this recognition, we feel injured, uncertain, and neglected. If this frustrating situation occurs too often, bitterness will develop.

It has become apparent that ward officers know of situations in which they have used rules to give themselves and others the impression that the officers, themselves, are valuable. An officer once explained in a seminar how rules are used in certain situations as a substitute for contact with superiors because "we get the impression" that the superiors "whom we may like do not like us, or do not recognize us sufficiently." Many of the officers easily understand that the criminals lack this opportunity of demonstrating their own value.

The great majority of the uniformed personnel have a positive attitude toward the treatment ideology of Herstedvester. However, on the basis of episodes that have revealed an adverse atmosphere in certain sections, this does not seem to be true of all of them. It may be that these attitudes are only present in temporary negative phases, activated by the weariness of many years of service and a series of difficult, repetitious episodes.

In spite of our trying to integrate all staff members' efforts, crises and differences of opinion have occurred periodically over the years. There have been times when a part of the uniformed staff was skeptical of groups of academic colleagues, or of one or more colleagues in a group. The younger, clinically inexperienced psychologists and physicians who show superior knowledge suffer, as do welfare workers who, because of the relocation of the social section outside the wall, are in an especially vulnerable situation.

Occasional differences of opinion occur between the uniformed men themselves. These are often quickly noticed and used by the inmates, even if the antagonism is not openly expressed. In seminars the personnel have said that they have observed how some inmates attempt to gain a short-term advantage from such conflicts, but the majority of the inmates only experience an uncertainty that makes their re-socialization more difficult. Officers often stress that we must endeavor to counteract this uncertainty in every possible way.

A common complaint is that the officers receive this more theoretical education too late and that it is insufficient. Much is gained by the participation of the younger members in routine meetings; however, we are aware that such participation encourages problems of prestige between the younger and older personnel, but these can eventually be overcome.

Various personnel groups have maintained that the number of asocial groups among the inmates is small. They admit the existence of a hard nucleus dominated by returned inmates but do not look upon it as a special risk. Ward officers and work instructors who know their groups are able to handle them. They find that weak inmates attach themselves to the strong ones in order to gain acceptance and guidance, but they believe that the officers and all other officials can

often influence the stronger inmates positively. These inmates may
then become a valuable support to the work of the different groups.
The personnel believe that the inmates cannot be designated as an
entity. The only truly common trait they see is that all of them are
marked as criminals and are therefore, to a certain degree, antag-
onistic to the staff. In reality, the inmates share no common interests
and have no great confidence in each other. The democratic environment of the institution, the individualized treatment in which the
officers themselves take part, and the indefinite length of the detention
period all counteract the solidarity of the inmates.

One group put it this way: there are three factors that discourage
the formation of negative groups—the small size of the groups in
each section, the quality and quantity of the staff, and the permanence
and stability of the personnel working with the groups. It is particularly important that the ward officer can obtain a thorough knowledge
of the individuals in his group and is therefore able to have a good
influence on them. Of course this works only if rearrangements of
personnel are not too frequent.

It is striking that discussions about inmate problems incessantly
return to personnel problems. From the uniformed men's point of
view, a better understanding of the problems of different personnel
categories is of utmost importance. It becomes obvious that, in spite
of our efforts, knowledge of the contributions of the specialists is
greatly lacking. The uniformed group needs a better knowledge of
the work methods of the nonuniformed groups and of our attempts to
coordinate the contributions of all the groups. Since we have established study groups and group conversations, the personnel have
become noticeably more satisfied with their endeavors.

A uniformed officer is often inclined to believe reports received
from an inmate that a therapist has criticized him. In a case illus-
trating this, quoted in one of my own seminars, the officer did not
attempt to discover whether the criticism that was irritating him had
actually been expressed by the specialist or had been invented by the
inmate. Such remarks provide an opportunity to hold valuable discussions concerning the need for cooperation.

A frequent criticism is that the group around the superintendent is
too small. This complaint occurs despite the officers' opportunity to
assert themselves by attending the Monday meetings or by applying
directly to the superintendent during his weekly visits to the wards.
As a result of such critical remarks by the personnel, we have frequently developed slight variations in both the administrative and

informative apparatus, and the entire staff now participates in a variety of staff meetings.

The so-called Nyborg meetings, organized by the central administration of the prison system, help to create a feeling of satisfaction for our general staff and contribute to the development of the entire prison department's orientation toward treatment. These meetings occur annually, and representatives of all levels of staff from correctional institutions and related fields participate. A topic such as discipline or asocial groups serves as the main theme for each meeting.

Seminars in each institution study this topic, and then it is discussed in groups at the final meeting at a hotel in Nyborg. Each group includes reprsentatives of different institutions and various degrees of training.

Because of the preparatory meetings, the Nyborg meetings encourage a "we" feeling in all individual institutions. However, they also give rise to criticism. During these discussions the personnel bring up many serious problems. The staff members who attend the meetings are apt to interpret their positive atmosphere as a promise of reform, and they feel frustrated if this is not followed up. Also, staff members often complain that the civilians have a better "gift of gab" and dominate the groups in which they take part, making the uniformed men become relatively reserved and frequently uncertain.

In order to achieve a deeper understanding of the opinions of the staff, I invited a series of groups of them—eight or ten at a time—to private meetings in my home. After a comfortable meal and some beer, we could relax and be at ease. Our conversation was recorded on tape. When such a group of staff members got to talking about their experiences and their attitudes to each other and the specialized staff members, it was difficult to stop them. In some cases I visited former collaborators and recorded characteristic viewpoints.

Each group represented different interests. The first group consisted of supervising officers—lieutenants, captains, the administrator, and the chief nurse. These are the connecting link between the ordinary staff and the therapists. The second group represented the management and some of the particularly active members of the officers' union, an organization of all staff members below the grade of lieutenant. The third group consisted mainly of uniformed officers who had acted as leave escorts and contact men for both long and short periods, so that both young and old men took part in the same group. These groups were followed by a group of present and former therapists and social assistants, and finally a group of work instructors.

In my invitation I suggested that we discuss inmates who had responded to treatment differently than the employees had expected and try to determine whether any elements of institutional life were especially significant. I also asked them to remember the impression they had of the institution during the first months they served here and, if this impression had changed, to give the reasons. Some employees later supplemented in writing what they had said at the meetings. In a written remark one asked, "Does the selection of one's life work depend on chance? I am thinking of those of us who have chosen to earn our living in the gray and sullen institutions of the prison authority. . . . We appear, superficially, to be highly dissimilar, but perhaps this only seems so. A study of this might prove interesting."

Selection of the Uniformed Staff

The uniformed staff has been selected in various ways. From 1935 to 1938 and off and on until 1943, Herstedvester was, in all respects, a branch of the State Prison. The officers assumed that their selection for work at Herstedvester was made by the State Prison, as one officer said, "for reasons that were, at least, human. We were promised good conditions 'over there,' which implied that everybody was nuts, so we would surely be able to get along. After all, among the blind, the person having one eye is king."

Another stated, "The great majority of the officers who came to Herstedvester only for a short time did not really want to go back to the State Prison. There were a few exceptions—those who were not suited for the work here."

An officer hired in the 1930's said, "We were scared of the work and scared of the conflicts. We were hired to serve in the State Prison and were afraid of having to serve at Herstedvester. It was mainly those who were in the habit of talking to the prisoners, a practice forbidden in the State Prison, who were chosen. They were found to be unsuitable in the State Prison, and therefore they were transferred to Herstedvester."

Another said, "Those who were interested in talking to the prisoners ended up here at Herstedvester. Those not interested returned to the State Prison."

Those hired later often express themselves differently: "When I returned to the State Prison after having served in a prison camp and having become accustomed to free conditions, I tried in desperation to get away from the State Prison to the detention institution. . . . Being allowed to talk with the inmates appealed to me, even though I often heard in the State Prison, 'Whatever are you going to do over there in that nuthouse?' We do not all like those arrogant colleagues over there who do not even condescend to greet us." One said he " . . . made a lot of fuss. I was not going to work with those 'half-freaks' over there. I was promised then that it would last for only eight days, but it has lasted for twenty years."

One expected to be discharged and said, "I was a very poor prison guard, but I was a craftsman and they suddenly needed someone with my skills over there, so I was transferred to the State Prison. When I had been there less than three months, I went to the Central School. When I returned, I was sent over here, where it has been the custom for many years to send the worst guards from the State Prison."

Another said, "Somebody said that the service conditions were better. I was a reserve officer and thought it might be a good idea to see how it would be at Herstedvester. I have never regretted it."

One officer " . . . felt as if I suddenly became somebody. I began to feel involved in the work, to have more contact with the local administration, and to take part in daily meetings. I started to view the inmates as human beings. I came with the others from the temporary section to Horsens, and, when we were discharged from there, I applied for Herstedvester. I was slightly disappointed, perhaps because my expectations were too high. Much of the pioneer work in the temporary section had already been done, and there was not the opportunity to take the same initiative in Herstedvester."

Another officer said, "Shortly after the liberation [1945], I was asked by the captain of the prison if I would like to serve in Herstedvester. This was done when it became obvious that some of us were more or less hopeless as ordinary prison officers. So I arrived at Herstedvester and discovered that the working climate was much milder here. Later, after serving a period in the State Prison, I realized that they are now much alike. The State Prison has changed considerably."

An officer who was hired directly by Herstedvester a few years ago said, "I got into prison service by accident. My first impression was good; I joined a good team who were very considerate and understanding. When I came to the second unit, I received another impression. I was now left on my own more. One is not fully qualified after a few weeks."

The total impression one gets from discussing these questions with the personnel is that they have been selected because they were interested in communicating with others or wanted to be public servants. The climate at the detention institution has, at least during the last few years, undoubtedly been a major influence on their wish to stay in the service.

Reception

The reception the new staff member receives is of great importance to his future attitude toward his work. Many small details are influential. As one has said, "At the hospital and institution for the mentally deficient where I was, the male nurse simply cleaned up and was always around. I had been in the last place for one and one-half years before I even talked with the superintendent. I had to take care of eighty-four patients as soon as I arrived from the outside. But here in Herstedvester, I joined the daily work. Where I worked before, nobody ever asked the male nurse about the patient as an individual."

Another told us, "One of the first persons I met at Herstedvester was a senior officer, X. He was a large and very congenial man. I proceeded into the staff office, where I met Y, who had changed my name. At the other institutions I had been named XX, and now I suddenly saw myself listed as ZZ. I said to Y, 'Have you given me a change of name?' He answered, 'Yes, for practical reasons.' I said, 'You don't know whether or not I am going to stay here.' To this he replied, 'For God's sake, I was sent here on loan many years ago. . . .' Well, time passed, and I think I developed a good spirit."

Another wrote, "The tone was different here. Just to be counted on as an independent individual with responsibility for one's own actions as well as those of the inmates gave me enough to think about. We should not just guard—of course, we must do that also—but we should learn to observe and evaluate. In the first period I was here, we made a report concerning two inmates who had been fighting. I was asked for a more detailed, verbal explanation of the circumstances that led to the fight—Were they regular enemies or did the incident occur spontaneously? This did not make my task any easier, but perhaps it made it more alive because it involved me in a different manner than before. We had to formulate observations and account for viewpoints that had been none of our business before. If you tended to become too clever, there was always the possibility of putting things back into their proper places. Naturally, at first you do many things the wrong way, but from all of this grows an understanding of the task and of its purpose. Skill slowly leaks in. There was not an essential difference, but different degrees of skill and knowledge did exist between the others and us. We had to grasp that we, who seemed so normal in our entire behavior pattern, revealed definite abnormal traits. The difference in behavior between us and the inmates is also a matter of degree. What have we not done during childhood and adolescence that might have caused trouble if it had been discovered? It became more a task of acknowledging oneself, than of belonging to a system."

Of special importance to a newly hired officer is the feeling of solidarity or esprit de corps, which must dominate the institution. As already described, there has been firm opposition to our experiment from outside. A number of colleagues have pointed out that, especially after Herstedvester became more distinguished, much aggression from both press and public appeared against our employees. Some of the staff were annoyed by this aggression, but all agreed that it welded the personnel together.

We give all new people a month of training in a particular department. The personnel already present have much experience, so the newly arrived officers are in good hands. This is where they learn the rules, the reasons for the rules, and why they must obey them. When they are placed in the general sections, there may be a tendency on the part of the older colleagues to watch for the young ones to make mistakes. The young staff member probably has only been able to understand the rule itself and has not been able to see how it is used in practice. To help him to become acquainted with the entire institution quickly, he is put to work in shifts, first in one department and then in another. In each department, the inmates have different needs, and different practices are followed. The advantages of this practice outweigh the disadvantages. It is well that the inmates and staff members alike understand, and adjust themselves to, the fact that different rules apply in different places, not only in our sections but in free society.

The solidarity of the corps can also make it difficult for a man who enters as a superior staff member. One wrote, "I had a strong feeling not of being badly received but of pushing myself into a freemasonry that existed among the others. They felt a kind of honor in this freemasonry which I thought meant that I had to qualify for admission. I was not turned away, but I was not helped. I believe that it takes up to one and a half years to familiarize oneself with the institution. This is probably because unwritten laws reign here. The motives behind the laws are not easy to understand and can only be learned through experience.

"When you slowly learn what lies behind the rules and what everyday practice is, then the pattern shows up beautifully, perhaps more clearly than in other institutions. It becomes easier to operate because one does not operate from the rules, but from a basic understanding of the principles behind the rules."

An older staff member told about difficulties during the early period when there were fights and ruined cells because "the policy of acting in accordance with the regulations was followed." There were many uproars, " . . . and we pressed for the establishment of a house order to be posted in the section. I can remember the superintendent saying that we ought to write such a house order, but we never did, and now I am able to see the tactics involved in not doing so. The object was to soften us up a little, so we would take the inmates in a slightly different way than we did in the State Prison."

The attitude of the staff depends on the information given them, among other things. We stress that one must beware of copying and saying the same things as the older staff members. The more experienced ones know how far they can go, but the young ones do not know this, and it must be pointed out to them at the very beginning. An inmate detects whether an officer is open and direct and he knows exactly what the officer means by what he says. One cannot expect a young officer to receive as much respect as an older and more experienced man. The inmates will have seen the older officer act in different situations—clearly authoritative ones as well as those of a more free and "professionally friendly" character. They know they can trust the older officers. "He may scold, but he is good enough at the bottom." It must be made clear to the young officers that they cannot count solely on the authority of their uniforms to carry them safely through any slightly irregular situations, whereas an older officer may be able to do so. He can go a bit further outside the rules because he is aware of what he is doing. This is not something which is easily learned, but requires professional, experienced evaluation of exactly how much flexibility a given situation needs.

Some younger officers have the impression that we handle the inmates very mildly, perhaps too mildly. One man, who has been at

Herstedvester for only a few years, claimed that there is "a tendency toward only getting everything to run smoothly." An older officer, who will not entirely deny this, answers, "We old ones do not just give an order. We chat a bit with the inmate, and with a smile we tell him what must be done. Then it sinks in. The young ones think they must give orders."

Another older officer says, "Being moderate and tolerant, we have the proper ballast necessary to act the way we do today. I can say to an old inmate that he must 'go to your cell and be quick about it.' The newer officer cannot do this, and I am afraid that, in too many cases, they do not criticize enough. The newer ones are scared of conflicts, and now some of the older ones have started to become scared. This causes palpitation that they are afraid of because of the effect it has on their blood pressure. It is perhaps dangerous that we do not raise the young ones to be a little more robust. It is difficult for them when they have to reprove and guide, even though they may be good at talking to the inmates."

When we started to talk about the problems of the officers' understanding of the real needs of inmates, one officer who had been in the service for about twenty years told about "a very aggressive, chronic polycriminal inmate who is now a good, sentimental family man. In an unbalanced state he once barricaded his door with his sewing machine (he worked in his room) and the officer said, 'I spoke to the captain and we agreed to allow it to continue.' The next day, around dinnertime, he unscrewed the observation glass and put out a white flag that symbolized peace. He avoided losing face because it was put out at a time when the corridor was empty of fellow inmates."

Another officer who knew the same inmate tells how he gradually learned to say to him, "Come here, we have to have a little talk." He said this whenever trouble seemed to be in the making. Among his friends, the inmate could not stand to be criticized, but later he realized it was foolish to feel that way.

In spite of the staff's over-all attitude, not everything is ideal. The older guards often become identification objects and are forced to function as father substitutes. It is regrettable that our system does not always grant them sufficient support in such difficult situations. We have made our daily life more and more democratic, but there must be a basic authoritarian element in a security institution. These dual attitudes produce strain. It is essential to stress that everybody is to some degree "equal," but, while some have more experience in one field, others have equivalent experience and education in other fields. Peace in the wards and workshops is the prerequisite which makes it possible to avoid anxiety and aggressiveness in both the inmates and the personnel. The sergeant of a house ought to feel sufficiently secure, but that is not always the case. In a given situation, he must feel free to deviate from a general rule and to tell others of his deviation and his motives. In some situations, he may immediately isolate an inmate in his own room or in the isolation section.

Other criticisms were voiced during the meetings; for example, "We neglect to develop the habits of the inmates. During service in the army, young men protest against all the things they are forced to do; nevertheless, this discipline leaves behavioral habits which are valuable in later life. When we give privileges, we should demand returns in the form of responsible behavior. This should be included in our educational approach. We have not yet succeeded in planning a sufficiently flexible system for relating privileges and returns. If we could, we would be able to pay normal wages to some inmates. It might be possible, in certain sections, to continue experimenting along these lines." All agreed on the idea, but no concrete, practical suggestions were offered.

Another sergeant told of an episode in which he felt somewhat endangered. "The incident ended when the inmate went into his cell without hitting me. Afterward, when I freed the two other inmates from the hobby room, I was surprised to discover that they had heard and seen the episode through a glass window in the wall facing the corridor. They told me that if the inmate had attacked me, they would have broken down the locked door and come in to help me. This created a certain relationship between my inmates and me, based on my trust of the inmates. This is a result of their willingness to back up a member of the staff, even a new one."

Another one said, "When I returned from the temporary open section, Lekkende [used for some years after the war], I felt that the individual officer was more or less put into a box. The happiness of creating something new was taken from us. Too many people share the honor of whatever we do. This is how the ordinary staff member feels. I want more independent responsibility. I shall never forget one doctor's words, and I still believe in them: 'We could get much more from the uniformed personnel if we used them differently by dividing the institution so that we still had small open units as in Lekkende, and a nucleus in Herstedvester.' In the open sections, the uniformed men could do much more on their own."

About the age problem, which is already serious when one is in the fifties, an officer said, "When we are older, we feel that security is most important and treatment appears not to be worth much. An older man backs out too often. Ten years ago, I would have called on an inmate and spoken to him for an entire hour. The older officers only talk for ten minutes. We begin to ask why we should take so much trouble. We know that, if we take an inmate into the office, another one will show up ten minutes later. Unconsciously you try to protect yourself."

The younger officers also have their problems. They are especially dissatisfied with their economic situation. "I find a certain crossness and dissatisfaction in the personnel. I think it is simply the result of the economic situation or our location on the pay scale. The young have an especially hard time. They often take their economic difficulties along with them to the institution, and this proves to be very annoying."

A session ended one evening with these remarks: "There is a lot of talk about problems of cooperation, but we make those problems ourselves. We say we are not clever enough or skilled enough, and are merely subordinates, but this is nonsense because no one is a subordinate in a treatment institution."

Coordination Problems

One of the main problems for the different types of personnel is that the members of each group often fail to understand the work of the other groups. Wherever several different specialized groups work at the same tasks, tension develops between them. An individual member of such a group, such as a doctor or a psychologist, feels obligated to assert special viewpoints as an expression of his group's position.

A member of the group of lieutenants claims that the officers' "failing to understand" is their main problem. The lieutenants must be sure that everybody is acquainted with developments in the institution. They have to act as interpreters to promote mutual understanding of what the others are doing and why they are there. As he puts it, "I try to explain to the officers that there is nothing degrading about being the one who has established the best contact with the inmate. You may know the most about him, but you have to pass it on to be used by the specialists. You cannot do their work yourself because you lack the proper education. If you educate yourself to observe everything and then pass it on in writing or orally, you fulfill your part of the task, and it need not be dull."

At the Wednesday meetings with lieutenants and sergeants, there are attempts to discuss these subjects.

At times we have attempted organized group discussions of problems of staff cooperation. This is important because it is often easier to be tolerant toward inmates than toward colleagues. If a man is able to cooperate with fifteen difficult inmates, we believe we are right in demanding that he also be able to cooperate with one colleague, even though they are not the best of friends.

In many areas, including six-hour leaves, the administrative lieutenant and the captain have the opportunity to give general and effective guidance.

For example, an officer asked to be excused from escorting a certain unfriendly inmate. The lieutenant granted this relief but warned him about the questions that would be asked by the staff member who took his place. He also suggested that someone might think he wanted to get out of difficult tasks. After this warning, the officer insisted on going on leaves and later told the lieutenant that he had learned a great deal from this incident. The lieutenant had started by saying, "Yes, you may do that. . . . " and proceeded to explain what consequences could be expected. This technique is also used often with inmates.

This kind of approach may cause trouble, however. When we discuss with an officer what an inmate should and should not be allowed to do, the officer may feel inclined to agree fully with us or with what involves him the least. Forbidding the act is not usually the first thing to be suggested. If you do not give staff members the opportunity to elaborate on their impressions, you can easily be misled.

For example, a problem arose in a discussion with a sergeant, a contact man, who, because of an interest in birds, had established a close contact with a homosexual on parole who was making some money selling birds and was receiving a disability pension. Asked if we should allow him to correspond with another inmate who was not a homosexual, the sergeant agreed. When we discussed more thoroughly the consequences of buying birds for the institution's inmates from the bird seller, the sergeant changed his opinion. The parolee would risk professional contacts with some former institutional "friends," whom he correctly did not wish to see. He had already complained once to the sergeant that the institution had given his address to a former fellow inmate. It had not, but he thought so because an escaped inmate had visited him. The bird seller left for just a moment to get bread and coffee, and when he returned, the escaped inmate was gone and so were 150 kroner ($20).

This demonstrates the need to use the knowledge of double expectations when dealing with staff. One should not be satisfied with an initial "yes" but should test whether it is based on an evaluation of acts and consequences.

Six-Hour Leaves

Now and then a young guard becomes nervous when he has to start acting as an escort for six-hour leaves. One guard said that he knew the inmate with whom he was going on his first leave was "something of an impudent fellow." He took the leave anyway because he thought it was a reasonable part of his job. He also thought he might learn something, which proved to be the case; the inmate was very polite the whole day.

Escape from leave is a problem that bothers both the inmates and the personnel. We are aware that the problem is a result of trying to find a balance between confidence in the inmates (which is necessary if the leave is to have any meaning) and the need for security (which we have to demand for the sake of society). One escort told us that he had been in the service ten years and had avoided being assigned to go on leaves. He was aware that the duty was not always enjoyable. When he was finally told to take a leave, he was especially unwilling because there were rumors circulating that the inmate in question would "skip." The escort was equipped with handcuffs, but he was not the least bit satisfied with his situation. When they arrived in town, he tested the inmate's desire to run by saying he had to go to the lavatory and going halfway down the stairs to a public one. The inmate shuffled along and stopped, causing the leave companion to go back upstairs. He asked, "What the devil! Weren't you going to run when you had the chance?" The inmate replied to this, "No, I am not such a fool. I know very well that I have said such nonsense, but I will not do that." They then had coffee together at a restaurant and later had many pleasant leaves together.

Another officer tells about an inmate who, during a visit with a family, asked permission to go to the grocery alone to buy some coffee. He was allowed to do this, as the grocery was just across the street. Nevertheless, the leave escort's conscience began to bother him, and he followed. The inmate came out of the grocery and headed directly for the doorway in which the companion stood. The inmate became angry when he realized what had happened and asked the officer if he really believed that he would run. The companion tried to explain that the weather was so nice that he came out to get a little fresh air. A few days later, there was an incidental inquiry from the police to find out whether the inmate had had a leave on the day after this incident. On the second day, a crime had been committed that was similar to the one this inmate had previously committed. The shock the companion experienced upon hearing this made him realize that one reason for him to accompany the inmate was to protect him from suspicion. Since then, he has never allowed an inmate to go anywhere alone.

The question of whether to let an inmate telephone during a leave also causes difficulties. Our rule states that an inmate may only make calls with permission, so that we know whom he calls, but the unexpected sometimes happens. For example, if someone who is aware that the inmate is visiting his home calls and asks to speak with him, it is almost impossible to deny him permission to take the call. The escort must always report such irregularities because even small ones may cause trouble, but his reports should not include information unnecessarily provocative to an uninformed reader. The officer is invited to discuss such incidents orally, as soon as possible after his return to the institution. This makes it easier for him to write a correct report.

An officer once allowed an inmate to telephone a person he did not know. By chance, this person, who was a former inmate, accidentally met me the same day and complained of being telephoned during work. A case like this calls only for a smile.

However, if a leave companion allows an inmate to visit a home where a newly released inmate is present and fails to report this, the situation can become quite dangerous. This occurred once, and a police report arrived later, saying that a radio had been reported missing at that home. It is mandatory for an officer who allows such a thing to happen to be transferred from the institution.

Another officer has said, "The fact that the concept of leave is so closely attached to the welfare work in the institution means much to us common prison workers. We gain a greater understanding of the entire work."

A former escort is often asked to stay in touch with an inmate and his family. This may prove to be of great help for the welfare work, as was the case in the bird seller incident. This practice may offer an opportunity to exert influence on the inmate's family relationships. However, it may also cause the personnel a great deal of trouble.

Funny situations also arise. An aunt who was present during a visit thought she should strike a jovial, straightforward tone. Because she supposed the companion was a friend of the inmate, she started to give each of them a ten kroner note while remarking that they should have some fun while they were on leave. The escort politely refused the note without revealing who he actually was, saying that he did not need any extra money. The inmate was sweating so profusely that moisture ran down his face. After the visit he asked his escort to excuse his aunt's behavior and was relieved to learn that it had not made a serious impression. The parents, both being hard of hearing, had not understood the scene, so nothing was said. But, during the mother's next visit to the institution, the inmate apparently explained the episode to her because the aunt, who was present again at the next visit, became stylish and eloquent and was considerably less natural than she had been before.

Working as a contact man assisting a social aide may irritate an officer. This practice was not brought about by good and clear planning, but, like much of the work now being done in Herstedvester, it arose from the personnel's practical experiences. When we abolished strait jacket methods which demanded absolute obedience to printed rules and instructions, a need for human contact was satisfied for a majority of the personnel and many of the inmates.

In certain complicated instances, the work of an officer as contact man has been of decisive importance to the treatment. One of the most exceptional cases was Jens, fifty-three-year-old sexual criminal (a pedophiliac, interested in girls). At the ages of thirty-three and forty, he had been accused of indecent exposure, but the charges were dropped. At the age of forty-three, he was sentenced to prison for seven months for a similar act, and at fifty-three he was sentenced again for indecency toward girls. During his trial he admitted that he had taken the initiative. He had strong feelings of guilt and inferiority which resulted in an attempt at suicide at the time of his arrest.

Later he convinced himself that he had been innocent and that the children had, as he said, "raped" him. He swore his innocence, and his depressed mood was strengthened and supplemented by obvious delusions. Because of this he was temporarily committed to a hospital for the mentally ill. When his psychosis was cured, he was transferred to Herstedvester.

It was extremely difficult to reason with him because he became very emotional and declared that he was persecuted. He misunderstood everything in a paranoid manner. During his mental observation, the possibility of castration had been suggested, but he firmly refused this. After a couple of years, in spite of his aggression toward the institution, we recommended a six-hour leave. In daily life Jens was harmless, peaceful, and industrious. Even though we found that he still had to be classified as a psychotic, it was rather hopeless to attempt to transfer him to a hospital.

Jens was fortunate enough to be placed in a section where the officer was willing to listen to him. He always talked about his problems, and, when his fellow inmates tired of his talk about innocence, right, and justice, the officer became his principal listener. This collaborator's complete report told that his statements were foggy and illogical. He admitted that he was liable to a penalty, but he said his sentence was "screwed and twisted." He also came out with the strange assertion that during his arrest he had been beaten over the head from behind, while he was sitting in church, but "they had not been lucky enough to knock me out completely." He also believed that someone was going to shoot him during his exercise period, so he always walked with the greatest caution.

At the mental hospital he had established a good contact with a nurse who convinced him that he was not going to be shot. The officer went through our records carefully and then told Jens that in his opinion the sentence was justified. After this, they started a chronological examination of his life, and, whenever the inmate tried to mix things up, the officer refused to talk with him. Sometimes Jens exclaimed that the personnel "should be able to understand right and justice," while at other times he thumped the table. After such fits of rage he would withdraw to his room for some time. A few days later he would start talking again about his case. After several months his line of thought became understandable and his violence subsided. His aggressive attitude toward the doctor was unchanged.

Jens had accepted his first sentence without appealing because he thought that, if the police said it was indecent to act as he had, then it must have been so. He had no doubt about it.

At one time he had been surprised while urinating in a place where it was illegal, and what he talked about most was the pains he felt in his abdomen when he "had been forced to stop without being quite through." He realized that he had been breaking a law, but he had been unable to control himself.

About his last sentence, he always maintained that the two girls who had accused him of being indecent had been rather aggressive toward him and had undone his trousers.

He does not recall much about the period after his arrest while he was waiting for sentencing, but he thought that there was poison in his food. And he barely remembers his stay in the hospital.

The central element in Jens's story seemed to be his complete, naïve confidence in the infallibility of the authorities and in the ability of the police to see and know everything. The officer went through our material on the case once more to make sure there were no holes in the information that Jens had given him. He slowly got the impression that he did not consciously lie, except about his relationships with women. The officer believed that Jens had never had sexual intercourse with a woman, but Jens insisted that he had done so once.

Eventually the officer succeeded in getting Jens to consider himself guilty. His ideas of persecution faded, but, when I tried to discuss his criminality with him, he still released a rushing, stumbling stream of words and asserted that we were against him and that he was not guilty.

Jens was a good workman and enjoyed his job. The officer appeared at a weekly meeting to plead his cause. It was obvious that he could control his basic paranoid attitudes under suitable conditions, but whether they would blaze up or fade away in free society could not be foreseen. After two and a half years had passed from the time of his sentence, we found that he had become more stable. We had to leave the decision about parole for Jens to the court, but the Medico-Legal Council was more cautious, and the court denied parole.

Jens gave a strange reason for not wanting to appeal: "When one judge still looks upon me as being guilty and another upon me as being innocent, one of the judges has made an unjust assumption, and this judge would not be worthy of the court. I would not take part in a situation like that." Nevertheless, his brother, who was his guardian, appealed to a superior court and succeeded in getting a parole for him. He then forgot his former argument against appealing.

His officer friend was working in our open section as a work leader at that time, so we put Jens there to get accustomed to more freedom. He was not in a hurry to get out and said, "The service and the treatment are first-class." After a month, the officer had to make him understand that we could not keep him there, occupying needed space. Work and board were then provided for him in the vicinity.

We kept in close touch with Jens during the next few years. He saved money for a holiday trip by getting some extra work. He developed a hernia, but we had to force him to go to a doctor, in spite of his pain. After that he used his savings so he would not have to seek public help which, he said, "was only for work-shy and lazy persons." The officer had to help him locate the social relief office and then had almost to force him to go there. After that assistance was finally begun, everything went all right and Jens was thankful later for the help.

He has often visited the officer's home. The officer has observed him closely, especially when children were present. Rather than being attracted toward them, he made a point of avoiding them.

Jens is very helpful toward those who help him. The officer concludes his report on his work with him by saying, "Even though I often have met with suspicion and tolerant glances when I have spoken of Jens's case, I do not regret what I have done. I am still uncertain about exactly how guilty he is and how much of what occurred was due to naïveté on his part and to exaggeration on the part of the girls." Thirteen years have passed since he was sentenced, and he was finally discharged long ago, but he still maintains contact with the institution and especially with the officer.

In this chapter I have made no attempt to isolate and describe typical defense mechanisms in either the inmates or the personnel. No permanent division between individual inmates, or groups of inmates, and staff members, or groups of staff members, shows clearly. As groups, they no longer oppose each other. As individuals, they may either like or dislike each other. We observe a delicate equilibrium that can easily be destroyed by interference that is too heavy-handed, though professionally correct. This balance, when it is first developed, is experienced as a therapeutic climate. This causes both satisfaction and dissatisfaction that often become apparent and are sometimes openly discussed.

This climate is one of our most profitable rehabilitation factors. The fact that the work seems worthwhile to the personnel can be seen from the following quotation from an officer: "Would I do it all over again? This is a question one often asks himself and others. Yes, I would. There have been experiences that I would have been very sorry to have missed. It really has been as stimulating as it has been educational. But it can also be hard—sometimes very hard. I have always seen the light sides of things—this is a gift of mine. It proves, I believe, to be a big asset in this work."

THERAPISTS AND TEACHERS

Many of our therapists and teachers are well able to express themselves, and part of the material in this section comes from their published articles. Other material has been derived from group discussions about their personal experiences in Herstedvester. The teachers, as a group, have not had many opportunities to assert themselves in their work since we have only recently been able to provide individual classrooms.

Twice psychologists have been promoted to better-paying appointments as chief teachers. One of these men, when asked to describe the role of the teacher, pointed out that during his last four and one-half years as senior teacher he found it difficult to separate the role of the teacher from that of the therapist. "The technique, or learning system, is the same. We attempt to change a pattern of behavior, either individually or in groups, and whether we use an educational model or a therapeutic model for our description is unimportant."

Like all other staff members, the therapists (psychologists or psychiatrists) undergo a certain change during the time they work in the detention institution. Some of these academically trained people stay here for only a few years. If they are slow to learn our basic, prevalent viewpoints, it will be difficult for them to make their own intentions sufficiently clear. They must know what the precedents and procedures are, in order to deviate from the standard when a situation requires it.

One of the first tasks of the therapist is to help the ordinary staff member acknowledge and accept the basic reasons for general rules and to help him dare to deviate from them when this is clearly necessary. Some therapists arrive with a very limited clinical psychiatric education. General practitioners have found it easy to merge into the team and quickly estimate what can be accomplished realistically in a given situation. In an effortless manner they establish contact with the general staff and the inmates. Even the therapists who come with an open mind, a complete, basic psychiatric education, and an unusual professional insight into psychiatric problems admit that at first they enjoy the peaceful atmosphere in which they live. As one psychiatrist wrote, "Nobody dares to ask me a question because a reasonable answer cannot be expected."[16]

However, in one case like this the tranquillity was brief, and, after six months, the therapist felt the strain of acting as superintendent for several months. Although this was a very heavy work load and responsibility, he admitted the year after he left that he often "caught himself missing the intriguing intellectual and emotional wrestlings with individual inmates."

Some psychologists and educators, as well as senior psychiatrists, may have the opportunity to follow the careers of the inmates for as much as eight to twelve years, not only while they are in the institution, but also during parole and after final discharge.[17] In this way, they obtain a thorough understanding of the inmates' lives. Somehow they are forced to expand their dynamic viewpoints by attempting to evaluate the eternal exchange between individual and environment.

We get the impression that psychopathic reactions are reactions of strain that are basically the same as neurotic reactions.[18] The mechanisms seem to be identical, but the symptoms are varied. We have recently looked upon them as expressions of disorganization, as described by Karl Menninger,[19] and we observe anxiety symptoms, as well as asthenic and psychosomatic symptoms, in a great number. We find neurotic traits such as insecurity, inferiority complexes, and immaturity. For Sachs, the clientele does not seem to differ from noncriminal neurotics except in the criminal aspect, and we all agree that the inclination to act-out is caused by the immediate situation. One may see several different reaction forms in a single person, each dependent on the particular time and place.

[16] B. Borup Svendsen, "En hospitalspsykiaters syn på forvaringsanstalten i Herstedvester i 1964," *Herstedvesteriana* (Copenhagen: Privately printed, 1965).

[17] Our contract with doctors' organizations makes such long periods of employment impossible for assistant physicians.

[18] Jan Sachs, "Om den neurotiske personlighed," *Herstedvesteriana* (Copenhagen: Privately printed, 1965).

[19] Karl Menninger, *The Vital Balance* (New York: Viking Press, 1963).

Alois Widmer writes that the aim of Herstedvester's treatment and environment form both an outward and an inward entity.[20] "From the beginning," he says, "psychiatrists and psychologists, along with the uniformed corps, have shared in shaping the concepts of Herstedvester. They have all been united under pioneering conditions by involvements, responsibilities, and fellowship."

After three years of work in Herstedvester, with previous experience as a general practitioner, Dr. Widmer worked as a psychiatrist for many years in our sister institution, an old-fashioned prison that he called "a big colossus," in Horsens. He has the impression that the best conditions for mental hygiene and communication exist at Herstedvester. "The sections are scattered and placed in individual houses, each easily accessible, and each with a varied and pleasant view from the windows. This counteracts institutionalism to a higher degree than Horsens's piled, laboratory-like sections, where the only differences in view are those of height." He clearly remembers how long it took him to walk through Herstedvester to his office, and how much direct and spontaneous contact with the inmates and other employees this caused. The fact that the entire institution could see that the therapist was present was valuable for mental hygiene.

Many therapists and teachers have felt that the pressure of work and indefinite sentences, the frankness and intimacy of the colleagues, the individual freedom to "get into hot water," and the unreserved, merciless discussion of everything and everybody were the principal factors that produced strain. These might, on the other hand, be taken as encouragement. One of our former colleagues, who is now in another kind of work, says he now feels " . . . limited and suppressed in a strange way. It is as if I have a smaller field of action in my social work. Everybody knows me as a 'psychiatrist,' and they all seem to see me as a person whose area of activity and competence is very limited."

Another therapist who had been at the institution for a few years wrote that he learned that one essential element in a psychiatric institution's treatment is teamwork. One of the teachers recalls that at first he spent a lot of time getting the officers interested in cooperating with the school, which he thought was close to being sabotaged. It took much work to counteract this, but he believes he succeeded. With the school sergeant and one of the lieutenants acting

[20] Alois Widmer, "Herstedvester set fra særfængslet i Horsens," *Herstedvesteriana* (Copenhagen: Privately printed, 1965).

as "interpreters," he got the needed cooperation, and the inmates could sense that "everyone was pulling the same load."

Some point out that their own impressions of the work changed and became favorable. They enjoyed the development of "the cooperation that eventually took place."

Others expected closer supervision, but they complained about the work load, feeling that the staff was too small. A physician "may be a little jealous of the psychologists, because he has to do routine medical work in addition to his therapeutic tasks." Another feels quite differently because he doubts that he informed his colleagues thoroughly enough about what happened in a discussion group he and a psychologist were conducting.

One psychologist says that when he was a newcomer, he "identified very much with inmates." He knows that he was accused of being naïve and optimistic, but he looks upon this as a therapeutic necessity or as something one is tempted to hide behind a "skeptical pose." He says, "We protect ourselves and become secure by saying that someone else will not succeed. This is something which is encountered in all institutions. This anxiety is sure to appear because we see ourselves as having such difficult jobs that we are not always able to support each other."

One of the special difficulties of the physician is that, when he arrives, he may feel "choked, because the usual medical viewpoints remain in the background. It took a long time before one got hold of the learning pattern." The person expressing this admits that during the first of the two periods in which he worked in Herstedvester, he barely achieved this. Five years later he returned, this time as a senior colleague, and "could feel the difference very distinctly. It was quite obvious to me that cooperation had developed and that there was much more contact between the different groups." At this time he formed the opinion that the uniformed corps was more active and took a more effective part in the treatment. "Something had happened to what, in Herstedvester, is called the cooperation upward and downward."

He thinks back with great pleasure to the time when he was given the task of starting "pre-meetings" for the collaborators who knew an individual inmate. They were to meet and plan an eventual parole. "I really got the impression that the personnel were inspired and felt this innovation to be valuable." He took the initiative to visit one of the sections once a week. He took along the records and went through them with the personnel of the section in question, further stimulating the staff's interest in collaboration. But he missed an interest in somatic causes and believed that medical treatment should have been stressed more.

Some former colleagues shrink from describing their viewpoints, and it seems to be just as difficult for them as it is for inmates to express what they felt when they worked under these conditions. Others, when prompted, often tell tall stories about extraordinary situations.

One of these stories will illustrate the agonies experienced. An aggressive inmate in a security cell broke the supposedly unbreakable glass and walked around barefooted in the cell, screaming about his intention to attack everyone who came near him and to injure himself. Preparations were made to bring him under control in as protected and safe a way as possible. Then his therapist, a woman psychiatrist who is usually very reserved, crossed the line of officers, pushed us all out of the way, opened the cell door, and surprised the inmate. Then, quite alone, she took him along to the sick ward where she worked for several hours to pick the pieces of glass from his feet. The rest of us simply hid away nearby, with bated breath, in case something should happen to her. Her help saved him many later troubles, and he never again got into such a violent rage.

Fifteen years later, I still remember my emotion when she demanded that we step aside from the corridor so that the inmate could go to the first floor without being troubled by the presence of the employees. When a happy ending was evident, my own tension was released in forced, short, and very unpleasant laughter.

One physician recalled a couple of escape situations that illustrate how a physician feels himself to be at the same level as other collaborators. Once he was driving around with an officer and saw an escaped inmate on the road, a good distance from the institution. "We drove alongside him and started talking, but he suddenly jumped into a field. I followed him, and we tumbled down fighting, but I held on to him. At this time a stranger with some horses turned down the road, and I said to the inmate, 'Karl, we cannot lie here fighting—he might see it.' Then all of us quietly drove home."

Doctors have stressed the intriguing psychiatric problems we encounter. The long-standing contact with our patients and the sometimes very slow development of psychopathological syndromes may cause great diagnostic difficulties, especially because of attempts at dissimulation. Reactions that are much more diverse than elsewhere are seen. All possible transitions, from grievance, repression, and denial via outward projection to real paranoic conceptions; from jokes, cheerfulness, and good-humored teasing via cutting, injurious personal remarks, to devious and hateful attacks may be seen in one inmate's behavior. His complaints may run the gambit from the poor quality of Danish pastry to a false accusation of a homosexual infringement.

Younger psychiatrists express themselves along the same lines. After a criticism of the institution's old-fashioned workshops, one of them admits that "about a year and a half passed before I started to catch onto some of the principles." Toward the end of his service at Herstedvester, he declared that the institution "is too little normalized" in relation to life outside—a criticism that is fully legitimate from the therapeutic point of view. But he also says he learned the value of "attacking problems and not postponing them or letting them continue while pretending to have solved them, as is often done in psychiatry and in many other scientific fields."

I cannot conclude this section without stressing the fact that there are experienced, nontherapeutic, senior staff members who believe that we do not live up to our reputation concerning cooperation. They say "at the official meetings, the therapists sit telling their own jokes and showing their own importance. Then there is a row of officers and welfare workers, applauding in the right places." This statement was answered in a debate by a therapist who said, "I cannot understand why you old trained hands have that damned inferiority feeling." Eventually it became apparent that what was being sought was "a little more inspiration" or moral support in the field work.

This illustrates some of our personnel problems in recent years. Enlarging the therapeutic staff has resulted in more changes. It takes some time for a new therapist to feel secure. He has to pass through a phase full of confusion, like any other newcomer, before he is fully accepted by the old hands. This makes it difficult for him to assist the social department with sufficient therapeutic expertise. A critical young therapist felt that he would have liked to serve for a period in the social department and to participate personally in visits with a social aide to the homes of former inmates. Unfortunately this might hamper the continuity of the therapeutic contact, a continuity which means much to the inmates involved.

THE SOCIAL AIDE

In many ways the problems of the social aide resemble those of the therapist, and Skriver was correct when he first described the welfare work at Herstedvester by saying that "it can be mixed pleasure to be a social aide."[21]

It was a long time before the employment authorities realized that social work was very time-consuming and that special education was needed, if the work was to be done well. During the first years, the parole work was spread among many different employees. Eventually there were firmer rules, the parole period was integrated into the institutional routine, and continuity was obtained in the therapeutic work. When we established the open section, and when inmates started working in private industries, their already broad contact with free society became even broader. This caused greater and more specialized problems for the social department. To solve them, theoretical knowledge is essential but not enough; practical training on the job would give a worker better preparation for the numerous questions he will encounter. Many decisions have to be made without warning, but sometimes an experienced person is able to foresee the nature of the problems and evaluate the difficulties as soon as he steps into a situation.[22]

Many times social aides have remarked that a long time passed before they were able to develop a feeling of sufficient personal security. Many felt that they were thrown into things much too fast. Some, when they themselves had become experienced, helped a newly arrived colleague who suddenly had to take over a group of parolees who had been taken care of by an employee who had transferred to another job. Instead of allowing him to take charge of all of them, these experienced colleagues took about ten of the most difficult ones for themselves. In spite of his helpful attitude, an older, more experienced welfare worker may still feel his own insecurity to be a strain. One said, "You often have to make a decision with your best judgment and with very short warning. The immediate attitude of calmness or cheer that you present to an inmate or parolee will often determine the confidence he has in you in the future. A clear stand, even though it is negative, and your statement to him that he must do what he thinks right may lead to a long period gratitude on

[21] Vagn Skriver, "Forsorgsarbejdet ved Psykopatanstalterne i Herstedvester," *Nordisk Tidsskrift for Strafferet,* 34(1946):151–65.
[22] *Ibid.,* p. 156.

his part, even if he acted against what the social aide thought was right."

Unfortunately, the distribution of clients is sometimes uneven. A single social aide, who has fewer clients than his colleagues, may suddenly receive a whole series of new inmates. This easily leads to an accumulation of parolees during a short period, overloading this particular worker for a few years or forcing him to give less time and effort to each parolee. This does not mean that an experienced welfare worker routinely makes a certain number of visits. In certain instances we clearly state that we are merely offering our assistance to each parolee and not controlling his behavior. Through this policy, we build up such conditions that the inmate feels a personal responsibility for his own fate.

Coordination and continuity do not always succeed, either. Therapists state frequently that it is not enough for a social worker to know the institution and its daily atmosphere but that he or she has to keep up with, and personally experience, the changes that go on. In the last few years, the social department's location outside the institution and its heavy work load have made it difficult for the social aides to take as much part in the institutional work as most of them have wanted to.

On the other hand, the social aides often complain that the therapists do not pay attention to the detailed knowledge of an inmate that the social section has obtained during a period of parole and that they put too much weight on the results of their personal interviews with him. At one time an experienced practitioner of fraud succeeded in convincing a therapist that he had not misused alcohol and that he ought to be paroled again, even though a social worker had arranged for him to be returned directly to Herstedvester, because he was unemployed and drank daily with a friend. The description in his case record of the number of empty bottles found in his room was not used to the satisfaction of the social aide.

For a long time we had a permanent welfare physician, and this was very valuable. It is somewhat awkward for the social aides to go to different physicians and ask for help—"like standing with your hat in your hand," one aide put it. Also, the younger physicians, who have been in the institution for only a short time, do not know the clientele of the social department.

A parolee with an alcohol problem is a great problem, not only to himself, but also to the social section. An aide has asked, "Should you go hunting for an inmate that you know is out drinking, or should you merely let him go until he is through? I think that half of my parolees drink, and the anxious, uncertain ones must have a prop now and then. Sometimes I cannot find it in my heart to take that consolation away from them."

It is not always possible to curb the basic, anxious uncertainty felt by parolees, but sometimes we do succeed. One man now looks back on the time when he could not make himself wait: "Everything had to happen at once—now I can get everything, if I just take time." He has also learned not to drink.

One difficulty that the social aide faces, more than other therapists do, is a sudden change in roles. If one has not seen an inmate for even a short period of time, his situation may have changed entirely. One man was often pressured to go to work, but he had to be supported and nursed. Then he disappeared, was searched for by the police, and found at a hotel, where he was working as handy man. We expected to find this forty-two-year-old man playing his customary role as a whimperer who could not take care of himself and did not dare to believe in anything. Instead of this, he had arranged the visit of the social aide so that, when she entered the hotel, she was told that the fine handy man was busy but would soon be back. Coffee was served, and nice things were said about him. The inmate then showed up, happy, smiling, well-dressed, and completely satisfied with life.

When an atrocious crime appears on the front pages of the newspapers, the social aides always discuss whether it might have been committed by "one of ours." Once, when a very severe crime was being discussed in public, I held a meeting with the social section, and we centered the discussion on evaluating danger. By going through a series of cases in which there might be a question of danger, the only conclusion that we reached was that we had nothing else to rely upon but our own vague feelings of what would be essential in each situation. However, the legal rights of the parolee must not be encroached upon by such subjective impressions, and we must realize that control of criminal activity by a social aide is practically unfeasible.

Occasionally a parolee may become aggressive and cause us to get into therapeutical contact with him. Alois was a mythomanic, disagreeable man, but he had not previously been aggressive. After a serious attack on a waitress, who later became his girl friend and then his wife, he thoroughly regretted what he had done. We used this emotional state therapeutically, and he soon became more respectable. Since then he has been quiet and does not show any of his former anxious uncertainty.

In this incident everything went well, but the social worker had a difficult time evaluating the situation and its possible risks. There had been serious problems of jealousy in Alois's first marriage, and these could have proven to be dangerous later.

When a situation culminates in a murder, as it did in Wulff's case, it may be very painful for the social worker. Wulff had constant difficulties from childhood on. At the ages of five and twenty-one years, he received head traumata. After the latter injury, he began to have epileptic attacks that were treated as traumatic epilepsy. His electroencephalogram record showed varying results, sometimes definite abnormalities and then nothing noticeably epileptic.

His situation at home had been difficult. He was the third of four sons; he felt that he was treated worse than the others and that his younger brother was especially favored. He had attended school irregularly. When he committed petty larceny at the age of twelve, he was placed under child guidance supervision. The year after that, he committed a burglary and stole a bicycle; then he was placed in a boys' home. A year later he committed a new offense and was placed in a youth home from which he escaped. Then he committed another larceny. He was eighteen years old when he was sentenced to imprisonment for one year and three months, and, at the age of nineteen, he began a sentence of three years in prison for 121 cases of theft. He was on parole at the age of twenty-one.

When Wulff was twenty-two, he married a sixteen-year-old girl, who was pregnant with his child at the time. Her baby was stillborn. Under later mental observation, he claimed that the treatment that was given to the dead child (he saw it casually packed in brown paper) gave him a bad shock. He said this made him very bitter and intensified his criminality. However, the record showed that the child was born when Wulff was twenty-three years old, and it was not until a full year later that he started a series of forty-nine property crimes, for which he was sentenced. He and his wife had two more children before he was arrested.

Because Wulff behaved strangely and appeared peculiar and spineless, he was observed several times. He was easily led astray and was misusing medicine. He was found to be mentally retarded, with an inclination toward depressive, dysphoric states, and had, according to the neurologist, a symptomatic epilepsy. He was then placed in detention.

During his stay in Herstedvester, he seemed to have normal intelligence, and he had no epileptic fits. On our recommendation, a new police investigation was made, and it proved that he had not committed some of the robberies for which he had been sentenced.

After only one and one-half years, Wulff's guardian started a parole case. His condition had improved considerably, and he seemed very stable in comparison to his earlier condition. He had been a steady worker in the open section. The court decided that it was time for his parole.

Wulff's two daughters had been living with his young wife but were placed in an institution because she was ill. Shortly before parole, he had visited her at home, and she had mentioned that she was going away for a holiday, intending to return home at the time of his parole. Later, however, just before he left Herstedvester, she wrote him to say that she had to think of herself first. After he was paroled, he went to pick her up as they had planned, but then she told him that she was not planning to come back home and that she would not resume their married life.

This was a hard blow to Wulff, and it was followed by a series of difficulties about his right to visit his children. He became depressed, and we took him back into the institution for one day. We found room for him at a rest home, and he met the woman who became his second wife.

He divorced his first wife. His social status improved, and she let him have their oldest daughter. He seemed to be deeply attached to his new wife, who was better than the first in administering their money but just as poor in raising the daughter. A child psychiatrist found that the five-year-old girl felt that her father was aggressive and that she felt herself to be outside the family. She was jealous of her little sister. The psychiatrist advised that she be placed in a special home for nervous children.

In spite of these problems, Wulff lived a crime-free life for a year and a half, although he had frequent fluctuations in mood. At the end of this period, he discovered that his second wife had been unfaithful to him for some time. He discussed his relationship to his wife with the social aide. Things were not really bad, even though, in despair, he had thought of committing suicide.

The social aide resigned at this time and took another job. A couple of weeks later, Wulff telephoned again and explained that his wife was going to be with the other man that weekend. He did not believe that life had any meaning for him, and he had taken an overdose of sleeping pills a few days before in an unsuccessful attempt to commit suicide. The long telephone conversation ended with their agreeing that difficulties like this often occur in marriages. When he said that he liked his wife very much (the wife had told the social worker a short time before that she liked Wulff), the social aide advised him to wait for some months before making a final decision. He did not seem excited, and he talked quite calmly about a new flat he and his wife expected to have within a reasonable time. He believed that his wife would not leave him now, because of his suicide threats. He did not think it would be useful for the social worker to visit the wife to discuss the problems at the moment, but he said he would call her when his wife was "easier to talk to." He was proud that he had undergone such difficulties during parole and had been able to take the strain. He said he would not dream of doing anything criminal again.

We will always wonder whether we could have interfered and prevented Wulff's murdering his wife the following noon.

Later it appeared that they had had a quarrel in the morning. The police had been called, but they left after the wife said she was not being threatened. The quarrel continued; she threw a cup at his head and stabbed him in the hand with a knife. After that, he killed her with several stabs of a knife. Afterward he did not recall anything about the murder itself, but he could describe the wounds he received. He said he then saw her standing with a broken knife in her back.

After the murder, he underwent a depressive reaction, which cleared up very soon. Again he was placed in Herstedvester.

THE SUPERINTENDENT

It is difficult to explain one's own situation, duties, and problems in an organization such as ours. The superintendent is looked upon by the staff and inmates at times as omnipotent and omniscient. To them, he becomes the man capable of doing anything, and the man upon whom all responsibility rests. In a short time he becomes a father figure.

This overestimation is far from a stable evaluation and is very far from my own impression of my role. It is obvious that I cannot disappoint associates very often without having situations which resemble the parent-child relationship, in reverse. They may reverse their opinions of me and develop aggressive thoughts. If I do not notice the change, I may easily misinterpret the reactions of the collaborators, both young and old.

It is a strange experience to be appointed superintendent while still young and have to guide people who are often older than oneself. The superintendent must take the lead if the stability and firmness that are necessary for correct treatment are to be maintained. Another essential element of his job is to avoid giving orders but to keep things going through the coordination of everyone else's roles. He must encourage cooperation and therefore receive and listen to all information necessary for proper administration.

To carry out his role, the superintendent must mingle professionally with both staff and inmates as much as possible. He must obtain many different opinions, sincerely accept criticism from the staff and the inmates, and permit free discussion in conferences and official meetings. He must let discussion develop naturally, so that administration becomes a realistic, shared process.

It is appropriate for the superintendent to lead one group himself, even though this will be mostly didactic, so that he can maintain a direct contact with inmates. At all meetings the superintendent's answers have to be given clearly and quickly and be well-motivated. He must never forget that the motives he gives can, and will, be studied and commented upon to a much higher degree here than in any other place.

It is often stressed that a leader ought to be mature and relatively free of personal problems. This is probably correct, but it is a very theoretical ideal. In an institution like ours, it is an invaluable advantage to have a solid knowledge of psychopathology and psychotherapy. A person who has mastered personal difficulties and has had rich experiences has great respect for the complications and mutual strain of therapeutic situations. If the superintendent has had such experiences, they help him to discover quickly and precisely where the shoe pinches when a collaborator contacts him.

A problem often proves to be in a completely different area than the one in which the colleague seeks help. The essential purpose of consulting the superintendent is often not the guidance for which a staff member asks or a request for official backing; he may also want to share a responsibility which he feels is too great a burden. At other times, a situation may closely resemble those which are experienced in a therapeutic relation with an inmate; that is, the colleague may be unconsciously seeking relief for another disappointment. The conversation has to be continued until he is relaxed.

Here we encounter one of the superintendent's greatest problems—the necessity for him to be realistic and foresee consequences, while also representing security. He receives confessions and carries a full load of responsibility. This responsibility is especially vital when he has to exert pressure on inmates in certain situations. If an inmate is not yet able to work out his difficulties constructively and reacts with such serious disorganization that he may become psychotic, the superintendent must carry the responsibility for an unhappy result of a therapeutic incident. There will be no one with whom he can share this responsibility professionally, and he cannot display his own problems. The importance of his having someone outside the institution who is able to listen to his problems is quite obvious.

It is the responsibility of the superintendent to represent safety in our exceptionally insecure institutional life, and this helps to keep both staff and inmates at ease. In spite of all attempts at sharing power and responsibility, the superintendent has to accept the fact that both inmates and employees look at him as *the* person with power, from whom prompt decisions and solutions to a myriad of problems are expected.

If unpleasant events take place while the superintendent is away from the institution, he will generally find a sign of reproach for his absence in a feeling that "this probably would not have happened if Daddy had been home." This role of "Daddy" cannot be isolated from the personality of the superintendent, and it becomes more and more obvious as he grows older. However, it is not certain that, even though this role eases the work, it is an advantage to the person himself. In any case, the leader's position inevitably carries with it a limitation of his free communication with other human beings. As superintendent of a security institution, with many hundreds of former detainees living in free society, he must be aware of the interpretations that are given of different sides of his behavior by employees as well as inmates, both inside and outside the institution. Even though his conduct has been very casual, even private, it is easily interpreted as being professionally conditioned. Outside the institution—on public vehicles, in restaurants, in shops, and in theaters—he is apt to meet one of the more than a thousand former criminals in whose lives he has been directly concerned. A number of these men speak to him, but others undoubtedly do not want to be recognized.

I have discussed this with former colleagues who have also held leading positions. One of them told me that, when he was going to take his first position as director, he remembered my telling him that "it can be lonely at the top." At that time he had not quite believed it, but now he realized that it was so. He pointed out that the superintendent's position is quite different from those of his colleagues. He is given his position by virtue of something outside the institution. He may transfer an employee, but the employee cannot dismiss him. In spite of the fact that he tries to use democratic procedures, he works near the limits of democracy, and, in spite of the close collaboration which the staff maintains, final decisions must be his.

This "loneliness at the top" means that the superintendent cannot refrain from talking about serious problems when he is at home, and, because his wife must hear this one-sided conversation, it is not always fair to her. However, the professional responsibility inevitably turns back to himself. An example of this heavy responsibility is the process of deciding whether a formerly aggressive inmate should be paroled, or whether he is still too dangerous. We discuss the question with one collaborator after another, in one conference after another, and among us we reach as correct a decision as possible. Our recommendation is evaluated by the Medico-Legal Council and presented to the court.

The judge and other authorities do not see the inmate regularly in the institution, do not have peaceful conversations with him, and do not sense whether he is experiencing any insecurity. But the superintendent later faces the difficult questions: If he was not paroled, were there other possibilities? Were we right in keeping him back? The decision may have been right when it was made, because he was too dangerous. But is this still the case?

The conservative element in an institution like this must be strong. If we are aiming at new methods of treatment, this conflict between the conservative approach, which gives easy answers that are not always correct, and our duty to look for other solutions, even though they may not be emotionally satisfying, may become very complicated.

The variety of these problems is illustrated by the story of Svend, a man now well over sixty years old. In his youth he received several sentences for larceny; then he was given fourteen years at hard labor for rape and murder. After this he had a long series of convictions for larceny and, finally, attempted rape. During his detention, which lasted for seven years, he had serious psychosomatic reactions accompanied by a considerable weight loss. This occurred in connection with a change in his attitude toward life. We discussed castration with him, but he did not believe it was necessary. We concluded that he was developing so successfully that he could adjust to society, and we recommended parole for him.

After Svend had been on parole for a year, he met a widow of his own age with whom he established a close relationship, and he went to live with her. A few years later, after a quarrel, she contacted Herstedvester. I called Svend in for a talk. I stressed that he must follow some treatment for alcoholism, and I suggested that he live alone for a while and keep in close touch with me. In one of our conversations, which we tape-recorded with his consent, we went over his entire life, including his involvements in serious crime. He expressed a belief in fate, and he understood that during detention he had not been physically ill, but mentally ill. He said that he had "been ill" for a long time, perhaps during all the years since his prison sentence for murder. He had felt entirely different during this parole. He added that he had never liked to hurt anyone and that he was good with animals. Then he referred to his last rape, of which he was thoroughly ashamed because he had been attracted to the woman while he was intoxicated and in a suicidal mood.

Three weeks after this conversation, Svend's woman friend called to tell us that she had visited him in the room to which he had moved after his conflict with her and discovered him in a very compromising situation with a former fellow inmate. Shortly after this he went to her apartment and tried to enter with his key, but she had had a new lock put on the door. He begged, but she did not dare to let him in. During the conversation he fired a shot through the mail slot. There is no reason to believe that Svend's woman friend was lying when she said that he had asked her to bend toward the mail slot so she could hear him better, although he later denied this. At this point he was arrested.

We had to recommend that he be placed in detention again. We had to admit that we had been wrong in thinking that he had fully understood the necessity of regarding alcohol as poison. He had put

himself in the extremely unfortunate position of appearing to be
preparing for homosexual relations. The difficulties which followed
had resulted in his suicidal threats and related aggressive acts.

As is often the case in such matters, Svend's woman friend felt
sorry for him. She said that he was "really a good human being," and
both she and his employer were very anxious to get him out of his
self-made difficulties. They pointed out that, in their opinion, the
shooting was a "momentary reaction" and that he had probably now
"learned his lesson."

Svend's case ended strangely. The public prosecutor decided to
drop the matter because of the nature of the evidence. Svend had
said at later hearings that he had not intended to harm his woman
friend, and she believed him. Dropping his case was especially
important because this decision made it possible for him to avoid the
"self-fulfilling-prophecy-situation." If he had been prosecuted and
the court had decided that the shooting had given new evidence of his
previously demonstrated dangerous pattern of behavior, it would have
been extremely difficult to effect a new parole. We would probably
have believed that our psychological evaluation had been wrong,
and it is unlikely that we would have dared to suggest a new parole,
at least not for many years.

Svend has lived a regular, peaceful life with his woman friend
during the past three years. He receives an old age pension and
works a few hours each day in a shop. He is now sixty-nine years
old and in good health, and the couple are doing well economically
and domestically.

Experiences like this make it difficult for us to accept the usual
resistance of the legal authorities to early discharges, after four to
six years, of young murderers with good prognoses, who only harden
in institutional life. Retaining these men causes a good deal of
agony. During his first years in detention, an inmate may receive
professional education, and the public usually forget about him.
Later we may become convinced that we are going beyond what
reasonable security demands and begin to feel our own inadequacy.
Of course it does help us to know that the problem is to cooperate
with the legal authorities. There has to be a balance between what
may be good for the individual, if our evaluation is correct, and
what may be bad for the institution, if our evaluation is incorrect.
We must also consider the likelihood that other authorities will

support us, or attack us, if an accident takes place. Such attacks may endanger our entire treatment program for long periods.

All these initially conflicting views are certain to cause a serious dilemma. On one side, the treatment of chronic abnormal criminals needs continuity, and this demands that the management be stable over a period of years. On the other side, the possibility of new methods demands a fresh attitude toward new ideas. The superintendent has to encourage optimism and open-mindedness in his colleagues, even though they are disappointed or tired. Concerning interpersonal problems, he must make it clear to the personnel that their own behavior influences the success of each inmate. He must strengthen their courage and optimisim when things are going badly instead of increasing their obvious annoyance by stressing mistakes which have already been made.

He will get great pleasure from seeing a colleague's pride when he says, "Have you noticed that nine months have passed since so and so (an apparently sure recidivist) was discharged?" If the superintendent has observed this, he will realize how sensitive people closely involved with their work often are. Sometimes a sensitive person's mistake should not even be mentioned.

Unfortunately, verbal guidance is not enough for the superintendent to give. The way he associates with the inmates is not only observed by the inmates, but also is taken as an example by the staff. Like everyone else, he learns clinical skills by observing and performing the work in practical situations. He cannot obtain this type of knowledge only by reading, but has to develop his own style.

In therapy such as that being described here, each staff member must "rest in himself," so that what he is doing does not seem artificial. Therefore the superintendent must warn his colleagues against too much copying. This causes him to be on a seesaw of saying both "Look and listen," and "Don't copy."

The superintendent's own observations are important, but often he has to be careful not to draw far-reaching conclusions from them. Conversations with the superintendent may, for some sensitive, anxiety-ridden inmates, be so burdened by authority that they do not perceive anything at all or do not remember later what was said. In such cases, man-to-man conversations may be difficult, and an interpreter is sometimes necessary. It has proven very valuable to have the chief nurse listen to a conversation and later repeat what was said. Sometimes it is necessary to have a witness to guarantee that what is said by the superintendent will not be grossly misinterpreted.

Perhaps I have spent too much time on the problems of the superintendent of an institution like Herstedvester, but sociological investigations often pass over them too lightly. Sometimes only the problems facing younger people are in focus, perhaps because sociologists identify with them more easily. The decisions of the superintendent may create difficulties for the younger employees. He often has to support therapeutic experiments, and he always has to protect the inmates against experiments which are not well-founded and which may hurt their possibilities of rehabilitation. A younger employee may regret that he is not given enough responsibility, but he fails to think of the superintendent's conflict when he wants to give responsibility but does not feel sure that his young colleague can master a situation. The bill will always be paid by the inmate!

Chapter IV

RESULTS

I would like to present a clear description, complete with statistical figures, of the final outcome of our work at Herstedvester, but I cannot do so. Criminals demonstrate more intriguing differences than similarities, and we have found no satisfactory way of classifying them according to criminogenic situations.

We do have exact figures on the number of recommitments. Of all inmates received during the years 1935 to 1942, except those who have died or been transferred to mental hospitals, 46 per cent relapsed within five years after their parole. In five three-year periods since then, the relapse figure has varied only between 40 per cent and 43 per cent. The shape of this curve shows that the relation between relapse and periods of time has been the same throughout all these years. (See Figure 5.) Half the recidivist group relapsed between thirteen and sixteen months after parole.

As I have already mentioned, our group is very mixed. Fewer of the aggressive and sexual offenders relapsed than the larger group of property offenders. The figures on the relapse rate of property offenders vary between 51 per cent and 59 per cent during the first five years after parole (counting only the first relapse). The number who are returned after the second parole is also about 50 per cent, and this rate is more or less constant for each successive parole group, leaving us with about 10 per cent of the original group after ten years.

During the period 1935 through 1957, the length of time spent in Herstedvester has been reduced substantially for the group of property criminals. From 1935 to 1941, less than 10 per cent stayed under two years, and more than 50 per cent stayed over four years. In the second period, 1942–48, the number of short-timers increased

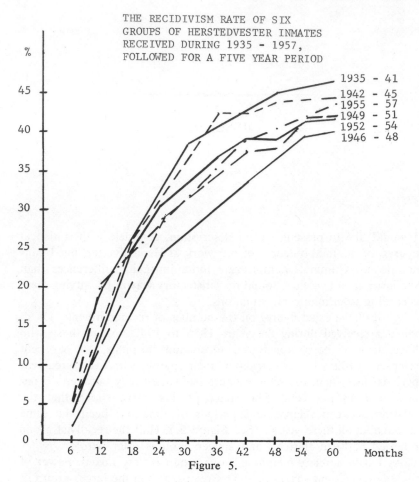

Figure 5.

to slightly more than 15 per cent, and the number of persons staying four years or more fell to less than 20 per cent. In the third period, 1949–51, the amount of time served was reduced even more, so that nearly 40 per cent left during the first two years of their sentences, and only 4 per cent stayed longer than four years. The significance of this shorter stay in the institution is not clear, but there has been a slight downward trend in the recidivism rate during these three successive periods.

The picture is quite different when we look at the aggressive offenders. In the same three periods, the amount of time served in Herstedvester remained relatively constant. That is, more than 50 per cent of these offenders continued to serve more than four years.

The same is true for noncastrated sexual criminals. In contrast, in the case of castrated sexual criminals, we have reduced the number of persons staying more than four years from 16 per cent to zero.

The length of time served is clearly and substantially influenced by our judgment of an inmate's readiness for parole because the court usually follows our recommendations, especially in paroling property criminals, who are ordinarily not very dangerous. Sometimes the court discharges inmates when we do not advise it, and at other times the court delays the discharge when we do recommend parole. It is rather common for the court to be unwilling to follow a suggestion for early discharge in the case of aggressive criminals, despite the fact that the recidivism rate for this group is quite low. The varied effects of the different elements that enter into the evaluation of each inmate for release, recommitment, and re-release would be worth a thorough analysis, but it would require an enormous effort to study and evaluate the materials we have in our files.

One should not attach too much importance to the statistics concerning "thieves" and "aggressives," such as I have already presented. Recidivism rates alone are not a proper basis for evaluating our work at Herstedvester. We are concerned with the short- and long-term elements of a man's life career, in crime, in institutionalization, and in postinstitutional adjustment. The possibility of gaining new and better knowledge of what happens to men engaged in crime for years and how to help them is worthwhile, even if our results do not prove to be statistically significant.

Serious difficulties have to be overcome if clinically meaningful comparisons are to be made. For many years it has been my hope to compile such statistics. To carry out this plan would be very time-consuming, for the results cannot be meaningful without a careful clinical scrutinizing of case histories.

However, a very simple and superficial analysis of the case histories of ninety-nine inmates, the total number of property offenders received in Herstedvester in the period 1952–56, shows that they stayed with us for two-three years. Six out of this group had been sentenced for other types of crime at some time in their careers, but their latest crime was a property crime. Six of the group were euphomanics; most of them had been sentenced for crimes related to misuse of narcotics. Three of these stayed with us only once, the other three recidivated, but only one remained with us in 1966. Four of the ninety-nine inmates developed a psychosis during detention. Several of them had—in our opinion—been psychotic when they came, but presented unclear symptoms. All four were in mental hospitals in 1966.

Of the rest of the group convicted for property crimes, received in this period, forty-one were in their twenties at the time of detention. In 1966 twenty of these had been with us only once, twenty-one had been with us two or more times, but only five were with us in Herstedvester in 1966 during one of their returns. Twenty-eight were in their thirties when they were first received. Eighteen stayed with us only once; ten were with us two or more times. Only four were with us in Herstedvester in 1966.

Fourteen of ninety-nine were more than forty years of age when first received. Of these two were staying with us in 1966. About half of the group of ninety-nine have been paroled for an average of nine to ten years, the rest in fewer years, and only a few have continued their criminal careers.

In the evaluation of single cases this information helps us very little and it does not tell anything about what elements in the process have been more or less effective.

If we analyze case histories, we see how varied the men's sociological and psychological characteristics are, even though there is some statistical conformity. It is extremely difficult to distinguish which life situations have been most important for the inmates' actual careers, and this leads to a new difficulty: Which parts of the information we have obtained should be tabulated? Our cases show that the first versions of a story of an inmate's life may be very different from the later versions, and this is not simply because the inmate is cheating. This is true even for such a "simple" problem as an inmate's relationship to his mother. In many cases this seems to be crucially important in the development of his personality and behavior disorder as we observe them at a given time in which we listen to his description of how he is experiencing this relationship at this time. But when we observe this relationship years later, sometimes in very different circumstances, the evaluation of this crucial factor becomes increasingly difficult. Only a limited number of our cases are capable of introspective observation and analytically trustworthy collaboration. Furthermore, it seems as if many of the criminals we have handled have been more influenced in their criminal career by other circumstances, such as those surrounding a crime or the reactions of their families to it. How he reacts to these circumstances must be seen in relation to his earlier difficulties and successes. Because we do not know what factors are the most important, we are not yet ready for a satisfactory statistical analysis of the interaction of the many factors contributing to the development of life careers as we have observed them.

Three very different case stories, each involving a dominant mother figure, will illustrate these points, and give a practical demonstration of how our work proceeds and what kind of information is available for any future evaluation of our results.

Stig was in his forties and had committed frauds periodically. In his first psychiatric examination, when he was twenty-nine years old, he was found to be spineless and emotionally labile, and he had hysterical fits. Seven years later a new psychiatric examination brought up the question of whether he needed detention, but, because he had been crime-free for five years, it was not strongly recommended. His ninth sentence was for fraud connected with misuse of medicine—Benzedrine and barbiturates. He had smuggled sleeping drugs into jail, as well as nicotine to kill himself. His suicide attempt was unsuccessful. When he came into detention, he was described as mythomanic and daydreaming. We kept him considerably longer than he had been held in his recent prison sentences.

In the beginning Stig was self-effacing and easy to get along with. His life-story showed a considerable problem concerning his relationship with his stepmother. His father had died in 1913 and left them in an economically desperate situation. They lived in a slum and moved from one bad flat to another, and he was deeply moved when he talked about how his stepmother kept life going for both of them. When he was nine or ten years old, he first heard that he was a bastard. Since then he has felt inferior. He went to many schools and had great difficulties in his school work because of his family's constant moving. He had only one close friend.

At the age of seventeen he was employed in a firm where he learned to swindle. After this, when he was without work, he talked eighty people into giving him loans. He told them that he needed money to help his stepmother and another old lady, and he easily obtained loans, mostly from academic people.

He was deeply disappointed by his prison sentence. He felt degraded and wanted to discuss it with his stepmother, but she did not want to talk to him. For this reason, he changed his name to his real mother's name.

Among Stig's records we found several good testimonials from different employers, but these he had forged. He never stole on the job, but his swindling continued, and he received one sentence after another. He was engaged during his twenties but did not dare to marry "without taking mother with me. And what would I do if she and my wife couldn't get along with each other?" Later he again considered marriage, but again he avoided it for the same reason. Finally, at the age of forty-three, he became involved with a woman with children. He was happy to have something more than "mother and myself to live for," but, when the woman was unfaithful, he felt that he had failed again and was of no use.

At this time his stepmother started drinking and Stig started using euphorizing medicine. For a time he used Benzedrine, barbiturates, and morphine preparations. Twice he attempted suicide. For some years he had no contact with his stepmother, but he started writing to her again and showed a strong feeling of guilt toward her. At the same time he wanted to be free of her.

During his stay in detention we concluded that Stig's first swindlings were really planned to help his stepmother. Then he discovered how easy it was for him to win the confidence of other people, and he could not resist the temptation to continue to obtain money in this easy way. The pattern became fixed. He was still very dependent upon his stepmother and considered his life to be one long failure.

After a year he visited home on a six-hour leave. His stepmother lived in an untidy house with a somewhat younger man who owned it. Stig did not think he would live with her again, but when she later became ill, he reacted in a very sentimental, hysterical way.

After four six-hour leaves, he was transferred to the open section where he was much respected, and called "Uncle," by his fellow detainees. He tried to help them in a sensible way but did so much that we had to advise him not to be too interested in individuals but to take a more general interest in social work. He had no homosexual interests. His inferiority feeling diminished, and his self-respect definitely increased. During this period he wanted badly to be paroled, and he had psychosomatic fits of dizziness. Careful neurological and otological examinations showed nothing abnormal.

After two years and three months he openly discussed the difficulties he had had in school, where he had been called "bastard." During psychotherapy he also mentioned that he tried to avoid military service in order not to hear about his origin. His later crimes had a definite relation to his misuse of medicine, which was rather expensive. During group counseling he obtained some insight into his own and other people's problems, and it was finally possible to discuss his self-pity with him.

When Stig was paroled, he was placed in a factory where he stayed for many years, although the work was rather heavy. Sometimes he lived alone, and sometimes he took care of his stepmother because he felt sorry when she was alone. She was now seventy-nine years old, spent too much money, and was tyrannical; thus he frequently had an opportunity to play the role of martyr. His escort on six-hour leaves stayed in touch with him, and a sort of family friendship developed between them. This was broken after four and one-half years because of a catastrophe in the life of the escort.

Stig still did not want a final discharge. He kept his contact with the social aide because "now only a few people visit me." His stepmother died when she was eighty, and he stayed for a time with a friend. Then he returned to his own flat because he preferred to be alone in difficult times. He still worked at the same job, and, six and a half years after parole, he sent us a happy Christmas greeting. In the following months we had no contact with him. As he had been paroled for such a long time, he had to take the initiative to contact the social aide. Five months after Christmas, nearly seven years after parole, Stig was hospitalized for cancer and died a few days later.

* * *

Joachim, thirty-three years old, was a property criminal who engaged mostly in housebreaking and sometimes in fraud. He was the youngest of five children, and his three brothers had prison records. One had been in detention, another committed suicide, and the oldest, who was probably the most criminal, had only been sentenced for war crimes. Joachim was enuretic until the age of eighteen. The relationship between his parents was very poor, and they were divorced when he was five. His mother then worked and kept the family going. She was very high-spirited, and she and the dominating oldest brother exerted a great deal of pressure on Joachim. His relationship with this brother was very ambivalent. He acted as a father substitute in the family, and, as the youngest, Joachim felt inferior and envied him. At times he hated and despised him, and at other times he admired him. He said, "When anything goes wrong I always run to him."

Joachim had the same puritan point of view as his mother, and the conflicts this caused in daily life led to serious problems; in school he had difficulties with both teachers and students.

During the time of his apprenticeship he managed well because he was not under the influence of his oldest brother, and he felt that these had been his best years. Then he entered into a platonic relationship with a young girl and felt very badly when she did not reciprocate his interest. At the age of twenty he again came under the influence of his oldest brother, and through him obtained a good job with the Germans. In a drunken state he joined the SS (Schutzstaffel), but, when he realized what he had done, he felt like a traitor. He stayed a short time in Germany and broke his connection with the SS. He continued to work for the Germans in Denmark for some time, then he associated with various asocial groups in Copenhagen. After he and a comrade attempted blackmail, he was arrested and sentenced for this and his German collaboration.

Joachim stayed out of prison for a few months after finishing his sentence as a traitor, and he married a woman he did not love. He was discontented, and again got in touch with his brothers and started merchandising. This period ended with fraud and housebreaking, and during his sentence for these crimes he had many disciplinary problems. He felt persecuted, and, as usual, he projected every problem onto his surroundings and was defiant.

After some time he developed some self-insight and obtained parole. For a year and a half he managed well. He and his wife worked hard, saved 10,000 kroner, and bought a car. Joachim became his boss's right-hand man, but, when he found out that he could not be promoted further because he had been in prison, he left his job without giving notice and without having a better one available. He started a private business, which soon ended in fraud, and at the same time he started drinking. Again Joachim got in touch with his oldest brother, who made big plans for him. These resulted in complete ruin, and this period ended with a series of housebreakings for which Joachim was placed in detention.

In Herstedvester he began by being very talkative, unreliable, sentimental, and bitter, and he felt injured by the punishment he received after the Occupation because he did not feel that he was a real traitor. Little by little he gained a better understanding of himself, and he realized that he was probably fooling himself. He could now see that his pattern of behavior demonstrated that he wanted to be more important than he was. Inferiority feelings had made him self-assertive during school and during the war, and he knew very well that this was childish. Joachim was eager to plan his stay in Herstedvester. He regretted that he had not finished his apprenticeship, and he wanted to continue it because he realized that he should not be a tradesman.

Using a more extensive summary than the one I have given here, his therapist, Wulff Feldman, presented this case at a clinical conference three months after Joachim arrived in Herstedvester. It was stressed that his need for change was already present. He had been troubled by his development for a long time but had not arrived at any solution to his problems. In his therapeutically oriented examination, he was surprised at first that the interviewer was not offended by his story but accepted him and took an interest in elucidating his troubles from different angles. Having a rational evaluation instead of the condemning authority that he had been used to was important to him.

In the second phase of the examination Joachim was very careful to explain conflict areas such as the German Occupation, his unjust treatment in court, and his relationships to his oldest brother, to his father, to women, and to his mother. He was still full of excuses and projections, as if others were guilty, but he repeated and varied his point of view so much and without receiving condemnation that we supposed he was already in a new phase and able to see something wrong in himself. It was important for him to realize that nothing serious would happen to him, even if he admitted that he had done something wrong. This seemed to be the way to show him his tendency toward self-deception and pretense; and to show him that he was continuing his mother's false attitude when she made the children behave as if they were not poor. "Even though Mother had no money, we always had to be just as nicely dressed as Director Hansen's children in dancing school."

Three months later he became cool to his family; he broke completely with his oldest brother and did not want to be visited by the other brothers. He said, "I don't want to be filled with lies." His relationship to his wife remained good, and she visited him regularly. He still said he did not love her but he felt close to her. He participated in group therapy and explained how he and all his brothers wanted to earn fast money and how he hated authority. He wanted to finish his apprenticeship as a cook, but it seemed that this was partly because the only way we could help him do this would be to transfer him to the open section very early.

At this time Joachim seemed to be developing well. After one year he obtained permission for six-hour leaves. When the social aide analyzed his practical possibilities, it was found that he had been apprenticed so short a time that he would need about four more years of training. This disappointed him, and for a time after this he was loud and haughty and felt he was better than his fellow detainees. His wife seemed to manage very well on her own; she saved money and lived with her family, but she felt sorry that his family had not accepted her.

In the group meetings Joachim's comrades attacked his somewhat forced moral attitude toward every question. They told him that he was right when he said that he did not get much out of his efforts, but they also pointed out that it was his own fault. Finally he gave up his apprenticeship plans and accepted the idea of taking ordinary unskilled work. After one and a half years he seemed freer during leaves, and he visited his wife and her family.

Finally Joachim was transferred to Kastanienborg. The distance between the level of his ambitions and his practical possibilities seemed to have shortened considerably. He was less stiff and forced, and more tolerant and human, in his attitudes. His tendency to inadequate, obstinate reactions was not manifest in the open section. His wife, who was his guardian, wanted him to stay in close contact with the institution but thought he was ready for parole.

Her application to the court was accepted, and, after two years in the institution, he was paroled and started working in a factory. He continued to visit his group of inmates in the open section, sometimes accompanied by his wife. Soon his wife told us that the oldest brother, who now worked as a baker, had suggested that Joachim open his own milk and bread shop. The brother would provide the bread. Joachim was dreaming again about independence, and his comrades attacked him severely.

Eight months after parole his wife phoned and told about a severe conflict between her and her husband. His mother had been present at some of the arguments and had not helped her; now Joachim wanted a divorce. Some days later he came to the group meeting and explained that he could not continue his marriage just out of pity for his wife. He stressed that he had not been unfaithful. His wife mentioned that he had beaten her but asked us not to mention that we knew about it. He himself did not mention it but talked about earlier conflicts.

One of his comrades critized him severely when he explained that it was his wife's fault—that she was in love with him but he was not in love with her. He was praised, however, for bringing his problems up in the group meeting. The meeting ended with his wanting to wait before getting a divorce and to continue living with his wife.

A year and three months after parole Joachim still came to group meetings. He had had an accident at work and still had a painful back. Then his wife was hospitalized and successfully operated on for cancer.

Both lived with the wife's uncle. After a year and a half, the uncle phoned the social aide to say that he wanted Joachim to move out immediately because he had beaten his wife. The social aide visited them immediately and met the whole family, including the brothers. They explained that the wife had threatened suicide several times. They found her unconscious in the cellar of the house, and she was hospitalized. No furniture seemed to have been broken, and the uncle was told that he must give the family normal notice if he wanted them to move out.

We found out that Joachim had been acting as chauffeur for his brother—a job which we thought very unsatisfactory. After a few months he again broke off his friendship with his brother, got drunk, and was apprehended by the police for drunken driving.

After two years he received some compensation for his back injury and used this money to buy a milk and bread shop. At the same time he was imprisoned for twenty days for drunken driving. He seemed to work satisfactorily in his own shop and his later life was peaceful. He was finally discharged after four years. Some time later he bought another shop in addition to the one he had.

When I visited him five years after his final discharge (nine years after his parole), Joachim received me in a very friendly way and seemed to be happy that I visited him. He had sold his shops and bought a better one. He saw me standing a little ostentatiously outside the window, came out, and called me in. His wife took care of the shop while we were talking together. He explained that he had felt it necessary to move because he had heard that there were rumors about his crimes in the district. He had seen a former detainee in the shop and later heard people allude to crime.

Speaking of his treatment at Herstedvester, he did not doubt that the personality of his psychologist had been most important in his career. The group work was important "because of the personality of the group leader." He still looked upon his first crime as a traitor as the one of which he was most ashamed.

His oldest brother was still the same, and he explained how this brother participated in one of his first crimes, and he said, "You cannot turn in your brother. He is still the person who, when you are in need, will give you a dollar and pat your shoulder, but only if he is sure he will get $100 back."

Joachim's mother visits each of her children four or five times a year and tries to keep order among them. He realizes that he is something of a tyrant in his daily life, and he tries to stop himself, but "everything has to be in order." He has learned that it does not pay to be irritated. With a smile he says, "One of the things I learned at Herstedvester is that when you don't feel unjustly treated, then you have nothing to work on." He uses this experience when customers complain. He stands peacefully and waits, and, when they have finished, he asks what they want without mentioning the inconvenience they have caused him. He does not misuse alcohol, and it is obvious that he has a good, solid social position. He has some contact with the oldest brother, who has also been in detention, is satisfactorily married, but still gets out of balance easily.

*   *   *

Anton was twenty-five years old when he was placed in detention sixteen years ago because of a serious attack on an old man and thefts from his mother and a woman he had visited. This is not an average case, but it will illustrate some of the problems we have faced during the years.

The case was complicated from the beginning. Anton was not sentenced for sexual crimes, but several cases of supposedly sexually conditioned aggression had been mentioned in his case records. Before he came to us, he had had psychiatric care and been in hospitals for epileptics. He himself had applied for castration, and a medical certificate had been drawn up. From the first version of this story, we may cite that he was healthy at birth and had not been ill during childhood. At the age of fifteen he was knocked unconscious for a moment while playing football, and soon after he had an epileptic fit which was described as being typical. These recurred once or twice a week in spite of adequate treatment (up to thirty centigrams of Luminal daily), and he was placed in psychiatric units several times. In the hospital no obvious epileptic fits were noticed, even when he was not given antiepileptic medicine. He was unreliable, he pilfered, and he was extremely absorbed in sexual matters.

As a shop clerk, he stole money (about 600 kroner or $100) and came under the care of a children's organization at the age of seventeen. At the age of twenty, in a drunken state, he joined the German army, but eight days later he was transferred to a psychiatric unit. The army did not want him back.

Anton's home was said to have been good. He left school when he was nearly fourteen years old because of being ill with scarlet fever. In the following three years he had three different jobs. At the age of eighteen he was transferred from a provincial hospital to a hospital for epileptics, and he stayed there for six months. He worked on a farm for two years, and then he was in a psychiatric unit again for six months and in a hospital for epileptics for another six months. At the age of twenty-two he was again in the psychiatric clinic and again transferred to the hospital for epileptics for another three months.

He worked for eight months, and at the age of twenty-three he was in the Danish army for eight months. He went A.W.O.L. and returned to the military hospital with a physical disease. Here his former hospitalization for fits was discovered, and he was discharged from the army. He had a variety of jobs for several years and then was without a job until the age of twenty-five, when he was placed in a psychiatric clinic and again transferred to the hospital for epileptics. He was described as unstable, unreliable, a drunkard, and sexually debauched.

He said his sexual life had been very hectic and confused. He had sexual relations for the first time at the age of thirteen with a girl of his own age and for the second time at the age of fifteen with a twenty-two-year-old girl. He was engaged twice and had sexual relations as often as three times a day. In a period of ten years he slept with about thirty different girls. He never paid for sexual relations. Two or three times he had had homosexual relations, and three times his sexual contacts nearly ended in murder.

At the age of twenty-five Anton choked his fiancée during an argument, but, when she started screaming, he stopped. Half a year later he planned to meet a girl with whom he was annoyed in order to choke her, but fortunately the meeting did not take place. The same night he wandered around and met a homosexual who invited him home. When the man started to be sexually active, Anton became angry and tried to choke him. The police were informed, but no action was taken. Another time, on a sudden impulse, he nearly choked a young girl whom he had followed home, but he gave up when somebody else appeared on the scene. The police were not notified in this case.

We noted that his explanation had been repeated several times in somewhat the same style at the psychiatric clinic as well as at the hospital for epileptics.

Anton had one son, born out of wedlock when he was twenty-one years old. When he was twenty-three, one of his fiancées became pregnant, but the pregnancy was terminated because of what was known about his disease.

Somatic examination did not show any definite abnormalities. A slight atrophic process in the left hemisphere was found on an airencephalogram. An electroencephalogram showed doubtful dysrhythmia; hyperventilation did not produce epileptic formations. During his most recent stay in the hospital he had no fits, although he received no antiepileptic drugs. The psychiatric clinic had advised castration, and Anton himself had expressed his willingness to have the operation, explaining that he was afraid that in sexual excitement he might commit a serious crime.

The conclusion of the recommendation for castration stated that he was a hypersexual psychopath who had planned or attempted three times, in sexual excitement, to choke his partner. There was reason to believe that he had slight brain damage which was probably significant in his abnormal sexual drives. Epileptic fits, which had not been definitely recognized, were mentioned. Permission was obtained for castration, but, just before it was received, he escaped and his case entered a completely new phase.

Anton and a comrade, who had also escaped from the hospital, stole a key from Anton's mother's flat. Later he went out with his mother, and, while they were out, the comrade took some of his father's clothing. Together they enjoyed the money they got from selling them. Anton slept with a girl friend, a former fellow patient, and stole her bicycle when he left her.

The two young men reported themselves to the police in order to return to the hospital, but instead they were put in jail, as the police had already been informed of some of their crimes. At this time Anton was charged for the attack on the homosexual man six months before. Because of his hospitalizations, the court found it doubtful that he was fit for punishment, and he was transferred to the psychiatric clinic for further observation.

Not much new data was found, but some facts were corrected. Anton's mother explained that he had had his first fit at the age of seventeen and that, since puberty, he had been unstable and very hot-tempered and had frequently told untrue stories. His first hospitalization was more clearly described. He was found lying on a street in a provincial town and was taken to the local hospital. Supposedly he had fainted. Here he told about a theft of twenty-five kroner from the shop where he worked, and the police were informed. He admitted that he had stolen from the shop—small amounts in the beginning and later a little more. The total came to about 1,000 kroner ($150). When the shopkeeper first heard about it, she considered it a small amount, and she wanted to have him back. She had been well satisfied with him and would not have notified the police because she did not want him punished. He used the money for dances, restaurants, and the cinema.[1]

When it was learned later that he had stolen a greater amount, she decided not to have him back. Another employer described him as kind, always correct, and never dishonest. The children's organization was notified, and he was allowed to stay at home, but one month later he was away from home and had another fainting spell. He fell off a bench where he was sleeping, hit his head, and started shaking in the legs, and was hospitalized.

Anton talked to the police about a sixteen-year-old girl whose home he had visited; there had been no sexual contact between them. Again he disappeared from home, and again he was hospitalized for fainting. But this time he was very disturbed at the hospital. He appeared to have epilepsy, and he was transferred to the hospital for epileptics, where he stayed for six months. At the hospital his lack of initiative and mental torpor were explained as epileptic dementia, and some of his acts were explained as epileptic fits. At the age of twenty his relationship to the Germans was characterized as the result of a fuguelike state which brought him to the hospital, and his pilfering was described as obsessive. In the psychiatrist's recom-

---

[1] Later he explained that he had had such a close personal relationship to this employer that this could have motivated her attitude and encouraged his pilfering from her. He agreed that this had not been very moral, especially as he had used the money for entertaining a younger girl friend. It is likely that this explanation is true.

mendation to the court, the incidents of attempted choking or attack were described and related to dysphoric states that were not considered really sexual; it was mentioned that he enjoyed being aggressive.

While in the hospital for mental investigation, Anton further explained how, as a boy, he enjoyed getting dogs to attack each other, and he said that when this happened his intellectual state became blurred and afterwards he felt relaxed. He felt that he was especially dangerous at times when he was without work, and once he mentioned that this aggressive mood appeared when he had not had sexual intercourse for eight days. In one choking episode he had been sexually excited and had sexual relations with a young girl. They had an argument and then had intercourse again. This time he became angry, and, before the sexual act was finished, he started choking her.

Anton himself started talking about these aggressions. In the beginning, the hospital staff doubted the veracity of his stories, but his attack on the homosexual man convinced them that probably all his stories were true. No epileptic fits were observed at the hospital, but his mother described typical absences (petit mal) and how, in such a state, he had shown a primitive aggressiveness, had struck her, and had attempted to choke his father. It had been nearly impossible to take his hands away from his father's neck because of his convulsion. In describing his problems, he showed no guilt feelings. He was intellectually well-endowed and peaceful, and he said that he told about his aggressions in order to avoid actually killing someone because this would result in life imprisonment. He had no thought for his victims.

In the hospital he went on to tell that he had been interested in films about the German gas chambers and the suffering of men and animals. When he saw sentimental films, the tears ran down his cheeks. He did not love any of the women he had known, and he seemed very shallow emotionally.

At one time he had told the police about his tendency to choke people, especially women, and repeated the description of the attack on the homosexual man. The police reports—known to the psychiatrist—did not furnish any further information.

The hospital psychiatrist diagnosed an epileptic disease with an epileptic personality change and a severe psychopathy of the emotionally cool type with a strong development of sexual drive.

In court nothing was said about Anton's women, although the police had found the different ones he had mentioned. The first one was sixteen years old when he was seventeen. They were together for about a year but had no sexual relations. He told her strange stories about his being nearly blind, about someone from the hospital having to help him to the tram, and he said that he had heart disease. He always had enough money. He never threatened her, and she was never afraid of him.

The second girl explained that he had impregnated her, but she obtained a legal abortion because of his disease. After that he visited her several times, but sometimes she did not want sexual relations. He never objected. In a letter he told her that he had attempted to choke girls and told about his attack on the homosexual. She had taken it all as fantasy. In one letter he said that clever people called him an erotomaniac. He continued, "But when I have been together with a woman one night and then some time after when I want to sleep with her again and she doesn't want it, and my mind goes blank, I get the idea that if I cannot have her again, nobody else should have her and then I attempt to choke her. That happened several times and I have been afraid of myself."

Another of the girls Anton said he had attacked dated him for some time. She said he could not differentiate between lies and truths. He visited her in her home. He kissed her, and suddenly he seized her around the neck; she struck him, and he ran away. She and her mother found him hidden in a ditch nearby. He said that he might choke someone, but they let him sleep in their house that night and the next day took him to Copenhagen and told his mother what had happened. The girl realized that he was ill and did not feel that she had been in any danger. When she was told that he could not be cured, she broke off their relationship.

The third girl had known him for nine months when he was twenty-one years old. They had normal sexual relations, but he was choleric and would hit her, even if other people were present. She had a child by him but did not want to marry him because of his disease. His parents had told her that he should not marry.

The last girl interviewed by the police knew him when he was twenty-four years old. She spoke of his hot temper, and said that he struck her and was jealous, but she had not found anything abnormal. He never tried to choke her. "What he told about that is not true," she said. However, he had threatened to kill her if she left him—a threat she did not take seriously. She stopped seeing him because of his lies and because he was not faithful to her.

The Medico-Legal Council concluded that Anton was intellectually normal, hypersexual, emotionally cool, and psychopathic with emotional lability and mythomanic tendencies. They found it likely that he also suffered from epilepsy and that some of the described psychopathological symptoms could be blamed on his disease; but his psychopathy and hypersexuality were supposed to be the most essential elements in his pattern of behavior. He was found not fit for punishment, and it was pointed out that still more dangerous crimes could be expected. Detention was suggested, and it was noted that castration could be carried out at Herstedvester.

In court Anton himself told about one additional instance where a girl had refused sexual relations, and he had suddenly jumped up and grabbed her around the neck.

He had told about the time he had tried to choke his father but stressed that this had been for fun and was not as dramatic an attack as his mother had reported.[2]

As I said before, the jury found Anton guilty, and he was sentenced to detention. At Herstedvester we reviewed his career. He still said he wanted to be castrated so that he would do nothing more serious. He stressed that he was a reasonably adaptable person if left alone. He had never had any friends, was easygoing in daily life, and was not depressed. He talked about his aggressive deeds in a cool way and with apparent objectivity, as if he were not talking about himself.

Six weeks later, in answering a question from the Minister of Justice about castration for Anton, I said that I was skeptical about his reports because in only one case was there agreement between what the detainee and the women had told; only one woman felt threatened. Because Anton was not sentenced for sexual crimes or sexual attacks, I felt that we must be careful and not advise castration too soon.

Three months later Anton's mother said that she thought that he was more relaxed and quieter, and he himself said that the seriousness

[2] The mother seemed trustworthy, but we found later that there was good reason to doubt what she said. The first doubt occurred to us after several six-hour leaves in her home, but it was a long time before it became clear that Anton tried to shield her. At my final interview with him, sixteen years later, he said about his relationship to his mother, "That's all right now, thanks to my wife. She has a strong character and she can manage her." But his wife confirmed that the mother-in-law was still not reliable.

of his situation now worried him. He still talked about his tendency to choke women after sexual relations, but admitted that he was not as engrossed as before in sexual thoughts. In psychiatric interviews he was more open and reacted more emotionally. A few months later it was my impression that he was not at all epileptic.

During anamnestic analysis Anton explained about his attack on his father. They had both been playing, but he agreed that it was reasonable to take it seriously because of his previous behavior. He also admitted that most of his stories about attacking girls were imaginary and that only one was true. That meant that he agreed with what the girls told the police. He thought he had been unreasonably irritable. He was unable to realize that he was emotionally cool, but he understood that people had thought that and that it was his fault they had done so.

Anton started writing a new life-story. In this he related that he felt "knocked out" when he returned to school after several months of an epidemic disease. He held some jobs doing errands, which he did not like, before he came to the lady who let him help in the shop. Then he found that he could easily pilfer money, and he spent heavily on young girls. He was found out and promised not to do it again. "But it wasn't so easy to stop, so after some weeks I started again. One day I thought, 'Now it won't work anymore. I will soon be found out.' I wanted to leave. I don't know why—maybe because I was afraid of the consequences, just as I have been several times since. In any case, I left and went to the town of O_____, where I stayed a few days. Then I felt tired and thought, 'How can I best get out of this?' I have always wanted to be interesting and to make people aware of me, so I suddenly let myself fall on the street." Then he was sent to the hospital, as has been described.

After that, he had another job and pilfered there also. "And then one day I again bought a train ticket, this time to F_____. Here I walked around for some days, and then one evening, while sitting in the railway station, I let myself fall from the bench. I was taken to the hospital, and there I had some hysterical fits. I was isolated in a single room, tied down, and got an injection every day. The longer I stayed, the worse it became. It was a nightmare. Then the doctor said one day that I would be sent to the hospital for epileptics because of my fits."

He also mentioned different girl friends. Concerning one choking episode, he wrote, "During the evening we were sitting together and were comfortable but I couldn't be satisfied with this and I started to be intimate. I was very surprised because she let me go a lot further than at any time before. Then I thought, 'Now she is mine.' Then she started defending herself and screaming. I became so afraid that I grabbed her around the neck and started to choke her. Suddenly she put her finger in my eye so I had to let her go, and I ran away but was soon afterwards found by her mother, who was very unhappy. I returned with her and explained what had happened. They let me stay the night, and the next day the mother and daughter both followed me to Copenhagen. We went to my doctor, and he sent me to the hospital. Still, to this day, I shiver to think what could have happened. I didn't want to choke her. I only became afraid when she started screaming."

Anton liked his military service and he was recommended for the school for noncommissioned officers. Later he met the sergeant who recommended him and was now an officer in the institution.[3] Because his criminal record showed that he had attempted to join the German SS during the war, he was not admitted for further schooling. Then he lost interest in military life, stayed at home without permission, visited a girl friend, and was discharged, as explained before, by the army.

Concerning the homosexual, he now explained that he knew very well that the man was a homosexual, but he thought that he could easily keep him at a distance. "We arrived in his flat and had some drinks. He told some dirty stories, and suddenly he suggested that we sleep together. I said, "No," but he insisted and started to make the bed. Now I could, of course, have left, but I got the idea of making him afraid before I left. When he returned, I had moved to another chair from which I could hit him in the head from behind with a candlestick. He fell over but got up again and wanted to go to the window. I put my hands around his neck, but only for a moment, because he kicked me in the groin. Then I hit him in the face and ran away. I went to the railway station where I washed up and bought a ticket to F_____."

Anton read about the attack by "the strangler" in the newspaper, but he did not dare go home because he had stolen there. He left the town and fell into a ditch, where he was found some time later.

---

[3] Contact with this officer has been of great importance in motivating Anton to a detailed anamnestic analysis and for his relaxed attitude in daily life. This he confirmed during my last interview with him, many years later.

He was taken to a hospital from which he was transferred to a psychiatric clinic. He told the doctor what had happened and believed that he phoned the police, but no police came. Three months later he was sent to the hospital for epileptics, and the discussion concerning castration continued. He accepted but found the waiting time too long and escaped with a comrade, as described before.

In Herstedvester we never saw Anton have any epileptic fits, and his electroencephalogram showed no abnormalities. His first fit in the hospital came after a fellow patient teased him. In a hot temper, he started to throw his dishes and was isolated, but he did not tell the doctors that his action had been theatrics. At the hospital for epileptics he observed other patients, and once he imitated their fits. However, the superintendent did not accept his as an authentic fit.

Anton found that the most foolish thing he had done was to tell the first young doctor about his ideas of choking people. "I did it in order to get peace and free myself of all the lies and hysterics from which I suffered." Now the possibility of castration was given up. Anton's so-called absences did not appear, and after two years he obtained permission for six-hour leaves and visited his mother, who was very happy to see him and praised his development.

After two and one-half years we reviewed his whole life career once more. Nothing new was added to this autobiography, which repeated his previous one. He now had a rather responsible job.

A short time later we found that he had carried on an illegal correspondence with one of our women detainees, and at the same time kept in touch with a former fiancée.

This situation was used for emotion-laden moment therapy. We found that he had not evaluated the consequences of this correspondence at all. I stressed that the letters, as such, were not important to me, but the lies in the letters and the consequences of his actions for another detainee were, and he ought to have thought of that. It was easy to relate this action to his earlier crimes and to future situations which might be dangerous for him. He felt badly, and we discussed how he projected his self-reproach to someone else, usually a girl, and then became angry at her. One week later he asked to continue this discussion, and after another ten days he agreed that it would not be wise at this time to discuss the parole which his guardian had planned to request. Anton himself explained to a leave escort that he felt happier and more relaxed and could even see his own foolishness. He thought maybe his fiancée was no longer important to him, but he did nothing about it.

On a six-hour leave Anton's mother confided to his escort that she had difficulties with her husband. She explained that her husband never had been able to talk with the children and that he was reckless and hit her. A few years before he also mishandled Anton. He was a drunkard, he had been unfaithful to her, and they had not spoken to each other for about a year. Anton did not know how bad the situation was at home, and she did not want him to know about it. Some months later he visited his home in the evening when his father was there, and nothing unusual was observed by his escort.

Three years later he committed a small theft at his job and was discharged. His mother said that he had changed for the worse and at this time it was obvious that there was some peculiar relationship between her and Anton. We did not take the situation too seriously but did not advise parole at that time.

Some months later he was transferred to the open section, and, when things went well there, parole was recommended. At this time his history was reviewed once more, and no change from his two earlier stories was found. He realized that he should not live at home, and he had found out that his parents' situation was not stable. His father had not been there the last time he visited his mother and was probably out drinking. He finally broke off his relationship with his fiancée.

I told Anton in detail why it might be difficult to convince the Medico-Legal Council that my optimistic evaluation of his future possibilities was correct but that I hoped they would accept it. A few weeks later, when everything seemed to be in order, he was found outside the area of the open section and sent to the main institution. He and a comrade had sold a watch, and they had been drinking in the nearby village. We discussed his situation carefully once more, and he admitted some fear about how he would manage when paroled. His mother also said that she was afraid that he would not manage well after parole.

In a letter to the prosecution, we suggested that his parole case be suspended for some time until the situation was better analyzed. For this new psychotherapeutical evaluation Anton wrote a new auto-biography which was again in accordance with the first. In the mean-time the Medico-Legal Council accepted my first point of view, but for some reason my letter requesting suspension of the case had not been taken into consideration. Anton was paroled after three and one-half years.[4]

After parole, he lived with his brother-in-law and worked with him at the same factory. We therefore thought it unnecessary to tell the employer about his criminal history. Three months later the factory shut down for a short time, and Anton moved to his parents' home, where he thought he could live without paying. He soon returned to the same factory, and we warned him that he should not live at home. He explained that he and his father had now joined forces in order to keep the mother in her place.

A half-year after parole Anton became engaged to a girl with a two-year-old son. I thought it was a bit early and told him that he needed a permit from the Ministry of Justice to marry. Before he had obtained this permission, the engagement was broken. A year later he became engaged again. He had visited this girl's parents in another town. His mother explained to us that she told the girl about her son's history and that this had not changed her view of him, but the same day he left home. He returned after two days and then left again. He and his fiancée had gone to redeem an overcoat and a ring he had pawned during his first escape. Then, in a bar, he asked her to wait at the entrance, telling her he would soon be back. He then sent someone out to tell her that now he had left by another exit.

We were afraid that it would make a "big case" if we asked for a police search, as they would not promise to help us secretly. Anton himself phoned us from a nearby hotel on the third day and said he had just left his room; he had started a fire in a mattress, and he was now afraid a more serious fire would develop. He wanted to come back to us. We notified the hotel and the police, and, shortly after, when he came to Herstedvester, he was very depressed and helpless, and he decided to stay with us.

Anton had known his fiancée for three months and did not take their relationship very seriously, but his mother had interfered and

[4] One of the difficulties of our parole system is the long road every application has to travel. The case goes to the lower prosecutor, the Medico-Legal Council, the superior prosecutor (State's Attorney), in some cases also to the Attorney General, and then all the way back, before it reaches the court. Also, the defense lawyer must have time to read the whole case and see what is new. When, in this case, we wanted to be careful, local "political" motivations were admittedly most important. Because we had no actual reason to believe that Anton was likely to commit aggressive acts, we did not intervene further.

invited her to live in their home. He wanted to tell her about himself in order to get rid of her, but, when he started telling her that he had a surprise for her, she became very happy and thought he wanted to get married. Then he stopped talking and accepted her invitation to visit her parents. At her home he became involved in new lies, promising that he could easily get a flat for some of her relatives. Then everything went wrong; he did not trust his mother; he could not explain anything about the arson (the fire had died out by itself), and he was terrified that he might commit some more serious crime. The police agreed that he should stay at Herstedvester.

Anton's brother-in-law said that his relationship to his mother was very difficult to understand. She had pressed him into living at home, suggesting that he could live nearly free, but the family thought it had been very expensive for him. His mother considered him somewhat helpless, and she had talked lately, with an odd smile, about whether "it wouldn't be better for him to go to a place where he could stay many years."

He was returned to Herstedvester by the court because of the arson and small thefts. We had advocated this, partly because he again had mentioned his thoughts about killing his fiancée, but this was not mentioned by the court. She loved him and wrote him heartbreaking letters. He wanted to say good-bye to her himself, but when she arrived both were too moved for him to do so.

Soon he was well-balanced. Some months later he asked his mother to stay away, and seemed to have realized the danger of her interference in the family's life. Six months later he was at the Hut during the visit of Professor William Lennox of Boston (the epilepsy expert), and they discussed the simulation of fits and competed in demonstrating for each other how this could be done. In the discussion Anton spontaneously said that he had been warned by us to avoid moving through small, half-truthful remarks which end up in lies, and then to new ones, until the whole labyrinth of lies would fall in on him.

His motive for the arson, he said, was that he needed to do something serious enough to be returned to Herstedvester.

His former comrade from the hospital for epileptics, who had now also arrived in detention, participated in the same therapy group. Anton's mother was invited to a group meeting, and she explained that as a boy he had been difficult in relation to comrades at school and that he was only interested in sports. He had felt lonely and isolated from the others. However, at the institution he had been very popular.

After two years Anton was again transferred to Kastanienborg, and he rejoined his original group. For a time he was very quiet. In the group the detainees discussed how hot-tempered he had been the first time, and now they teased him about not even taking the chance to talk to a young girl when he had the opportunity. His family relations were carefully worked out. He visited his home when his father died, some time later. He did not show any clear sorrow, but he talked to the group about his confidence in his therapist.

After this he told the group that he would not let his mother interfere any more in his life. He told his comrades that his mother had sold some of his father's clothing that had been promised to him. When his sister behaved strangely, three and one-half years later, he asked the social aide to help her family. In therapeutical interviews his attitudes toward women were carefully discussed and related to his attitude to his mother. He sometimes avoided visiting his mother when he went on leaves and said he could not stand her. Because he was very clever at market gardening, we tried to give him a complete apprenticeship in this field. He attended the nearby technical school and managed the examination very well. After four years he was paroled and got a job nearby as a market gardener.

He remained in the discussion group for some time and explained how he had told his colleagues at work where he had come from. They had been curious for only a short while and then did not talk about it any more. For a time he started using a little too much money in bars, but we discussed that with him, and he stopped

He found a girl friend who was very economical, and this probably helped to stop his beginning drinking pattern. In any case, once when he and his fiancée were having guests at her home, he brought liquor. She sent him back to the store with it. She did not drink, none of her friends drank, and she thought it would be a bad idea to start a tradition of drinking when they had guests because neither she nor her family could afford it.

Anton worked for six months, then disappeared from his job, saying that he would go to Jutland. The next day he turned up at Herstedvester, depressed and weeping. He had used his mother's address as his official address but had lived with his fiancée, and now his mother had pawned all his winter clothing. He did not have enough money to get them back. He had left his job but behaved as if he went to work, and he came home at the normal time. He had tried to call our social section, but by chance the social aide had been engaged.

He was transferred to Kastanienborg and by the next day he was pacified, and his fiancée, to whom he had told part of his story before, visited him. Now she heard more details. After a week he returned to the same job and lived again, now officially, with his fiancée. Three months later they married, and half a year later they had their first child.

One and one-half years after Anton's last parole, the police called on him routinely because of a series of arsons, but he was ruled out as a possible suspect. Some months later he left his job, and his employer phoned Herstedvester the day after because he was afraid Anton had met bad company. The social aide visited him, and he said that he had obsessions about choking a woman. My deputy found it necessary to take this seriously and sent him to the psychiatric section. Here he was soon pacified, and he returned to his wife. It seemed that he had been given more responsibility than he could handle. It was later found that he had taken thirty kroner belonging to a colleague when he first left. This was found out two weeks after he returned to the job, and again he disappeared. His wife was nine months pregnant, and he had some financial difficulties. He received some economic assistance and found another job with less responsibility.

A few months later everything was in order again. Some irregularity with installment payments had been discovered and cleared up. He did not drink, but instead he started eating sweets so that he became too fat. As he had not had fits for many years and probably never had really been an epileptic, he obtained a driver's license, which he did not need for anything but his self-esteem. We still found it necessary to classify him as severely psychopathic. When his wife became pregnant for the third time, she had a legal abortion because of his condition and because it was unlikely that they would be able to bring up a large family with reasonable success.

Nothing special happened to Anton during the following four years. Then I visited him in order to get his story as he could tell it then. I arrived without warning. Both he and his wife received me very kindly. They had three rooms and a kitchen, and their flat was well furnished. He talked about the help he had received from the officer who had been his sergeant, saying, "You never know how much that means at a later time when you are on your own." He also talked about the help he received from the escort when his father died and about being "moved after two years, even though I didn't

live up to what I promised the first time—that helped me enormously."
He remembered a great deal of help that one of the market gardeners
gave him with his school work, and also assistance from the local
director of the open section. He compared the hospital with Herstedvester and felt that the freedom at the hospital, where he could do
what he wanted, had been too dangerous for him and added with a
smile, "You remember it also proved dangerous for me to be at
Kastanienborg." He talked about the American doctor. About his
criminal period, he said that probably his anxiety about what would
happen when he had done something wrong made him have other
problems.

Most important in his re-socialization was that he quickly found a
girl friend, so that he did not have to be alone.

He said he sometimes became angry, especially when the newspapers wrote of some psychopath who had done something serious.
"Then your comrades think that he is all mad, and then you sit
there, and they don't know that you have been there. Then you get
mad. Then you hit the table and say they do not know what the
word psychopath means. All together we are psychopaths. What's the
difference between criminals and noncriminals? Then you can hear
how clever these comrades are. They know how it works much
better than someone who has been through it. Then you don't want
to tell them that you have been there. You get afraid, but it would
be nice if they once and for all knew that you have been there. Once
it nearly happened."

One of Anton's colleagues had been in the State Prison, and he
told about how the prisoners had seen the people from Herstedvester
coming to church and how the prisoners talked about the "mental
defectives" who came to the institution. And the former prisoner told
him that those were the psychopaths from the other side of the
road. "They are a little mad," he said. "Then," Anton said, "I got
angry and told him that they are neither insane nor mentally defective
and that many of them are very intelligent, more so than the
prisoners. It was all a lie, what he said. Then the others wondered
what had angered me, but I left without explaining." He did not dare
tell his comrades at his new job where he had been before and he felt
it was better to keep away from all of his Herstedvester comrades.
"After all, I believe that comradeship there is somewhat different
from that outside. At Herstedvester you were comradely in order
to obtain something, in most cases. That's, after all, something

different than what you share with your comrades. It is quite another
atmosphere. The most important thing is to find a new group of
people to meet with when you get out."

At the age of forty-three, Anton was finally discharged from
Herstedvester.

* * *

CONCLUDING REMARKS

This book has not given a systematic analysis of the reasons that
the many more than a thousand men I have handled during my
years at Herstedvester developed the way they did, and I do not
apologize for this. Other psychiatrists have attempted to understand
the development of character abnormalities, but their sometimes clear
understanding of some important mechanisms has not produced
practical action. It seems to me that their studies have more frequently
hampered attempts at treatment than resulted in clinically satisfactory
results or prophylaxis.

When this book was nearly finished, I read the following comment
by Norman Cameron:

> If such an adult [one with a character disorder] and those who are
> close to him accept his peculiarities as simply his nature he is not
> likely to find them disturbing or seek to change them. He may be
> proud of them and consider them, not incorrectly, as signs of his
> individuality.
>
> It is only when a person with a character distortion realizes that
> something is wrong with him, with his attempts at adaptation, defense,
> mastery, and satisfaction, that he experiences his difficulties as ego-alien,
> usually without knowing precisely what they are or why he feels as he
> does. The realization often comes with repeated failures and dissatis-
> factions which a person cannot explain away. It may come because
> new circumstances force a person to compare himself with others, and
> the comparison raises self-doubt, dissatisfaction, and perhaps anxiety.
> He may even recognize that some of what he has regarded as his
> special virtue or his mark of individuality may be in fact a pathological
> need, fear, or incapacity. He may find, for example, that his vaunted
> firmness rests upon a rigidity which keeps him from changing even
> when a change is necessary, or that his widely known affability is
> actually a fear of displeasing anyone, or that his willingness to com-
> promise stems from an inability to take a firm stand.[5]

[5] Norman Cameron, *Personality Development and Psychopathology* (Boston:
Houghton Mifflin Co., 1963), as quoted in Jay Katz, Joseph Goldstein and
Alan M. Dershowitz, *Psychoanalysis, Psychiatry and the Law* (New York: The
Free Press, 1967), p. 520.

This description seems to me to fit the inmates we have observed at Herstedvester. The bending of the life tree of childhood distorts the form of the adult personality. How the personality trees of our inmates can be reshaped and made acceptable to themselves and to society depends upon the local culture. As we see it, the realistic and rational practices we have established in our institution cannot simply be reproduced in another setting. It should be stressed that our methods are based on what we felt was realistic and rational in the Danish culture, in the middle of this century, in this institution as it was built, and with the legal requirements that were given to us.

Whether the basic principles of our realistic, rational, and humane general approach to the problems of our inmates can be carried out in other cultural settings depends on the laws of the country and on close cooperation with the courts. When the courts discovered that our inmates felt that they had been helped, it became easier for the judges to understand that many people with severe character disorders do not have to continue their criminal lives. Justice does not need to destroy the future life of an offender. Justice in our time must be based both on traditional principles and on the requirements of each individual case. A sentenced criminal is still a citizen, and he will usually, often after a very short time, become a free citizen again. When we limit his freedom, we have an obligation to try to motivate him to live a life acceptable to himself and to others. We condemn his criminal acts, but we want to help him to regain his self-respect and live as a noncriminal citizen.

The relevant questions are these: What can we, as fellow members of the same society, do to prevent his stumbling again, and what can we do to prevent others from stumbling as he has? How can we study his problems and learn by his mistakes?

I am convinced that even criminals with severe character disorders are able under special circumstances to obtain an insight into the way their behavior has been twisted and bent. Sometimes, by means of their peculiar way of perceiving what goes on and what is important, they can be persuaded to accept help if it is offered to them in a form that does not threaten their self-respect.

Most of the cases that come to us are considered to be hopeless, and it is true that many of these inmates have lived in situations that have made a crime-free life impossible. Nevertheless, it is possible to obtain positive results in cases like ours, and efforts to do this are humanitarian as well as scientific necessities.

While criminals are in the institution, as well as after they leave, many difficult interpersonal situations occur. Such difficulties are a strain on inmates as well as staff. However, I hope it is evident by now that this work may give great personal satisfaction to anyone who becomes deeply involved in it. Staff members and inmates alike must try, with dignity and realism, to strike a balance between ideals and social and personal realities.

We have seen that continuity in this kind of work is essential for the inmates as well as the staff. Only through continuity of contact with persons in the institution will the staff be able to experience the great variety of situations which, combined, reshape the careers of chronic criminals. Only continuous effort makes it possible to integrate custody, treatment, special rehabilitation, and social aid so that they will blend into what we call therapeutic climate. This climate makes it possible for the inmates to obtain and use the varied kinds of assistance that they need at different times.

Continuity of contact with our criminal fellow citizens teaches the staff to comprehend the destructive effects of life in an institution and stimulates us to try to overcome these handicaps. However, we still have to remember that in many cases society's need for protection makes institutionalization of a criminal necessary.

Through our attempts to reintegrate our inmates into normal society, and through careful and prolonged study of criminal careers, we obtain clinical experience and valuable new insights into socialization processes. The problems here in Herstedvester have a magnitude which makes it possible for us to observe them. It is important not to work solely with the minor criminal situations. Our handling of chronic criminals, including the aggressive ones, ought to be such that in the future we may at least state that we do not, through our approach to them, augment the risk they present to society.

APPENDIXES

History of the Herstedvester Detention Centre

1912: A law proposed by the Kriminalistforeningen, an organization of criminologists including lawyers, psychiatrists, penologists, and others interested in crime problems, included the first complete plan for a special institution for psychopaths.

1924: On October 27, on the order of the Minister of Justice, K. K. Steincke, a pedophiliac sexual criminal who had relapsed several times, was not released when he had finished his last sentence. As he was supposedly dangerous to society, and no suitable place could be found for him, he was retained in a prison infirmary. A political storm resulted in a temporary law.

1925: On April 11, a law was enacted concerning internment of especially dangerous persons whose defective development, "more permanent" weakness, or disturbance of mental faculties—including sexual abnormality—resulted in criminal acts and/or threats indicating an obvious and serious risk of considerable violation of the public safety (Retssikkerheden).

1925: On December 23, a temporary unit for detainees opened in rented rooms in Sundholm, a municipal institution for vagrants in Copenhagen, giving the three detainees, who had been kept in cells until then, a more pleasant Christmas.

1930: On April 15, a new penal code was enacted.[1] The most important sections for our work are:

Section 16: Acts committed by persons being irresponsible owing to insanity or similar conditions or pronounced mental deficiency are not punishable.

[1] Published in English as *The Danish Criminal Code* (Copenhagen: C. E. Gad, Publishers, 1958).

Section 17: (1) If, at the time of committing the punishable act, the more permanent condition of the perpetrator involved defective development, or impairment or disturbance of his mental faculties, including sexual abnormality, of a nature other than that indicated in Section 16 of this Act, the court shall decide, on the basis of a medical report and all other available evidence, whether he may be considered susceptible to punishment.

(2) If the court is satisfied that the accused is susceptible to punishment, it may decide that a penalty involving the deprivation of liberty inflicted on him shall be served in an institution or division of an institution intended for such persons. If appropriate, the Prison Commission may alter the decision as to where the penalty of imprisonment shall be served. If, during the term of imprisonment, it becomes evident that continuation of such imprisonment will be useless or will be likely seriously to aggravate the condition of the convicted, then, at the request of the Director of the Prison Service, the case shall again be brought before the court which passed sentence in the last instance. This court shall decide, on the basis of a medical report, whether the penalty shall continue to be served or not.

(3) If a person in respect of whom preventive measures are taken under Section 70 of this Act (cf. Subsection (1) of this section) for an offence committed by him has committed another offence, and if he is considered susceptible to punishment for offences of that nature, then, where the latter offence is of minor importance in relation to the offence in respect of which preventive measures are applied, the court may decide that no penalty shall be imposed.

Section 70: (1) Where an accused is acquitted under Section 16 of this Act or where punishment is considered inapplicable under Section 17 of this Act, while having regard to public safety it is deemed necessary that other measures be applied to him, the court shall decide on the nature of such measures. If public safety is unlikely to be guaranteed by imposing less rigorous measures, such as sureties, directions as to or prohibition against residence in a particular place, orders of the nature dealt with in Section 72 of this Act, appointment of a supervisor or relegation to a state of minority, the person concerned shall be placed in a mental hospital, an institution for feebleminded or other curative institution, an asylum for inebriates or in a special detention centre. Within the limits set by the court, the competent administrative authority shall decide upon any further arrangements that may be required by such measures.

(2) Where the accused is likely to be sentenced to placement in a hospital or an institution, the court may appoint a supervising guardian for him, if possible one of his near relatives, who is qualified for that task and has accepted it. The supervising guardian shall, on the one

hand, assist the accused during the proceedings together with the counsel for the defence and, on the other hand, keep himself informed of his condition and see to it that his stay in the hospital or the institution be not extended beyond what is necessary.

(3) At the instance of the Public Prosecutor, of the director of the institution concerned or of the supervising guardian, the court which passed sentence in the first instance may at any time alter the earlier decision made concerning the nature of the measure or may, on the basis of a medical report, cancel it temporarily or absolutely.

If a request on the part of the supervising guardian for cancelling or modifying the measures of security is not allowed by the court, the supervising guardian may submit a second request only after the expiration of one year: provided that, if warranted by special circumstances, such a request may be submitted at the expiration of not less than six months.

1933: On January 1, the new penal code went into effect. The number of inmates rose and another temporary unit for detainees opened in the State Prison in Vridslöselille.

1935: On March 30, the newly built detention institution, Herstedvester, received its first detainee transferred from the temporary institution. It was directed by the warden of the State Prison across the road, aided by a part-time psychiatric consultant, Max Schmidt.

The institution is surrounded by a wall 5 meters high. The area is rectangular, 250 by 120 meters. Inside the walls (see frontispiece) to the left there are 2 two-story buildings, each with 40 rooms and divided into 4 sections. In 1938 a new two-story building with 4 units and 60 rooms was built to the east. Across the middle, east to west, are two buildings. The southern one is a workshop and gymnasium and the northern one holds offices, the infirmary, and the security section.

1936: A social aide was employed.

1938: The psychiatric superintendent, Dr. Paul Reiter, took charge of treatment at Herstedvester. He was employed full-time and was aided by a medical practitioner. He also had to act as physician for the State Prison.

1940: A royal decree stated that:

The goal of the institution is to safeguard society against the dangers to law and order (retssikkerheden) the persons detained in the institution would present if they were on their own, and inside these limits submit them to a treatment adapted to their psychological peculiarities in order that they become suited to return to free life. During the detention, which is not a punishment but a security measure, the treatment ought to have in view the individualities of the detainees.

1942: Dr. Georg K. Stürup succeeded Dr. Reiter as superintendent.

1942: A teacher was employed.

1943: A psychiatrically trained assistant, Jan Sachs, was employed. The superintendent was exempted from the general medical work at the State Prison.

1944: The open section, Kastanienborg, was established. The section for women came under our supervision. Extra social aides were employed.

1945: The section for women was transferred from Vestre prison in Copenhagen to Herstedvester and from there to a section in Vridslösellile State Prison. After the German capitulation the male detainees also were temporarily transferred to the State Prison and severe difficulties developed. These were solved after some months when a group was transferred back to Herstedvester and another group to an open section in a fenced manor house in southern Zealand. This section was used until 1952.

  In the following years the number of persons sentenced to detention grew, and even though the detention period was shortened, the number of detainees and staff continued to grow.

1948: It again became necessary to establish a temporary unit, this time in a prison in Copenhagen.

1950: A psychologist, Erik Hoeck–Gradenwitz, was employed.

1951: A sister institution was established in Horsens, Jutland. Herstedvester's women's section was moved to a section of the Women's Prison at Horserød.

1952: Horsens became independent of Herstedvester.

1960: Name changed from "Psychopatforvaringsanstalt" (Detention Institution for Psychopaths) to "Forvaringsanstalt" (Detention Institution).

1967: A new office building was added.

Placement of Criminal Psychotics

Psychotic patients sentenced under Sections 16 and 70 of the Criminal Code are not usually placed in a detention institution. However, this may occur in a few borderline cases or in cases where psychoses have become stationary. Normally, criminal psychotics are placed in local mental hospitals. This is an old tradition.

In 1910 this line of thought was well developed in a report from a medical committee that stressed that many psychotics are taken into custody because they have committed a crime but that they ought to be treated like any other insane person instead of being sent to a prison. In many cases it is "to a high degree an accident that they happened to commit a crime. An earlier alertness to their surroundings, a more sensible evaluation of their particular state of insanity, which could have been brought under suitable care, could have changed this and placed these patients in the same category as all other patients in a mental hospital."[1] It is up to the medical superintendent of each mental hospital to evaluate the amount of freedom he dares to allow each patient.

A special security institution for a very small group of dangerous patients was opened in 1918. In the beginning, this institution also admitted some of the psychopaths who were later transferred to Herstedvester. Shortly before this, mental defectives had been removed from the security institution to a hospital for mental defectives.

From 1925 to 1955, the number of inmates in the security institution varied between forty and fifty. After the use of psychopharmacological drugs began, the number fell considerably. In 1960, there were twenty-five inmates, in 1965 only 12.

[1] From "Medicinalkommissionens Betænkning København 1910," as cited in "Betænkning om psykisk abnorme lovovertrædere," nr. 450, Copenhagen 1967, p. 10. Statens Trykningskontor.

In the 1940's the group of criminals placed in mental hospitals were examined and it was decided to consider the establishment of an institution for the treatment of a large part of the psychologically normal offenders.[2] It was found that some inmates in Herstedvester who are sometimes psychotic, sometimes not, are not suited to the treatment that we have worked out, but there are too few of them to justify establishing an institution for treatment suited to their condition.

Such an institution must have several sections so that persons who cannot live together may be separated. We had hoped that an institution for this group could be combined with an institution for criminal patients who have a high escape risk and those who are decidedly dangerous to society. Together, these two categories of patients could perhaps make up a special institution with closed and open sections, giving treatment that would be independent of, and different from, the system used in detention. If such an institution could be established, it would avoid the upsetting shift from mental hospital to detention institution and back again and establish the necessary continuity in treatment.

Since this suggestion was accepted in a committee report of 1949, nothing more has been done about it, but the problems have undergone considerable change. The court now seems to be more inclined to send offenders with severe borderline psychotic deviations to detention in Herstedvester. This makes it easier for the mental hospitals but more difficult for Herstedvester. Also, in recent years the court has obtained greater leeway. It can either sentence a man to stay in a mental hospital, order him to receive treatment in a mental hospital, or be under the care of the hospital (which means that the hospital may parole the patient and keep contact with him, but that it must not discharge him without consent of the court). Moreover, the court may sentence a person to stay under some sort of supervision with assurance of hospital care if it is needed.

In some cases it is still difficult for the court to decide who shall go to a hospital and who shall go to detention. Although this borderline group is not very large, it has been our experience that the

[2] Georg K. Stürup, *Om behandling af kriminelle personer på sindssygehospital* in *Betænkning om oprettelse af et krimininalasyl for psykisk abnorme lovovertrædere* (Copenhagen: Schultz, 1949), pp. 32-44.

dangerous kind of criminal patients with common psychotic phases which need treatment in hospitals ought to stay there as long as these psychotic phases appear, even though there may be intervals of as much as a year between them. The most important criterion for the court's decision ought not to be the formal diagnosis but the consideration of the patient's need for a "strain-relieving" treatment as against the "strain-producing" treatment of Herstedvester.

Placement of Criminal Mental Defectives

Care for mental defectives developed along with care for psychotics. The first hospitals for mental defectives were developed by Hübertz in 1855, and since then institutions for mental defectives have cared for children as well as for adults. These hospitals have been managed by medical men with psychiatric training and have a huge aftercare system.

One of the psychiatrists of the Medico-Legal Council must have suitable experience with mental defectives.

Until recently, it has always been easy to have the criminal mental defectives placed in the proper institutions. There is now, however, some objection to receiving the criminals, who are more difficult to handle (especially the borderline cases), but there has been no real change in policy.

We have in Herstedvester a number of borderline cases, and we have had a substantial number of cases that were considered mentally defective for many years, before it was discovered that this was not the case. We usually call these inmates "former mental defectives." Some of them have proven to be of normal intelligence, and many of them have needed our long term social support in order to survive in normal society.

Psychopathy and Insufficiency of Personality or Character

It has always been difficult to get psychiatrists to agree on the concept of psychopathy. In the 1920's and the beginning of the 1930's, the Danish professors of psychiatry Wimmer and Helweg stressed the disharmony of the personality structure in these cases but warned against placing too much stress on single abnormal elements. For a time, Kurt Schneider's opinions were dominant in Denmark. He considered psychopaths as persons with abnormal personalities which, under any circumstances, must cause inconvenience for themselves and/or society. Schneider also stressed the inherited basis of the personality and unsystematically classified psychopaths into ten groups.

Our attempts at using the Schneider classification system were not very successful. In the first 300 inmates, we found no one classified in the depressive or fanatic group. In the hyperthymic group we found 17; sensitive, 15; self-assertive, 55; emotionally labile, 31; explosive, 10; emotionally cool, 12; spineless, 26; asthenic, 3; mixed, 58; and without clear classification according to Schneider, 73. We found it especially difficult to classify pedophiliacs and exhibitionists; 25 per cent of the property criminals were found to be mixed types and still more, 30 per cent, of the aggressives were in the mixed group.

In the same period we attempted to classify a group of inmates in the State Prison. As we had only known these prisoners for a period of about an hour during an interview and had before us a carefully prepared life-story, it was much easier to classify this group in an unambiguous way. However, persons we knew in Herstedvester were followed in the institution, as well as outside, and observed in many different situations. Because we knew them much better classification was much harder. The longer we knew a detainee, the more difficult it became. We encountered more and more "mixed types," and finally we gave up trying.

Rather early we realized that psychopathy was not a uniform phenomenon calling for a uniform treatment of all cases.[1] A very individualized approach was needed. We could not diagnose which clinical states depended on inherited elements (Sachs, 1946) so we stopped paying special attention to this as being important to diagnosis.[2] For legal and other interdisciplinary use we have tried since 1948 to establish a simple classification of variations in personalities.

For administrative and legal purposes it is necessary to know whether a person is mentally defective. The biological etiology is important for research but not for nonmedical purposes.

Conflicts between law and psychiatry would be substantially lessened if only the results of our investigations of an inmate that are relevant for the court were elaborated in the conclusion of a medical recommendation. Etiological speculations and divergent opinions as to the importance of one or another etiological factor in the observed personality pattern does not belong in courtrooms.

To handle a person who is not insane, the court needs to know if he fits any of the following personality patterns:

  I. Defective intelligence
      A. Borderline cases.
      B. Mental defectives (insufficiencies of intelligence).
      1. Debiles (morons).
      2. Imbeciles.
      3. Idiots.

 II. Defective personality
      1. Personality peculiarities (with some possibility of managing life in a reasonable, acceptable way—a sort of borderline case).
      2. Insufficiency of personality.

In order to call a man "insufficient in character" or "insufficient in personality" it is not necessary for him to show symptoms of insufficiency under all circumstances. It is enough if his deviation is so

[1] Georg K. Stürup and Karl Johan Ebbe, "Særbehandling af kriminelle psykopater i Danmark," *Nordisk Tidsskrift for Strafferet,* 33(1945), pp. 71–117.
[2] Jan Sachs, "Psychopathic personality traits terminological considerations," *Opuscula Psychiatrico-Neurologica Hjalmaro Helweg* (Copenhagen: Einar Munksgård, 1946), pp. 699–714.

severe that it is obvious that his disharmonic personality is causing great inconvenience to himself and people surrounding him.

Special immaturity symptoms such as misuse of alcohol or drugs may be noted and any sexual abnormality must be described.

We consider it important for the court to have an opportunity to evaluate the basis on which this sociopsychiatric diagnosis rests. Therefore a report gives an elaborate outline of the investigated person's life-story and present condition. In this part of the recommendation it is suitable to include a discussion of different kinds of biological and psychological facts which are more or less independent of personality sufficiency or insufficiency. These we have categorized as follows:

I. Inheritance
    Disharmony in gene structure has recently become important because of the demonstration that double X chromosomes and double Y chromosomes are found in a higher than normal proportion in people having social problems.

II. Psychic "scars"
    Milieu-effects, effects of strain, psychological development, neurotic symptoms, and so forth.

III. Organic brain diseases
    Traumatic, encephalitic, and intoxicatious.

IV. Hormonal and other physical disorders

Court Decisions Affecting Detention at Herstedvester

Decision by Østre Landsrets (Eastern Superior Court) on January 13, 1955:

" . . . the Superintendent of the institution is authorized to place the detainee outside the institution under family care so that he can be brought back to the institution for a short or long period of time if need be and again be placed outside when circumstances call for it. It is the duty of the Superintendent of the institution upon his return to advise the supervising guardian and the prosecution without delay so that these people have the opportunity to bring the question before the Superior Court."

Decision by Østre Landsrets (Eastern Superior Court) of March 13, 1958: After setting forth the standard conditions for parole, the decision stated, " . . . and that he submit to outpatient treatment for alcoholism under the supervision of the institution and that, if he commits new offences or his circumstances in general motivate it, he must expect to be returned to the detention institution.

"A further special condition for parole shall apply: that the detention institution is authorized to let the sentenced person return to the detention institution at the first moment when it is possible to doubt if his state may contain risk for new offences on the condition that within five days of his return the State's Attorney is informed about this for his presentation before the court of the question if the return is estimated to be sustained."

For a narcotics addict it is commonly required ". . . that he only uses one physician who previously is informed by the institution concerning his circumstances and so that he does not exchange physicians without previous agreement of the supervision of the institution."

The Parolee's Guide[1]

Parole. Discharge occurs only after you have been paroled by the court and on conditions set by that court. You will be given a copy of your parole sentence with the conditions for your parole. Before you leave us, we will discuss the conditions thoroughly with you.

When you leave, you will also receive a parole pass in which the conditions are set out. This pass is meant as a legitimation for you for the first few days after parole.

The Conditions. Parole nearly always includes the conditions that you accept the institution's supervision, that you follow the directions of your social aide (supervisor), and especially that you not change work or lodging without having obtained permission of the institution through your social aide.

The court may order other more special conditions such as the arrangement for treatment for misuse of alcohol or the requirement of a direct return to the institution in certain situations.

If such conditions are not changed by the court, they are in effect during your whole parole period and until your final discharge.

Return After Parole and Direct Return. If you break the conditions of parole, it may result in your being returned to the institution. New offenses will nearly always result in your being returned to Herstedvester. Return can only occur after a court decision. Direct return can be used if your conditions—or a later order from the court changing the conditions—provide for it. A direct return in such a case may be ordered by Herstedvester and be reported immediately to the State's Attorney who will bring the case before the court for its acceptance.

Duration of Parole. The length of your parole period is not determined but it will usually be not less than four or five years. It may be somewhat shorter or longer depending on how your situation

[1] Translation of a printed folder given to each parolee.

develops during the period. Final discharge occurs after an order from the court.

Supervision. Supervision is planned as continuous collaboration between you and the institution and is primarily a standing offer to help in managing the difficulties which may come up during your parole period. Because of this, it is very important that you are prepared from the beginning to participate in an open and trusting collaboration with your social aide. Supervision is a duty for both you and the institution and cannot be dismissed until the court decides so. Supervision has two goals: (1) to give you advice and support and, (2) to exert that type of control over your circumstances which the court finds necessary.

How frequently you will be in contact with the social aide is decided by the aide. The form of this contact will be decided in each individual case. Most often, contact takes the form of a visit from the aide to your home or a visit by you to his office. Between visits, telephone calls and letters may be used.

The Social Aide and Other Contacts with Herstedvester. One of the social aides of the institution is assigned as your special supervisor.

In individual cases a special contact man may also be appointed. He will be a member of the staff—a person in whom you have had special confidence during your stay and with whom it may therefore be opportune to keep contact.

It may also be desirable for your therapists to continue your treatment during your parole period. Whatever happens, you can always contact your therapist, doctor, or psychologist.

In special cases, such as your being located at such a distance that direct contact with the personnel in the institution is difficult, it may be possible to appoint a special, local contact man for the daily work.

Income. The amount of money you have saved in the institution will be administered by us and paid to you when deemed necessary. Should you be returned, the amount will be transferred to your new account, and, when you are finally discharged, the remainder will be paid to you.

You will have to administer your own income after parole if other arrangements are not made, but you will always be able to get assistance from your social aide. This is also true for those receiving disability or old age pensions.

Borrowing money and buying on installments must usually be approved previously by your social aide.

The institution has a small amount of money available to loan to parolees who have been unable to obtain needed financial support through private souces or public authorities (social relief offices). We emphasize that such loans must be taken seriously. Repayment of each loan makes it possible for others to be helped at the right moment.

Acquaintances and Marriage. In principle you are free to select your companions, but there are exceptions to this rule.

The institution stresses that you must not stay in contact with fellow detainees or their relatives if you have not obtained special permission to do so from the institution. Furthermore, it is possible for the institution to advise you to avoid circles which have previously proved dangerous for your future. Finally, you must remember that the marriage law includes special rules and that you may be affected by them.

Therefore, if you consider marrying, you must ask your social aide if you are covered by these rules and have to obtain permission from the Minister of Justice to marry. The institution will advise you in the case. If the rules in the marriage law are not followed, your marriage may be annulled, and it is therefore in your own interest to have all requirements in order before you finally decide to marry.

Your Occupation. When the institution actively participates in providing work for you, we have to give your employer the information that you are, or have been, at the institution. In special cases it may also be our duty to inform later employers, but this will not happen without your knowledge. In all normal cases the institution will *not* call upon your employer. Neither will we usually inform your landlord.

As already mentioned, you must not take a new job without having obtained permission from your social aide because the court wants us to be fully informed at all times about your situation, and it wants us to intervene if you are changing your life in a way that it may be dangerous for you.

When the court agrees to parole you, it is because it believes that you may be able to manage a crime-free life. However, we know that you will have many difficulties when returning to a normal way of life after a stay in an institution. Therefore, when you leave us, you will be supervised under conditions aimed at lessening the risk of your getting into difficulties which can result in new offenses.

It is important that you realize that even though there may be disagreements now and then between you and the social aide, the goal is the same for both of you—to ensure that you keep your freedom in the future.

You should also remember that not every offense necessarily results in punishment or return to Herstedvester. The closer and more open your collaboration with the institution has been, the better will be the institution's basis for reasonable advice to the court and prosecution.

We know that you, yourself, will have to do the work of making a new and satisfactory way of life, but we hope and believe that we will be able to help you.

Life Charts

These charts begin at the top line at point zero with the man's arrival in Herstedvester.

To the left of this zero point are marked on the top line: ten, twenty, thirty, and forty—meaning years before his arrival. Between thirty and forty a mark on the line shows when this person was born. His periods of internment in different kinds of institutions are marked with different symbols. This makes it possible to visualize the years each person has been interned because of his criminal activities.

To the right of the zero point is marked ten, meaning ten years after arrival in Herstedvester. The first man stayed with us for less than two years—the black square—and did not return.

On the left half of the life charts is reproduced a line for each one of the property offenders, from thirty to forty years of age, who spent only one period in Herstedvester, and they are arranged in the order of length of stay. Shortest stay in the first, longest stay in the last line.

The right half of the chart is made in the same way, but here we see the property offenders in the same age group who have spent more than one period with us in Herstedvester. These are arranged so that the first man has spent the shortest time, and the last man the longest time in the first period he was in Herstedvester.

Four of these persons were here at the time of this study. This is illustrated with an arrow-shaped symbol.

The vertical single lines illustrate arrests or short periods of direct return to our institution. Most of these have been preceded by some minor legal infractions.

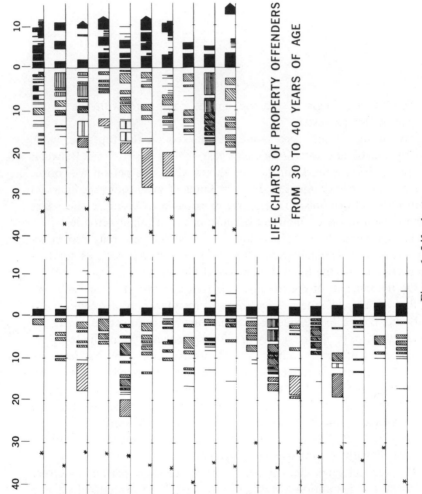

LIFE CHARTS OF PROPERTY OFFENDERS
FROM 30 TO 40 YEARS OF AGE

Figure 6. Life charts.

 THE JOHNS HOPKINS PRESS

Designed by Arlene J. Sheer

*Composed in Times Roman text and Times Roman Display
by Baltimore Type and Composition Corporation*

*Printed offset by Universal Lithographers, Inc.,
on 60-lb regular finish Tosca Book*

Bound by L. H. Jenkins, Inc. in Columbia Riverside Linen